Social Work Under Pressure

of related interest

The Survival Guide for Newly Qualified Child and Family Social Workers
Hitting the Ground Running
Helen Donnellan and Gordon Jack
ISBN 978 1 84310 989 1

The Post-Qualifying Handbook for Social Workers
Edited by Wade Tovey
ISBN 978 1 84310 428 5

Social Work with Children and Families
Getting into Practice
Ian Butler and Caroline Hickman
3rd edition
ISBN 9781843105985

Handbook for Practice Learning in Social Work and Social Care
Knowledge and Theory
2nd edition
Edited by Joyce Lishman
ISBN 978 1 84310 186 4

A Practical Guide to Working with Reluctant Clients in Health and Social Care
Maggie Kindred
Illustrated by Cath Kindred
ISBN 978 1 84905 102 6

Being White in the Helping Professions
Developing Effective Intercultural Awareness
Judy Ryde
ISBN 978 1 84310 936 5

Competence in Social Work Practice
A Practical Guide for Students and Professionals
2nd edition
Edited by Kieran O'Hagan
ISBN 978 1 84310 485 8

Social Care Management, Strategy and Business Planning
Trish Hafford-Letchfield
ISBN 978 1 84310 986 0

Social Work Under Pressure

How to Overcome Stress, Fatigue and Burnout in the Workplace

Kate van Heugten

Jessica Kingsley *Publishers*
London and Philadelphia

First published in 2011
by Jessica Kingsley Publishers
116 Pentonville Road
London N1 9JB, UK
and
400 Market Street, Suite 400
Philadelphia, PA 19106, USA

www.jkp.com

Library of Congress Cataloging in Publication Data
van Heugten, Kate, 1959-
  Social work under pressure : how to overcome stress, fatigue
and burnout in the workplace / Kate van Heugten.
       p. cm.
  Includes bibliographical references and index.
  ISBN 978-1-84905-116-3 (alk. paper)
  1. Social workers--Psychology. 2. Social service--Psychological
aspects. 3. Job stress. 4. Burn out (Psychology) I. Title.
  HV40.35.V36 2011
  361.301'9--dc22
                                       2011001446
British Library Cataloguing in Publication Data
A CIP catalogue record for this book is available from the British Library

ISBN 978 1 84905 116 3

Printed and bound in Great Britain

Acknowledgements

First, my thanks to the 14 social work practitioners, supervisors and managers who shared their insights into how, despite its pressures, a career in social work can be enormously rewarding and enjoyable.

Thanks to my research assistant Jaimee Kleinbichler, without whose excellent literature searching and proofreading I would have been hard pressed to meet my deadlines. My appreciation also goes to Professor Ken Strongman, for his encouragement and suggestions on a draft of the book. Muchas gracias, to Dr Maria Pérez-y-Pérez, in particular for her support of my storytelling in the concluding chapter, and for many other stimulating conversations. And to Stephen Jones and Caroline Walton from Jessica Kingsley Publishers, London, whose advice, answers to questions, and kind messages in the aftermath of the 2010 earthquake in Christchurch were much appreciated.

Finally, thank you to Charles for countless hours spent critiquing and reading drafts. And to Jack and Hanna for allowing me to write about some of our family experiences, and for ensuring I remember the importance of living every day.

Author's note

In Chapter 5 I describe the immediate aftermath of the 4 September 2010 earthquake in Christchurch, New Zealand, that measured 7.1 on the Richter Scale. Subsequent to that, on 22 February 2011, Christchurch was struck by a more devastating earthquake, this time measuring 6.3, but at a shallow depth and located close to the city centre. Thousands of homes and businesses were destroyed and close to 200 people lost their lives. Family, friends and colleagues from within New Zealand and around the globe provided support and extended their good wishes to our community. At the time of my writing this author's note, not all of the deceased have as yet been identified, and the grieving of losses is interwoven with the beginnings of a recovery and rebuilding. The events of 22 February have left a profound imprint, and will, eventually, make most of us more resilient and compassionately attuned to human suffering.

Kate van Heugten
22 March 2011

Contents

Part 1

Workplace Stress

Chapter 1

Introduction to Concepts and Models of Workplace Stress

Introduction

It will not come as a surprise to the readers of this book that workers in human service occupations experience high levels of stress. Yet until very recently, there has been a lack of attention to what may be causing this and how it can be overcome.

Occasionally, beginning practitioners are fortunate enough to be assigned a confident mentor or buddy who normalizes the impact of work on the worker. When I think back to the start of my career as a social worker nearly 30 years ago, I recall how I was assigned an 'old hand' for those first weeks. Matt (not his real name) inducted me into the official, and not quite so official, finer points of working in the child welfare service. I well recall his words to me that 'we have mental health days here,' and that taking a little time out and doing something pleasant when I felt overly stretched, whether physically or emotionally, could forestall illness. He reckoned this should not be classed as time wasting. I am not sure that his views were sanctioned by management, though I suspect they were. The message let me know that it was normal to feel that this was a tough job. It helped me tune into my physical and emotional wellbeing, and let me know that actions to take care of myself were a mark of professionalism, rather than personal failure. My mentor's words to me were heartfelt, well timed, and always remembered.

Other social workers, with the help of a sympathetic supervisor, stumble upon the discovery that the distressing effects of working too many hours with traumatized clients have names, such as *vicarious trauma, compassion fatigue* and *burnout.* Timely support may forestall the loss of some of our most sensitive and passionate workers from agencies or from the profession. However, whilst some individuals receive good support, lack of concerted attention to the problem of stress overload means too many social workers are left to struggle on their own.

In the process of writing this book, many people came forward and offered suggestions and recommendations. Amongst those, 14 social work practitioners, all resident in New Zealand, responded to an invitation to participate in interviews about what they find most stressful about social work, and how they believe this may be overcome.

Phoebe was one of these. She had this to say about the lack of attention to ameliorating stress:

> **Phoebe:** It's like a culture of stress and anxiety maybe, that you are kind of just supposed to deal with, not really supposed to talk about out loud. And, kind of, the toughest survive. But what that does to a person and what that does to their practice from what I have witnessed is not that great. I had this thing where, to be a good social worker I had to learn how to get over it. I should learn how to manage the stress better, I should learn how to manage the workload, and that would make me a good successful social worker. ... and I considered seriously not ever doing social work ever, ever again [crying] – which is like a calling for me rather than just doing it to make money.

Phoebe left the agency, but not her profession. She came to realize that 'being tough' in the face of high workloads, clients' aggression and public disrespect was detrimental to her wellbeing, and that 'toughening up' was not the answer and might harm her capacity for empathy or her health: 'Maybe I could have stayed, but what kind of person would I be, oh my God, I think I'd have had a heart attack by now!'

There are probably several reasons for the lack of attention to the needs of people working in human service occupations. Human service workers are employed to care for others, and in doing so they are expected to put the needs of others before their own. They are required to function well at a personal and interpersonal level, and they may worry that they will be considered inadequate if they reveal that they are struggling to cope (Lonne 2003). Managers too may worry that if they accept that there is a stress-related problem for their staff, this may amount to an admission of liability that could be costly to the organization. The unfortunate effect of all of this is that workers suffer in isolation, never realizing theirs is not an uncommon problem. When problems are de-contextualized and individualized, remedies are less than effective and rarely preventative or with benefits that can be generalized to the wider workforce.

Too much stress and too little support ultimately lead to a high turnover of staff, increased rates of sick leave, and 'absenteeism' where workers are present at the job, but absent in terms of attention and commitment to their work. In a report commissioned by the International Labour Organization, the total cost of workplace stress and violence was estimated to be between 1–3.5 per cent of a country's Gross National Product (Hoel, Sparks and Cooper 2001).

This knowledge, combined with an international crisis in recruitment and retention of staff in social and human services, means we can no longer ignore workplace stress and its impact on workers, colleagues, service users and organizations. In November 2009, a government appointed Social Work Taskforce reported on wide ranging problems in social work in England. Morale was found to be low. Following on from the Social Work Taskforce's (2009) report, the Social Work Reform Board (2010) recommended that workplace 'health checks' should be carried out by the end of 2011.

The focus of this book

This book recognizes that social workers face *particular* pressures in their jobs that need a specialist focus. It is written for managers, supervisors, and frontline social workers, although people in related social care or human service occupations will also find much of the content applicable. The perspectives taken are broadly ecological, considering personal and contextual contributors to stress, and are strengths-based. Strengths-based perspectives do not ignore difficulties, but remind us that there are many qualities on the positive side of the ledger: By and large, the combination of life experiences and reflective education of social workers means that in terms of resilience (the capacity to bounce back from stress), they have a head start.

People who choose social work as a career tend to do so actively and it is not uncommon to talk about this choice as a 'calling' as Phoebe did. Although they expect to find work meaningful, they do not assume that they will meet all of the expectations of others. They do not tend to be driven by public and status demands but are instead motivated by public good related considerations. In fact, despite the difficult nature of their jobs, most social workers still find their work enormously satisfying (Collins 2008; Lonne 2003). This message was reinforced by all of the 14 participants I interviewed, who said things like, 'I think I've had the most amazingly rich working life' and 'My work is extraordinarily rewarding.'

More recently, people have begun to ask what we can learn from social workers such as these, who show resilience and remain enthusiastic and hopeful, so that we can understand better what leads to satisfaction in the face of so much pressure (Carver 1998).

How the book is organized

The book is organized in two parts. In Part 1, this first chapter introduces important concepts and how they will be used throughout the book. It also introduces some highly influential generic models of workplace stress. These models provide us with guidance on how we might think about what is happening in our workplaces and how we can intervene. For example, it is important to know that relaxation exercises have not been shown to effectively reduce negative stress. They may still be nice to do, and if your organization provides related training it at least appears to be making efforts to assist you, but this is not the best investment of time and money when staff are heading toward burnout.

The second chapter looks more closely at the typical work pressures faced by social workers and what research and workers themselves identify as being helpful in overcoming these. The third chapter considers stress in the context of personal experiences and addresses the importance of work–life balance. In Part 2, chapters cover issues such as the pressures encountered in frontline practice, trauma work, and the impact of encountering violence from clients or colleagues.

More than a thousand research articles and books were reviewed to establish the basis for the materials in this book. In addition, 14 social workers offered their reflections in audio-taped semi-structured interviews of about one hour duration. Their stories were transcribed and analyzed with the help of qualitative data analysis software 'Nvivo8'. Quotations are sprinkled throughout the text to highlight various themes and ideas. The participants were promised anonymity, and to maintain that, certain potentially identifying details are omitted from the discussion. They signed ethical consent and they have all been given, or have elected to choose their own, pseudonyms. They are Anthony, Phoebe, Margaret, Rachel, Amanda, Teina, Joe, Ella, Joy, Kris, Steve, Rewa, Val and Cathy. Collectively they have over 200 years of experience, individually ranging from 18 months to over 20 years, with the majority having over ten years experience. They chose to tell their stories in the hope that this endeavour would go some way to overcoming the problem of workplace stress.

> **Kris:** Basically I like the idea of doing things for the greater good. And what happens to each individual is not always isolated, and unless we put it out there we don't make the links. So that's part of any research, you know, ... speaking out. And that's part of social work principles of attending to bigger matters and working as a collective. So there's solidarity if we do bring things out, and, bearing in mind that we're all unique as well and there's different perspectives on what is stress and my experiences of a situation, so I don't say this is an absolute truth is what I'm saying either, so bearing that in mind, I thought, yeah, if any use can be made of experiences that can be quite challenging, that's all good. It's telling something, it's that transformation of things that happened to me.
>
> **Margaret:** I think for me it is important to participate in this sort of thing, so that we can learn from each other how to understand that we will experience the level of stress and the impact of the traumas that we work with. And we need to take care about that so that we don't sort of give up on the job and leave, because I know a lot of people, I have experienced a lot of people leave. And certainly I have left jobs in the past because it wasn't handled as well as it could have been. And really it is not about me it is about the systems that support me to continue in the work that I do.

Throughout the book there are prompts to assist you to reflect on how the information presented may relate to your situation or that of colleagues or staff for whom you provide leadership and support. Each chapter ends with a 'stocktake' or 'toolkit' section and a list of additional resources.

What is stress and is it always bad?

In discussions, and even in writing, words such as *stress, vicarious trauma, compassion fatigue* and *burnout* are often used interchangeably. But because different pressures may lead to particular effects that may in turn need different measures to prevent or mend them, it is helpful to have these concepts differentiated.

It would be fair to say that we probably all think that we know what stress is. The colloquial use equates stress with the distress that we experience when we don't feel we can cope with the demands placed upon us. But sometimes we also use the term to refer to the demands themselves, which, in the literature are more commonly called *stressors.* Some writers, wanting to avoid possible confusion for readers, try not to use the word *stress* at all, but it is so embedded in our common language that those attempts to reshape the way we talk have not been very successful.

To keep matters simple, I will use words like *stressor* or *pressure* or *demand* for work events, tasks and requirements that impact on workers. I will use the word *stress* to indicate the effects of those impacts, which may be physical, cognitive, emotional or behavioural. It is important, however, to note that neither the demands, nor the consequences are necessarily negative. Some degree of pressure can be a motivator, and even relatively high levels of pressure may be felt to be challenging by some social workers. An example of a straightforward neutral definition is the following: 'Job stress is the mind–body arousal resulting from physical and/or psychological demands associated with a job' (Quick and Nelson 1997, p.10).

Dr Hans Selye was an important person in the history of the study of stress. Selye was a Canadian endocrinologist who studied the biological effects of stimuli on the body and first coined the term *stress* to denote those effects in the 1930s. The concept was expanded over time to include psychological responses, and by the 1960s, Selye's writing identified two types of stress, whereby *eustress* was the term he used for 'good' stress of the kind we experience when we are energized, focused and excited as a result of demands we experience (Le Fevre, Matheny and Kolt 2003; Selye 1976). When we experience eustress, our hearts may beat faster and we may experience a surge of hormones, but this is to good effect as our cognitive capacities are enhanced and we express ourselves confidently. There is a sense of balance in terms of what we are asked to achieve, and what we can manage within our available resources of time and skills. We feel supported to learn any new information we may require. Afterwards we may feel relieved or pleased by our achievements. We recover our resting state relatively quickly. Joy gave an example of such a challenge.

> **Joy:** It was tremendously interesting, challenging and exciting. ... We would work through the night because suddenly ... we would be told, 'Look, you can't go home tonight because this paper has got to be read, we need costings,' or whatever. And we would be drinking coffee all night and we would be there absolutely wired getting this stuff. But we were on a journey together and we were going to give birth to something that was going to hopefully change the course for kids or, you know, whatever. And so I did all of that as a single person and it was wonderfully challenging, interesting.

By contrast, *distress* happens when our inner or outer resources to manage pressures are out of balance. We feel overtaxed, either by the size of a problem or its unexpectedness, or because demands have gone on over a long period of time without satisfactory resolution and we have not had time to recover our energy or replenish our resources. Perhaps, unlike Joy above, we have to balance competing work and family demands. That kind of stress has a negative effect on us and we may begin to feel discomfort, tension, tiredness or negative thoughts and feelings including self-doubt and anger.

Over time, tiredness, anger, frustration and irritation can all weaken the immune system. It is natural to try to avoid or withdraw from situations that cause such discomforts, or to block the feelings themselves, which can lead to behavioural impacts like absenteeism, job turnover, tardiness, poor job performance, and substance use (Caverley 2005). There is a link between the use of coping strategies such as disengagement and depersonalizing of clients, and eventual burnout. However, at least in the early stages, professional people often manage to contain their behaviours and feelings at work, but find they are more inattentive or argumentative at home.

Models for considering workplace stress

This discussion has brought some important questions to the fore: Are there job situations that tend to create heavy pressures or *demands*? Can we identify any particularly helpful *resources* for mitigating the impact of those pressures? Are there particular combinations of those factors that are more likely to result in the stress balance swaying to the positive or negative, toward eustress or distress? Are there models for understanding how these factors combine that may provide us with guidance on how to examine and improve the safety of workplaces?

There are indeed a number of generic workplace stress models that have been developed to provide frameworks for addressing these questions. They are not mutually exclusive, and combining them may enable us to achieve a more comprehensive overview than considering them in isolation.

One of the best known models of job stress is Karasek's (1979) *Demand–Control* model. This model has more recently been expanded to include considerations of support and has therefore now become the *Demand–Control–Support* model (Karasek and Theorell 1990).

Karasek's original hypothesis was that stress increases when high job demands in the form of workload or skill requirements are coupled with lack of control over decision-making. The model helps to explain how highly demanding jobs that offer autonomy and flexibility are found to activate and energize workers, whereas high demands and low levels of control lead to illness. This model has been tested in various cultural contexts, including in Europe, the United States, and the People's Republic of China. The theory that stress is mediated by control or job discretion has been found to hold true across these cultures (Landy and Conte 2007). When it persists over an extended period of time, lack of control over work can lead to learned helplessness and eventually to burnout (Collins and Parry-Jones 2000).

In applying the model to social work, we can see that social workers often become disheartened and dissatisfied when they lose the capacity to determine the scope of their role and the nature of their engagements with clients.

Since the concept of support has been added into the model, this now also recognizes the importance of adequately resourcing and encouraging workers, for example, by providing opportunities for learning and professional development, and supportive supervision.

Siegrist's (1996) *Effort–Reward Imbalance* model suggests that when people make efforts for which they do not feel rewarded, this creates a stressful imbalance. However, what counts as reward is clearly different for different people. Beyond adequate financial compensation, social workers may not be intrinsically motivated by monetary gains. They may prefer to forgo these if, for example, they can achieve a good moral fit (Vagg and Spielberger 1998; van Heugten 2002). Although this model is somewhat limited on its own, it helpfully draws our attention to rewards as resources, and feeling valued as nourishment.

Participants gave examples of situations that caused an imbalance of effort and reward including: Constant criticism in the media; risk averse supervision that appears more aimed at ensuring the organization will be safe from complaint; and time spent on fulfilling administrative requirements that have no clear benefits for clients.

French, Caplan and Van Harrison's *Person–Environment Fit* model (1982) emphasizes that stressors are not inherent in either an individual or in the work environment, but relate to the level of 'fit' of a person's abilities and needs and the demands from the environment and the resources it supplies. This is close to the familiar *ecological* perspective of social workers. Simply put, demands are stressful when they outweigh (*or* seriously under-utilize) a person's inner and outer resources including abilities, material resources, and support. An imbalance in person–environment fit can lead to distress, but it can also encourage coping. Coping can be achieved by altering the person or the environment; cognitively reframing the person's perceptions of self or environment; or withdrawing from the situation, including by leaving a job.

Aspects of the Person–Environment Fit (P–E Fit) model can be seen to be used in motivational recruitment techniques. Some questions are used to ascertain person–job fit: How well is the person equipped for the tasks of the job? How well does the job meet the worker's interest? Others are aimed at finding out whether the person–organization fit is good, for example by checking that the person's values match the organization's values (Landy and Conte 2007).

The differentiation of job and organizational fit is clearly relevant to thinking about social work. A social worker may be well suited to a job as the profession defines it, but less well suited to working in some organizations than others. The following experienced practitioners had very different views on working in the health sector.

> **Rachel:** I'm not good in a health setting. I don't like the hierarchy and all the things that come with it. And I left there and I went to an NGO [non-governmental organization] and … that was an amazing experience.
>
> **Joy:** And it's been, for me, really refreshing to come out of welfare and go into health again. I found health to be, it feels much more pro-active, positive, and with willingness to reflect and change. And not driven by people sitting up on high, but a real listening to the ground, the grassroots, you know, and tweaking and being willing to change from that level up.

The naming of the *environment* in the P–E Fit model should also draw our attention to physical and emotional comfort and ambience issues that may otherwise be overlooked. For example, participants found that noisy open plan environments with little private space to undertake conversations with clients or supervisors increased stress levels.

P–E Fit can also be impacted by uncertainty and change, which are currently features of many workplaces. Public services are frequently restructured, reformed and retrenched in the wake of economic recessions or a change in government. Workers in NGOs are uncertain about their ongoing employment or the retention of services that are provided under annual contracts. Uncertainty can be more distressing than certain negative events (Luckyj and Campbell 2009). Whether we find change exciting or frightening depends not only on our personal dispositions, but on the contexts of our lives, on whether we have some control over the direction and pace of changes, and whether we believe the changes are likely to lead to improved outcomes, in particular improved lives for clients.

> **Joy:** We restructure and we change things, and often it's the clients who are missing out while we try and forever get this right. And there is no right, you know, but we keep trying all of these things and meanwhile the frontline often suffers.

The P–E Fit model has been criticized, however, for the difficulty of testing the multiple factors that may be relevant. The concept of person–environment fit may also let employers 'off the hook' when it comes to considering why workers are unduly stressed, as they can claim that there 'was just not a good fit'. In at least some respects these criticisms, that the model is too broad, or too oriented to adaptation rather than radical critique, befall any ecological model that considers persons in context. The benefits of the P–E Fit model include that it enables us to take into account the broader context of work, for example the relationship between family and work demands, and laws that affect the domain of work.

The three models of job stress discussed above are relevant to thinking about what circumstances provoke eustress or distress for human service workers. In addition, it is helpful to understand how individual workers process pressures, as this too can help us to identify useful interventions.

From an ecological perspective, it makes sense that some demands would tax most, if not all, human beings *and* that people have different thresholds at which demands become distressing, depending on inner and outer resources. Lazarus and Folkman's (1984) theory of *cognitive appraisal* holds that the way we view a situation, for example as either a challenge or a risk, plays an important part in determining whether we will be energized or distressed. For example, when we think of a situation, such as a review of our services, as potentially harmful or likely to cause loss, this will be experienced as more distressing, than if the review is interpreted as likely to lead to rewards. Levels of stress are also impacted by what Lazarus and Folkman (1984) call *secondary appraisal*, being our assessment of the resources and coping mechanisms available to us for dealing with the situation (Oliver and Brough 2002).

Le Fevre *et al.* (2003) draw attention to the fact that we appraise stressors in a context when they write that:

> ❝ ... a stressor can be characterized according to its timing, whether it is perceived as desirable or not, whether it is beneficial or not, whether the demand is self-imposed or imposed externally, and if imposed externally, what that source (a friend, a manager, a policy, an institutional norm, etc.) represents to the individual. (Le Fevre *et al.* 2003, p.730) ❞

Responding to a stressor with positive cognitive appraisals minimizes the likelihood of distress, whereas negative cognitive appraisals maximize the chances of this. Maintaining hopefulness and making meaning are therefore associated with eustress (Le Fevre *et al.* 2003). We can learn about thriving by being alert to these messages from the field of cognitive psychology about how people sustain eustress. We can work on our thinking habits to reform tendencies to, for example, predict catastrophic outcomes or to notice only criticism rather than praise. However, whilst providing us with some buffers to stress, positive thinking is not a panacea.

More recently there has also been increasing recognition that job demands, environments, supports and rewards are experienced differently by people from different cultures (Pal and Saksvik 2008). In the human services, workers from ethnic minorities are sought after to provide culturally competent practice, but are not always appropriately resourced to undertake additional face-to-face work or attend to community networking. There continues to be overt, covert, and unintentional discrimination with respect to gender, ethnicity, age, sexuality, and abilities, aspects of which will be discussed in later chapters.

Pause for reflection

At this point you may like to make some notes about how you think your workplace conditions measure up when considered in the light of the above models. You may want to work in a linear fashion from one model to the next, or you may prefer to draw an eco-map with concentric circles depicting micro to macro environments, paying attention to demands, resources, supports and rewards within each. Consider and note how much control you or your staff have over situations, including over the pace of change. Is the concept of cultural diversity relevant? Don't forget that seemingly small demands or vexations can add together to be considerably exhausting.

The impacts of stress overload

Latterly, it has been realized that not only eustress, but even short-term negatively experienced stress may in fact have health benefits. Humans are adapted to experience many bursts of short-term stress lasting between minutes and hours. As long as the stress response system returns to a restful state following the bursts of activity, this is not necessarily detrimental and may in fact be beneficial, for example to our immune systems (Firdaus 2009).

Beyond such occasional short-term challenges, however, stress overload impacts on our physical, psychological, and behavioural functioning.

Physical signs of stress overload include skin irritations, allergies, under or oversleeping, headaches, muscle tensions (sometimes leading to chronic neck pain or repetitive strain injuries), and gastrointestinal upsets. Health risks are further exacerbated by smoking, drinking, and other substance use. Accidental injuries may also increase (Leka and Jain 2010).

Cognitively, we may find we have more difficulty prioritizing. What might be a series of challenging tasks under normal circumstances now becomes an overwhelming disorganized pile and we are unsure where to start to deal with it. We develop self-doubts, and might begin to think negatively about our competence.

The impact of stress is felt in all spheres of life, as performance and mood decline, not only at work but most frequently also at home. This may lead to relationships becoming less supportive just at a time when we need them most.

Participants talked about the ways in which they had learned to identify that they were overly stressed by tuning in to certain physical, psychological and emotional signs.

> **Joe:** I start having quite early morning waking, staying up late at night. Often when I wake up I'll be thinking about work stuff, so I'll be thinking about clients at work and, you know, issues at work and things like that. And I'll sort of wake at three or four in the morning and not be able to get back to sleep, so that's my warning sign that I kind of mainly look out for. I probably get a bit irritable with people around me and the family and stuff, mm. And when I get to that stage I usually try and make some changes that help affect it.
>
> **Teina:** Some people eat heaps. I don't eat because I just physically find it very difficult to eat. I usually sleep okay but I just can't eat. I lose weight, yeah, yeah, so that's how I know when I'm stressed.
>
> **Margaret:** It's quite a balance really and you can't always get it perfect, you can't always get it right. But when you see it's out of kilter, when you recognize – oh I'm not

getting any time to do the paperwork, I'm not getting a breather, I haven't been taking lunch because I'm working through ... so you can't even go to the toilet ..., for me, when I feel I haven't got enough time to pay attention to the detail I think, 'No, you need to reign back and take notice of that!' **"**

Pause for reflection

- Do you recognize yourself in any of these examples?
- Do you remember times when you felt particularly stressed? Where were you? What were you doing?
- What are the early warning signs of stress overload for you? Do you stop exercising, eat at your desk, and withdraw from your friends?
- Are there any early warning signs in your body, your thoughts, feelings, and any behaviours that you get into when you are alone or with others?

When we fail to take note of early warning signs, or lack the resources and support to moderate or meet demands, more serious problems can begin to develop. Stress may impair immune systems. Some of the serious illnesses that have been identified to increase in incidence in chronically overstressed workers include cancers and cardiovascular disease. Cognitively and behaviourally, a vicious cycle may develop whereby repeated experiences of lack of control can lead to learned helplessness and hopelessness, and giving up trying to change situations any further (Collins and Parry-Jones 2000). Job satisfaction can be negatively impacted, resulting in anxiety, depression or burnout.

Special types of distress: Vicarious trauma, compassion fatigue and burnout

If there is confusion about the use of the term 'stress', there is perhaps even more confusion about the meaning of *vicarious trauma, compassion fatigue* and *burnout*.

Vicarious trauma

Vicarious trauma occurs as a result of observing, hearing or reading about, commonly violent, trauma that has been experienced by others. It is therefore something that befalls human service workers more often than other professions, although, for example, train drivers who are unable to avert the death of a person attempting suicide by driving across train tracks, or engineers whose designs fail to safely support users are also liable to experience it.

Vicarious trauma is sometimes called secondary trauma, or secondary post-traumatic stress disorder (secondary PTSD). It does, in its symptoms of flashbacks, intrusive thoughts, avoidance, and hypervigilance closely resemble PTSD. Workers with vicarious trauma often experience a change in worldview, as do sufferers of PTSD. This change in worldview usually relates to the type of trauma – workers may for example see the world as a more violent place. Views of clients or the profession are not usually negatively impacted unless these are implicated as perpetrators.

Moosmann (2000) notes that burnout and vicarious trauma may have some symptoms in common, such as mood changes and irritability. However, the difference between them is that in vicarious trauma empathy is retained. Indeed, emotional responsiveness to trauma may be especially acute, and some authors think that when social workers are encouraged to be reflective and empathize without being taught how to also distance or otherwise buffer themselves, they are made vulnerable to vicarious trauma (Yip 2006).

The topic of vicarious trauma will be further explored in Chapter 5. At this point, it is important to note that, although 'diagnoses' often involve a set number of criteria, it is not helpful to think of vicarious trauma only at the most serious end of the spectrum because doing this precludes early intervention.

Compassion fatigue

Compassion fatigue also more commonly arises in helping professions. It does so generally speaking in the context of an overload of demands on our compassionate feelings over an extended period of time. As a result of this overload, our capacity for such responses becomes depleted. Figley (1995) wrote that compassion fatigue was 'a state of exhaustion and dysfunction, biologically, physiologically, and emotionally, as a result of prolonged exposure to compassion stress' (p.34).

To prevent compassion fatigue it is important to ensure that workers have a varied workload, privacy and space to process responses, and that they are educated about the impact of working with disadvantaged and sometimes difficult to assist clients. Weariness and a need for self-care should be normalized so that concerns can be discussed without shame (Bell, Kulkarni and Dalton 2003). In the early stages of compassion fatigue, workers are still able to empathize but begin to feel burdened and experience exhaustion at bearing the suffering of others. Rest, respite and a change of work pace or content may relieve compassion fatigue, but if it remains unrelieved, compassion fatigue may lead to burnout.

Burnout

Burnout is a gradual process that occurs over time, as an accumulation of fatigue leads to a state of exhaustion. The defining characteristics, which are a loss of the capacity for empathy and compassion and a growing cynicism, distinguish burnout from other types of stress reactions such as vicarious trauma. In addition people experience emotional exhaustion and a reduced sense of professional accomplishment. Since Freudenberger (1974) first coined the term, it has entered the common language of helping professionals, and there is a good understanding of key symptoms as shown by Joe.

> **Joe:** I would say that probably heading towards not having empathy for people would make me quite stressed. And so I was getting quite distressed about work and upset about things and I probably didn't have the perspective that I'd normally have. My perspective was probably out. Definitely irritable at work as well.

Burnout has received a significant amount of attention in the research literature, not least because it has been shown to result in many negative outcomes for workers and organizations. Workers who are burned out show increased health problems, less job satisfaction and loss of organizational commitment. They are not as productive even when they are present at work, and they are more likely to be intending to leave in the near or intermediate future (Thomas and Lankau 2009). At the organizational level, research has linked burnout to financial losses, accidents, and reductions in the quality of patient care in health care organizations (Demir, Ulusoy and Ulusoy 2003).

Similar impacts of burnout have been noted in child protection/ welfare services and were commented on by participants like Phoebe in the extract below. Although the term 'child welfare' is preferred by some authors and in some jurisdictions, I often revert to the term 'child protection' in this book. This was how participants tended to identify the aspect of their work with children and families that caused them most concern.

> **Phoebe:** And some people that stay [in the job], like a colleague, she has become so hard. ... And when she first went there it was like – wow, she is going to be a fantastic social worker! She really cared, she was there for the right reasons. But maybe burnout affects everyone differently. ... It's like the fire goes out, and it really pisses me off. All these social workers are coming out of [university], or wherever they are coming from if they go into [child protection work], and then they come out the other end probably not really wanting to be a social worker or not being as good as what they could have been.

Research suggests that the causes of burnout are related to job situational rather than worker personality characteristics, and so it is generally thought to be more helpful to focus on features of a job or workplace rather than on characteristics of a person when seeking to prevent this costly problem.

Maslach and Leiter (1997) identify six environmental sources of burnout:

- Work overload.

- Lack of control, including due to rigid regulations and tight monitoring.

- Insufficient rewards.

- Lack of fairness and respect in the workplace.

- Breakdown in the sense of community with colleagues.

- Value clashes or conflicts with respect to workplace missions.

You will find these issues reflected in the words of the participants throughout this book. For example, six participants said they had burned out or come close to burnout during their careers. They emphasized workloads as contributing factors.

> **Joe:** I went through burnout a few times. Well actually, I think for maybe a year or two I was perpetually in burnout with one of the roles I had. Most days I was working about 12 hours a day and ... I was also on call most nights as well, so I'd quite often get two or three calls a night. I was working for an NGO.
>
> **Cathy:** I was actually put in a position being kind of sole charge ... which was far too soon to be put in that kind of position basically. And although I enjoyed the work, I just burned out basically. It was just too hard. I was too young and too inexperienced to be able to look after myself adequately in that kind of position.

More recently, as part of the positive psychology movement, research has begun to attend to how burnout is avoided, and engagement and involvement are fostered. Job satisfaction, having a sense of being able to do a quality job, has been found important (Griffin *et al.* 2010). Job satisfaction requires a good enough fit between personal professional and organizational goals and the resources to be able to carry out a role to a satisfactory standard. Supportive teamwork and work atmospheres also appear to provide a buffering effect. Positive team experiences have been found to reduce intentions to leave in child welfare and mental health workers (Kyonne 2007; Lasalvia *et al.* 2009).

Participants who had experienced burnout or had observed its effects on their colleagues, pointed to the importance of managing workloads assertively, even in the face of a manager's demands that they take on more cases. They also set boundaries and avoided intrusions of work into home life, reduced work hours, and endeavoured to keep fit. Several participants were grateful that they had not been financially reliant on a well-paying job that no longer provided a fit with values or a sense of meaning, and had therefore been able to pursue alternative work options.

Starting a stocktake

Let us now review the above information by undertaking a beginning 'stocktake'.

- Have you had a physical health check lately? Yes, it is possible that your symptoms of stress, anxiety or exhaustion have physical causes, such as thyroid or cardiac disorders, or are due to substance use. Those extra coffees you drink to push yourself from one meeting to the next may be counterproductive. Participants emphasized that they did things to keep up their fitness levels and that exercise and healthy eating were helpful to them.

- How is the demand–control–support balance in your job? Is there a workload management plan in place? Are workers encouraged to have a say in your organization, especially about matters that fall within their professional purview, such as when clients should be referred or who should be employed to join the team? Are they micromanaged?

- Is adequate and relevant training provided? Is there sufficient support from supervisors, or do only line management imperatives get dealt with?

- Do workers feel rewarded for the work they do, financially, via development opportunities or by being otherwise recognized for their efforts?

- Are new staff members inducted into the organization's culture and mission and do you know if this mission still fits today?

- Are teams cohesive and communicating well?

- Is the work environment satisfactory for a diverse range of people? If not, what can be done to fix this?

- Are workers able to attend to important family matters? Does your employer allow you to take time off for important meetings with your children's teacher, or to accompany your mother to her health checks? Are you encouraged to take such time, or grudgingly allowed it?

- Are there regular workplace health checks or audits? The Social Work Taskforce and Social Work Reform Board have provided some helpful guidance (see the additional resources listed at the end of this chapter).

- Do staff members who express distress have ready access to confidential counselling services, for example Employee Assistance Programmes?

- When staff members leave, do they receive an exit interview and are their comments considered in efforts to improve human resource practices?

Staff members who are constantly in overload, not taking time out to have lunch or go for a walk, dreading coming to work, or feeling flat and deflated about work accomplishments are not experiencing a healthy work–life balance. Unpleasant work environments and lack of team cohesion negatively impact on communication between colleagues and on service to clients. This can have damaging consequences well before burnout is diagnosed in any team member. If a reduced or altered workload, additional support or a vacation no longer help to remedy the situation, or the problem returns or worsens soon upon return to work, then depression or burnout may be present (Canfield 2005).

By contrast with popular self-help books that emphasize personal change, most of the research emphasizes the need to make organizational changes to overcome high levels of workplace stress. In terms of individual approaches, generally positive results can be expected from maintaining a healthy lifestyle, supportive social relationships, and a positive goal-oriented approach to work. Cognitive behavioural interventions which seek to reinforce active coping skills may be best at reducing anxiety and enhancing coping and work satisfaction.

In this first chapter, we have begun to examine the causes of workplace stress, and sought to define some commonly confused concepts such as vicarious trauma and burnout. There has been some consideration of what may be helpful in preventing stress overload in general terms. In the next chapter these themes will be elaborated as we delve further into what is particularly stressful and conversely most resilience building for social workers.

Additional resources

The impacts of workplace stress

Leka, S. and Jain, A. (2010) *Health Impact of Psychosocial Hazards at Work: An Overview*. Geneva: World Health Organization. http://whqlibdoc.who.int/publications/2010/9789241500272_eng.pdf

Recent reports relating to pressures in social work (UK)

Social Work Reform Board (2010) *Building a Safe and Confident Future: One Year On*. Progress Report from the Social Work Reform Board. London: SWRB. www.education.gov.uk/swrb

Social Work Task Force (2009) *Building a Safe, Confident Future*. The Final Report of the Social Work Task Force. London: SWTF. http://publications.education.gov.uk/

Chapter 2

Stress in Social Work

Introduction

In Chapter 1, I introduced models of workplace stress that emphasize the impact of factors such as workloads, intellectually challenging work coupled with lack of control, and lack of resources, rewards and supports. But there are particular pressures on social workers along with many other human service workers, and these are discussed in this chapter.

After identifying some typical and current pressures in human service organizations and the impacts of these, this chapter will begin to explore interventions that have been found to be helpful. Different individuals and teams will require different approaches to preventing stress overload, but common to almost all is the benefit of support from colleagues, supervisors, mentors, families and friends. This chapter stresses the importance of managing workloads and involving workers in planning for change. Practical self-care techniques include cognitive and mindfulness-based approaches.

Worldwide, some of the pressures facing social workers are more common today than they were even a decade ago. The complexity and size of caseloads have increased, while at the same time, from the 1990s, human services have been impacted by a shift to neoliberal economic perspectives that favour market-driven policies and have led to reviews of welfare spending. The start of the global recession in 2008 significantly worsened financial situations and has led to further efforts to contain or reduce social spending. Frequent organizational restructurings, sometimes accompanied by redundancies, put pressures on human service staff as they endeavour to ensure service users are not disadvantaged by these changes. Efforts to reduce costs have resulted in the loss of some services, reduced time for client contact and networking with colleagues, and increasing competition for scarce resources between professional groups.

Participants in the book interviews spoke of a pervasive risk avoidant orientation that increased their administrative burdens, such as reporting requirements, without clear benefits to clients. Whilst research shows the benefits of providing supportive supervision, participants noted that some supervisors spent more time ensuring that they could verify that their supervisees had complied with expectations and met competency-based criteria.

Reports and initiatives, including from the Social Work Task Force (2009) and the British Association of Social Workers (2010), highlight the need to relieve the pressures on social workers, and provide some helpful guidance.

Is social work especially stressful?

We have been aware of stress in social work anecdotally for a long time and studies began to emerge from the 1980s (Bennett, Evans and Tattersall 1993; Dhooper and Byars 1989). For a time, until the 1990s, the literature focused on personality characteristics that were thought to contribute to difficulties in coping, but from the 1990s that emphasis began to shift to looking at organizational factors. Since then, there have been numerous surveys, and some smaller qualitative studies aimed at identifying levels and causes of stress overload.

Across the human services, social workers have been found to be unduly stressed. Child protection and mental health services stand out as being most stressful. In the health sector, the stress levels of social workers have been compared to stress levels of other human service providers such as nurses, psychologists, psychiatrists and occupational therapists (Coyle *et al.* 2005; Lloyd, McKenna and King 2005). Overall, it appears that the difference in stress levels between social workers working in different settings is less than the difference in levels of stress between social workers and other disciplines in the same setting.

Some research, including that by Evans *et al.* (2006) of mental health social workers in England and Wales, finds that job satisfaction is also lower in social workers. There are conflicting results and as some authors point out, workers can still find satisfaction despite high stress levels, because satisfaction comes from being able to help service users and doing something valuable. In such circumstances, job satisfaction may help to prevent burnout (Collins 2008). What can be expected then, is that when workers' ability to do meaningful work with service users is undermined, their capacity to deal with pressures will be negatively impacted. This happens when social workers doubt that they are making a difference, maybe because they have too many cases or too few resources, or because the ideals to which they subscribe are not given a high priority by their agency (Dollard *et al.* 2003; Lait and Wallace 2002).

In all, a conservative estimate would suggest that about one-third of social workers experience significant mental distress at any one time. More than half experience stress levels that are too high for comfort. As a consequence workers commonly report a lack of wellbeing, absences from work due to stress or sick leave, and wanting to leave work (Coffey, Dugdill and Tattersall 2004; Huxley *et al.* 2005).

In some fields such as child protection, high staff turnover and recruiting problems result in a vicious cycle of increased workloads for those who remain. This can lead to entire services developing a reputation for poor employment conditions. Nevertheless, some turnover is healthy. Moving sideways within a larger organization or moving to another agency is a way in which workers manage stress or avoid burnout.

> **Joy:** I guess the way that I've managed avoiding burnout, or if I've detected that I'm getting stale in the job, is that I've moved. I have never lingered and lurked about in work that I haven't felt passionate about and ... that's worked incredibly well for me. I feel like I've had a very rich and wonderful social work career and very varied. ... And that's been wonderful for me, and perhaps enabled me to stay in it, keep going, and feel like I'll keep going for as long as I choose because I love it!

But when too many workers change, negative consequences start to outweigh positive ones. There is more likely to be a lack of continuity of knowledge and consistency in approaches. It is generally accepted that an annual turnover in excess of 20 per cent indicates a problem. In statutory child protection agencies rates commonly exceed 30 per cent (Nissly, Mor Barak and Levin 2005) and as a consequence, as Joy also said, 'a kid might have ten social workers because they're constantly moving on because of the stress.'

Typical stressors in social work and human services

Prime stressors that were identified by participants are discussed below. Many of these pressures are interrelated. For example, when the values or the mission of the organization are not a good fit with our own, it is difficult to feel that our efforts are respected. It also becomes less likely that the work we believe in will be well resourced. The stressful impact of dealing with conflicting work and home life demands has received better recognition in recent years. This will be the focus of the next chapter.

High workloads and administrative demands

High workloads often come to mind when considering likely stressors, but this does not always need to be so. Several participants said that they thrived on being busy – within limits. Being busy is energizing when we feel our hard work is bringing good results that are being recognized. In addition, when we can trust that we will be supported to cut back our workloads if they do get too high for comfort, we may be able to take a fairly full load.

However, almost all of the social workers interviewed for the book said that workloads had increased to become unreasonably high over the last decade. Rachel thought a greater public willingness to report family violence was one of the causes of this increasing workload. Not only are there more cases to attend to, but people present with more complex problems, especially addictions and other mental health conditions. The associated administrative duties, such as documenting and reporting on investigations, may lead to overtime without any adequate compensation.

The need for careful documentation was well understood. However, some of the reporting requirements were considered to stem more from external demands to quantify 'outputs' that social workers thought peripheral to their roles, or from a risk management approach to ensure that the agency could demonstrate that practice had been 'safe'. Kris and Steve noted that the increasing administrative workloads do not provide a good fit for many social workers.

> **Kris:** I was warned to it on placement when a woman from [the UK] said that the admin and the hands on was about 70:30 … I've been active and out there most of [my working life] and now I'm behind a computer. Mm, that's been a big shock. It wasn't what I wanted to do.
>
> **Steve:** People don't enter the social work profession to be doing paperwork. I mean a physiotherapist probably has more people contact and time than a social worker!

Line managers with practice experience in the human services, not necessarily in social work, were thought to be better able to offer staff some protection against administrative overload.

> **Joe:** Management's probably quite keen on working out what we're doing day-to-day, trying to sort of keep our time schedules tight, making sure that we produce a lot of paperwork. Those sorts of things is probably what they're interested in. Whereas I think my line manager is much more interested in finding that we're helping people, that we're involved in doing clinical practice, thinking about what we're doing, keeping people safe. So I find that that's quite supportive for me.

Administrative requirements can be particularly onerous in non-governmental organizations (NGOs), where multiple contracts require reporting on services.

> **Steve:** I was working with an NGO and we had three different funders, so you had to do three separate forms of [statistics]. I think that hopefully they've collapsed it by now, but yeah, we had to do three different sets of stats for three different funders. Crazy!

As a manager, Amanda was well aware that reporting formats do not necessarily 'count' or fully value the work that practitioners believe to be most important.

> **Amanda:** I know what work is being achieved with the clients and I know it's phenomenal and I know that the outputs don't measure it accurately. I know that you are being given the contract based on the outputs but that you're not getting given the opportunity to accurately

report [efforts and outcomes]. And we can try to gather that information ... hoping that if someone comes along at least we can say, 'We know what we've done – we are doing that. We know what we're achieving – here's what we're achieving.' **"**

Workload management systems were not always in place. Poor workload planning not only led to distress in individual workers but raised tension levels in teams where colleagues felt case distributions were inequitable.

" **Ella:** I really think that it's very hard to do, but managers should try and have some sort of way of managing [and] measuring caseloads so that it is equitable, and that's something I didn't see at [the agency] at all. No, I don't see any attempt, not even just the basic, 'You can only have so many cases,' never mind weighting them for type of case or whatever. And it is something that is known to be really really hard to do. There's different [systems], there are time-based systems, and points-based or whatever, but I think, however imperfect, you need to have some way of doing that. Because you have to say, 'Well, this is the limit.' **"**

At times social workers were expected to be available in ways that exceeded their resources, and several participants pointed out that poor regard for boundaries could lead to exhaustion and eventual burnout.

" **Margaret:** They were grassroots NGOs so you are expected to be all things to all people, and when I tried to say, 'Well no, I'm not going to be answering the door at 11 o'clock at night to a client, I'm not going to let them have my home number,' and things like that, there was pressure ... because people felt if you said no, you were not helping people. Whereas I always said, 'Well in all reality you need to teach people to work within systems as well because the next worker may not be as available as I have been, and people need to understand there's differences in people and in agency criteria.' **"**

Expectations for indigenous workers can be particularly high because their cultural capacities are in great demand and scarce supply. Rewa was a Māori practitioner who said:

> **Rewa:** There's more expectations on you. ... You've got to be a lot more disciplined than mainstream [social workers], because the chances of you getting overloaded are so much easier because you're a 24/7 worker unless you can say no. And I can certainly say in earlier times I was a 'yes', because you want to change the world.

Huxley *et al.* (2005) found that, especially for women, working long hours poses a risk to mental health. They note that women, more often than men, feel pressured to work long hours. Women are also more likely to need to juggle work with family responsibilities. If workers can have control over workload planning and a say over what jobs are priorities, then satisfaction is higher.

Role conflicts and lack of clarity about the social work role

In multidisciplinary teams, especially in the health sector, social workers are found to experience more role conflicts than other workers. The reasons for this include a lack of clarity amongst other staff, generic managers and the public about the main roles of social workers. They may be expected to undertake only relatively menial tasks, such as filling out benefit forms or assessing people for rest home care, that do not draw on their full range of abilities.

The problem of lack of clarity about their roles and potential contributions is significantly upsetting for many social workers (Carpenter *et al.* 2003; Coyle *et al.* 2005; Evans *et al.* 2006). This does, however, improve with age and experience as social workers gain confidence and learn to articulate their capacities (Wiener 2006). Anthony noted that when there is trust amongst colleagues, they can learn from one another without feeling threatened by their disciplinary differences.

> **Anthony:** And we all sit around the table and we talk about casework and we are just all going, 'Oh is that what you do?' And it is actually not just challenging, I think it is really respectful. It is very very interesting how I think I have felt as a social worker. I am not somehow down the bottom of the knowledge hierarchy anymore. I am not kind of relegated to some position which means you get paid less and you get regarded, as my old supervisor used to say, 'Well Anthony, if you are going to do mental health work

you just have to understand you are a handmaiden. You are going to change your gender and you are going to go right down to the bottom of the scale.' I find myself delighted to pick up many good ideas [from other disciplines]. **"**

Lack of status and remuneration or other rewards

In addition to a lack of understanding of the social work role in health services in particular, social workers may experience a devaluing of their status. They may be doing similar work to other professionals, but be paid less, or receive fewer allowances.

" **Joe:** Nurses have been really vocal and so there's been some changes towards offering them more support. Sometimes we're not eligible for that. They might get free study, whereas we get quite heavily subsidized but not free study. They probably, for doing the same role they probably get paid 10 to 15,000 New Zealand dollars more than us, and that's around the way the contract's been negotiated last time ... So I think that's sometimes a bit difficult for the fact that we're doing the same role. **"**

Although pay may not be a primary motivator for social workers, inequalities in pay are experienced as a symbol of disrespect and unfair treatment. Furthermore, when pay rates within the occupation also vary, and in some agencies these are so low that workers struggle to make ends meet, they may feel forced to work longer hours or in less favourable circumstances than they would otherwise be prepared to accept. Resentment can then begin to be felt.

Value conflicts

For participants in this project, lack of clarity about roles became less stressful over time as confidence improved. Rates of pay led to some grumbles but did not appear to be a significant stressor. By contrast, however, value conflicts and loss of a sense of being able to carry out meaningful work that helped service users had caused debilitating levels of stress and were implicated in burnout. In discussing value conflicts, participants referred to concepts such as alienation, neoliberalism and managerialism, to explain how quantitative 'outputs' increasingly took precedence over quality attention to human needs. These concepts were also referred to by English social workers interviewed for the Social Work Task Force's Workload Survey (Baginsky *et al.* 2010). Amongst New Zealand social workers, Rewa had begun to question whether she should remain in the profession.

> **Rewa:** For me, as a practitioner, I get a bit sad about that. Because I wonder, why did I study, why did I work? … It's a bit disillusioning and that causes me a stress at this mature age. So I wonder – what the hell should I do? Do I want to stay in a social work profession that is not compassionate in my opinion but is task-centred and outputs driven?

Lloyd, King and Chenoweth (2002) undertook a literature review and found that for social workers, tensions between job demands and workers' values or philosophies impact on levels of stress. They note that social workers' ideals are more often in conflict with workplace expectations of outputs than the ideals of other professionals. Especially in health settings, social work ideals, such as ensuring clients have sufficient time to consider their options, are not always seen as being cost effective. Struggles with professional values that are at odds with organizational priorities contribute to burnout.

Inadequate resources to meet clients' needs

The most painful situations, which had kept social workers awake and were recalled by them over the years, had occurred in positions where they lacked resources to help their clients adequately, especially when those were children. Participants thought that, had they not left, they would have begun to feel hopeless and depleted. Resource problems cited included lack of adequate foster care placements; lack of social worker time; turnover of workers leading to discontinuity in services; and changes in government funding for services. Anthony summarized the sentiments of several other participants when he said:

> **Anthony:** But what is probably the most distressing thing, is how do we go home and sleep at night when we know our children are alright and some other child that we know is relying on us isn't. We just kept on saying to ourselves, 'Well it is the best system we've got, the Family Court system is the best system. It is very tricky but it is the only one we've got.' Huh – which is never quite okay.

Other researchers note the stress inherent in working with chronically impoverished clients. They suggest that social workers can experience a parallel process, whereby they begin to feel despondence and hopelessness like their clients, which is then further reinforced when no change occurs in the circumstances of those clients. Over time, as part of a coping mechanism, despondency can lead to withdrawal and depersonalization of clients. Israeli researchers have noted that workers may begin to blame clients, rather than socioeconomic circumstances, for their failure to emerge from poverty. They suggest that adopting a strengths-based perspective, and creating active partnerships with clients may buffer social workers from developing hopelessness (Krumer-Nevo, Slonim-Nevo and Hirshenzon-Segev 2006), which, as we also saw in Chapter 1, has been linked to burnout.

Lack of control or job discretion

In Chapter 1 we saw that when jobs are demanding, having a lack of control is predictive of workplace stress. Looking a little more deeply into this suggests that human service workers feel particularly troubled when they are not included in decision-making about matters that impact on service delivery. They may be happy to have certain decisions made without their involvement, but not clinically pertinent ones.

Margaret felt frustrated because the work that her NGO had been contracted to undertake failed to properly match the needs of service users. She went on to say, 'The challenge of that is somewhat out of our control because you can't necessarily drive to change another system. … But you know that … the system is not a human system … it's not really working.'

While the above comments about the stresses resulting from value differences, lack of resources and lack of job discretion arise in the New Zealand context, they are strongly echoed in international research. For example, McLean and Andrew (1999) report on results of the analysis of a sub-sample of 451 managers and 512 social workers amongst a total of 2031 social service workers across England, Scotland and Northern Ireland, who had taken part in face-to-face workforce surveys in 1993–94 and again in 1995–96. Whilst managers and social workers derived satisfaction from feeling they had done a good job, helping people and having satisfied clients, four out of five had experienced undue levels of stress in the last year. Stress was increased when workers' values were out of step with those of the organization, and when they were not able to obtain what service users needed due to a lack of resources. Having responsibility but no power was a common theme.

Poor image and excessive public and political criticism

Social workers receive much criticism from a broadly defined 'public', including politicians, and other professionals. This can be painful to workers who are already inclined to self-evaluate their efforts with the wisdom of hindsight. The problem of the degraded public image of social workers has also been noted by the Social Work Task Force (2009). The Task Force's report recommends improving public education about the social work role. This may offer a partial answer, but, as Ella noted, the kinds of situations in which social workers are required to intervene, can give rise to so much anxiety that there is a tendency for people to search for someone in a position of responsibility to blame.

> **Ella:** I would say the perception of schools, some health professionals, you know there is a general saying, 'Oh they just don't do anything' or, 'They will do something that is too extreme.' And obviously in situations of child protection other professions are trying to manage their own anxiety about the situation so they'll be maybe wanting the child removed or not wanting a child removed, and the social worker's sort of caught in this bind of trying to manage how they're feeling in the situation and keep some sort of professional judgment around what is actually happening, and then that's really really stressful. And on top of which then, if you have in the wider media and in the wider society, which you do have in New Zealand and in the UK, that sort of [perception], 'Well you know social workers – aren't they terrible!' I mean, that hugely adds to people's stress.

In Chapter 8 we will look more closely at the stresses experienced by social workers who need to make balanced decisions in a context of uncertainty and in a culture increasingly saturated by risk, blame and complaint.

Aggression from service users

Participants noted that aggression from service users has become more prevalent. Violence directed toward human service workers by clients and their families or friends is a significant and serious problem, and is the subject of Chapter 6. Violence is anxiety provoking and can be traumatizing to the extent that workers may develop post-traumatic stress disorder (PTSD). It is more likely to lead to burnout when coupled with lack of support and work overload.

Team conflict and lack of supervisory and managerial support

Team conflict is distressing and prevents social workers from gaining access to resilience building opportunities that arise in supportive cohesive peer groups. For participants, conflict arose in child protection teams, for example around workload distributions. In health sector interdisciplinary teams it arose around such issues as the social worker's opinion that resources needed to be put in place prior to a service user's discharge.

In Chapter 7, bullying and mobbing are discussed as some of the most distressing and debilitating encounters experienced at work. Several participants in the book interviews also discussed experiences of bullying. However, most were currently in supportive teams and they found this greatly enhanced their enjoyment of work. Teams provide opportunities to debrief and learn as well as to socialize. The use of humour is clearly an important tool for stress relief. Humour also expresses trust and a shared understanding of the difficulties of work.

Whilst most participants were happy with their current supervisors, most could reflect back on unsatisfactory arrangements.

66 **Joy:** I would go to supervision and she would talk more about herself, about her agenda. And it wasn't about me being able to go and actually being able to discuss my work, reflect on it, and you know, think about a context, about what I might currently be doing or whatever. It was railroaded constantly by her needing to talk about herself really. ... But people get promoted into management roles but they've never been taught how to be a supervisor, they don't do the training and it's just assumed that because they're experienced as a social worker they will now be

> effective in a supervisory role or a managerial role. And often social workers don't make really effective and good managers. They weren't trained as managers, they haven't been in a business model or whatever was required. **,,**

By contrast, excellent internal supervisors or line managers insist on workload management plans, protect workers from unwarranted criticism, offer praise, and, importantly, listen first, before making recommendations. External supervisors may be well placed to support clinical and professional development, but it is more difficult for them to impact specific workplace stressors and to ensure workloads are contained or training opportunities are funded. They may more frequently encourage their supervisees to leave an agency as a way of overcoming difficulties.

Physical work environments

Several pertinent issues were raised in relation to physical work environments. The need for high levels of security in some workplaces could make these appear unfriendly or even intimidating. Also, in both the book-related interviews, and in my research into bullying, open plan social work offices were generally considered to afford too little privacy. I was surprised to hear that these settings are sometimes used to carry out the bulk of supervision sessions. Ella said, 'Lots of managers will do most of the supervision like the casework supervision at their desk so they can input it straight into the computer because [the separate interview] room wouldn't have a computer.'

Teina, who was a Māori practitioner, did favour the companionship she found in a more open office setting, where colleagues were more likely to visit and talk informally with one another.

Lack of work–life balance

Approximately half of the participants had children. Others cared for parents or other family members. They stressed that family took precedence over work demands. Several had made career choices in an effort to protect family members, for example from potential violence when threats were made. Family and friends also provided support, interestingly, often by *not* asking about work, but instead allowing the participant time to unwind and focus on other interests.

An important message from participants, from my personal experience, and from other research, is that loyalty is built when workplaces enable workers the flexibility to attend to family needs. The next chapter explores the interconnectedness of stress in personal and professional lives in more depth.

What to do about stress for social workers

Links can be seen between the stressors identified above and the models of workplace stress that were introduced in Chapter 1: The *Demand–Control–Support* model, the *Effort–Reward Imbalance* model and the *Person–Environment Fit* model. What is also evident, however, is the particularity of what count as demands, rewards, and fit for social workers.

The need to feel that one is doing a good enough job for service users is paramount. Beyond reasonable pay rates and allowances, the most significant rewards and satisfactions are found in being able to help service users. If provided with adequate resources for clients, social workers will be less stressed, even if their offices or transport are less than salubrious. Ethical and value conflicts can drive social workers out of agencies to seek alternative employment, enter private practice, or even abandon the profession (van Heugten 2002).

To protect them from stress overload, social workers need to be supported to strike a balance between caring for their clients, ensuring they represent clients' needs and have adequate resources to support them, and keeping boundaries on excessive demands from those same service users, their employing agencies and the wider public. In the next part of this chapter we will examine measures that have been found helpful in assisting social workers to achieve or maintain that balance.

Workload management and workforce planning

Internationally, workloads have reached critical levels in some organizations, notably in statutory child protection services (Evans and Huxley 2009). Not only are caseloads high, but the complexity of the work is increasing.

Stevens (2008) notes workload management for social workers has received increasing attention in the UK in recent years. This followed on from the recognition that workloads are implicated in increased stress levels and burnout and hence impact on job satisfaction, wellbeing of workers, turnover rates, and practice outcomes for clients. In the UK, The Department of Health and the Department for Education and Skills as well as the Social Work Taskforce (2009) and Social Work Reform Board (2010) have called for better workload management systems in social care agencies in order to improve worker effectiveness and outcomes for service users (Stevens 2008).

Before workloads can be managed, they must be measured. As Ella noted earlier in this chapter, workload measurement should not rely on a simplistic counting of cases but assign weightings for complexity. In addition, it needs to take account of staff characteristics such as skill levels and experience (Stevens 2008). Types of work done also differ across services and some approaches, such as intensive early intervention programmes, clearly require more investment of time and emotional energy. Intensity of administrative requirements, such as court report writing and recording of detailed case notes all need to be taken into consideration. Whilst this is why we can't devise a 'one size fits all' workload formula, there is no excuse for failing to tackle the issue. The finding that some organizations have no workload management systems in place, that staff worry about becoming sick or taking leave because there is no backup plan, that some are working full days only to go on call over evenings and during weekends, is unacceptable. It may be in contravention of labour laws.

High workloads are distressing because they prevent workers from providing timely, consistent and reliable services. They may lead to poor practices, such as the neglect of cases that are progressing well but still need support (Juby and Scannapieco 2007). Several participants thought that managers who had not worked on 'the frontline' were less often aware of the importance of a balanced workload that allowed room for dealing with crises. Unexpected assignments of cases, including via the computer rather than in face-to-face allocation meetings, led to additional stress and were thought to be unacceptable, but they continued nevertheless. One manager had noticed that whenever she was ill and not present at allocation meetings to forestall it, her team would have cases 'dumped' upon it.

Transparent workload measurement tools can help workers hold their line managers to account, with less fear that aspersions will be cast on their professional capacity to cope with demands. They can also assist line managers or supervisors to protect their teams.

In addition to the immediate need to measure and manage staff workloads, workforce planning is both crucial and difficult, due to high levels of sickness-related absence, failure to recruit new staff and an ageing workforce. Some authorities are paying high wages to attract locum agency staff, including from overseas (Evans and Huxley 2009). Referring to her experiences in the UK, Ella noted this is doing little to improve stability for service users, and increases dissatisfaction amongst permanent members of staff who are paid significantly lower wages. This concern is also reported in the Social Work Task Force's workload survey (Baginsky *et al.* 2010).

Education, induction and ongoing training

Social workers may increasingly find that the reflective work that they were educated to do is considered less desirable by employers in today's workplaces. Many writers point to the neoliberalization of workplaces whereby financial imperatives override social considerations. An associated technocratization of work fragments social workers' roles and tasks so that they are required merely to provide their assigned part of a service. Social workers have expressed concern that the coherence of their practice, and their relationships with service users, are disrupted by these changes. An example of this is when needs assessments are separated out from service allocation in health and social care for older persons (van Heugten 2011a).

Given these pervasive shifts in the way social work is constructed, students and new graduates have a right to be forewarned that there is likely to be some discrepancy between the ideals they have been taught and what they may be asked to do in practice (McDonald 2007).

Similarly, students should not stumble upon words like 'vicarious trauma' and 'burnout' for the first time when already in practice. When I introduce students to these issues their responses are overwhelmingly positive: They feel cared about and better prepared to look out for warning signs of stress. They enter the workplace understanding that to be impacted by human service work is normal, and it is hoped that they will not feel too ashamed to tell their supervisors if they struggle to cope.

Bronstein, Kovacs and Vega (2007) surveyed 179 members of the National Association of Social Workers in the USA who worked in health care to find out about the fit between education as portrayed in standard texts and social work practice. They found that social workers wanted to be better informed about teamwork, including the ways in which other disciplines function and are trained; managed care (short-term interventions); crisis interventions; organizational dynamics; accreditation and business-related content; ethics; death, dying, grief and loss; diagnosis (including mental health) and treatment; administration and supervision; and cultural diversity.

The Social Work Task Force (2009) emphasized that educators, employers and professional bodies should consult with one another about educational imperatives. This is sensible advice, but perhaps less straightforward than might appear at first glance. Tensions are likely to exist between the beliefs of educators who maintain that pre-professional education should focus on developing a capacity for critical analysis, and the demands of employers for work-ready graduates (van Heugten 2011a).

In addition to pre-professional education, the training with which workers are provided in their transition from education to work is therefore also of vital importance. The Social Work Task Force (2009) emphasized this point by recommending that the first year in practice should be better supported and assessed. When there is a shortage of workers and high turnover, investments in induction can be patchy and enshrinement of its importance into regulations may encourage adherence. But even when in-service training does occur, high workloads can soon deplete enthusiastic new workers.

> **Phoebe:** They have great training, they have great training aye. And they send you on all this great training, and then you come back to reality and within a week or two it's just like, oh I can't even remember I went there.

Jaskyte (2005) considered the means used to socialize newly qualified Master of Social Work graduates from two university programmes in the southern USA into human service organizations. She found that beginning social workers lack knowledge about their role, the roles of colleagues and the way in which these fit together in organizations.

The bureaucratic structure of the workplace can bewilder them and they don't yet have the experience to practically step through value conflicts. Organizational socialization can assist with this by increasing familiarity with expected roles in the organization for the worker, improving understanding of line management, and of policies and processes required to be adhered to.

Socialization can consist of formal training or informal mentoring, and be individual or group-based. Sequential socialization, which builds knowledge of tasks and of how one role leads to another, may be especially helpful. Orientation programmes and orientation job assignments that are delivered to small groups can also assist in the building of supportive networks in cohorts.

Interestingly, some research has suggested that *not* asking new workers to change, and instead telling them that the values and knowledge they bring are respected, leads to lower role ambiguity and conflict. Ensuring social workers feel valued by their colleagues for what they can contribute to the organization, and helping them to transfer perspectives and values from their previous role into their new one is supportive (Jaskyte 2005).

In view of the frequency with which good intentions with respect to socialization and induction give way to shortcuts due to workload management problems, written induction manuals should be developed and the provision of adequate induction should be audited as also recommended by the Social Work Task Force (2009).

Continuing education is a requirement of registration for social workers in most countries. Practitioners are sometimes sceptical about the support they receive from in-service training when this is overly geared to their agency's needs and requirements. Externally provided training may enable attendees to ask more critical questions. Training can also become a burden when it is not carefully matched to workers' needs or when workers have to frequently retrain to use systems they consider to be of questionable benefit (Beddoe 2009; Williams 2007).

In all, appropriate and timely education and training build knowledge and confidence, and, if undertaken as part of a group, encourage the establishment of a supportive network of peers. The latter may be especially helpful in lowering emotional exhaustion (Cohen and Gagin 2005).

Supervision, mentoring and team support

Supervisors, line managers, mentors, teams and professional associations are all vital to the provision of instrumental, emotional and social support.

Supportive supervision relates positively to job satisfaction even when workloads are high. Appropriate *instrumental* support from knowledgeable supervisors guides workers in 'what' to do, 'when' and 'how' to do it. It assists workers to realize what resources and networks are available, and encourages them to appropriately refer service users. This can help to reduce workloads (Juby and Scannapieco 2007). In addition to demands on time, there will be client expectations that cannot be met, and scarce resources that have to be distributed. This requires social workers to develop a capacity to accept that their reasonable efforts are 'good enough'. Internal supervisors and line managers can protect social workers from excessive demands from service users and from the organization itself, and help them to set limits.

Emotional support from a supervisor is one of the strongest buffers against occupational stress and yet the need for this gets easily overlooked in busy, risk obsessed workplace environments. Supervisors who first listen and help workers unpack their emotional responses to difficult situations are more helpful than supervisors who immediately analyze and critique what has, could, and should be done about that situation.

When imperfect resources do not allow social workers to do as good a job as they know they could, supervisors need to be willing to hear about workers' regrets and allow the worker to grieve. The difference between intention to leave and actually leaving lies in management practices and satisfaction with immediate supervisory relationships. The care and attention paid to workers as human beings are critically important (Davys and Beddoe 2010; Tham 2007).

Dollard *et al.* (2003) suggest that doing emotional work is especially stressful for human service workers. Emotional work involves coping with one's own feelings when confronted with difficult situations at work. They propose that the capacity to balance emotional engagement and disengagement is a valuable tool in moderating stress, and emotionally competent supervisors play a key role in teaching this. In addition, whilst external supervisors and mentors have less control over internal resources and workloads, they too can assist workers to develop boundaries and manage expectations and emotions.

Basic cognitive tools for developing the capacity to balance emotional engagement and disengagement are introduced in the stocktake toward the end of this chapter. The topic of setting emotional boundaries will also be revisited in Chapter 5, where we will look more closely at coping when working with trauma.

Several participants expressed a concern that social work supervisors and managers might not have received training for their current position and were ill-equipped for it. In view of the clear message from research about the vital role that supervisors play in ameliorating stress overload, there should be more investment in training of supervisors, a lessening of the ratio of supervisors to workers, and careful consideration of how we might reduce turnover of supervisors (Nissly *et al.* 2005).

Social work managers similarly need support and training about matters such as budgeting, including for staff development, and education about different management approaches and how these fit into the organization. In the USA, the National Network for Social Work Managers is an organization that was set up in the mid-1980s to establish a resource for social workers involved in agency management in recognition of the complex nature of this role (Wimpfheimer 2004).

Mentoring by people at a more advanced level of professional development may be additionally helpful for workers at all levels and not just during induction. This could help prevent rather than merely endeavour to treat burnout. It has been found that mentors who sit outside the line management or internal supervisory structure are able to help improve socialization to a profession, but not reduce role stress. This is probably so because they have little influence over the actual job done in the particular settings. Mentors may be especially helpful to overall career development and can be chosen for particular qualities or capacities that the mentee wants to enhance. Several of my participants referred to mentors as resilient people who modelled a capacity for occupational achievement without compromising high levels of integrity and professionalism. Because mentoring demands different skills and a different relationship with mentees, supervisors and line managers are not usually able to fill that role. Strong leadership by supervisors and line managers, coupled with external mentoring may be the most effective combination (Thomas and Lankau 2009).

On a day-to-day basis, colleagues fulfill most instrumental, emotional and social support needs. Assurances from colleagues that support will be available, even if it is rarely necessary, creates a resource surplus that provides a buffer against distress (Dollard *et al.* 2003).

Colleagues are particularly well placed to offer one another *social support*. Social support provides a sense of being connected and appreciated in the communities in which we live and work. It counters isolation, is vital to a sense of wellbeing, and may reduce turnover even when stress levels are high (Collins 2008; Nissly *et al.* 2005).

Team cohesion is built when members work together on problem solving and participate in cross-disciplinary training. Organizations further enhance the sense of inclusion of all staff when they pay attention to a diverse range of needs, and recognize these differences in human resource policies and practices (Acquavita *et al.* 2009). By contrast, unfairness, including in allowances, leads to envy and communication problems.

There is also strong positive payoff when workplaces encourage teams to engage in social activities.

> **Rachel:** It becomes hugely important that the team culture, that team environment is 'wow'. ... And the site leadership makes a huge difference, because it lets the bakeoffs and the bits of fun happen but keeps the momentum going with all the other [work], yeah.
>
> **Val:** We have fun, we do fun things together ... so she has organized for us to take time out to do that ... There is not a lot of money or a lot of time spent on those things but they make a difference to enjoying the job.

Several participants had joined the Aotearoa New Zealand Association of Social Workers, or continued their membership even though this was not required by their workplace. They noted that they did this so that they could retain professional links.

Other support avenues that have received some attention in the literature include online chat groups, bulletin boards and Listservs (electronic mailing lists). At present, research suggests that as an ongoing avenue for support they are overly time consuming, can lead to message overload, and the burdening of some members by others. Advice may be poor, and security can be a problem if confidential material is inappropriately posted (Meier 2002). However, these methods of networking may be helpful around particular topics, and may also facilitate the provision of continuing education via a distance. I expect that more recently educated social workers may engage more strongly with such resources. The potential uses and problems associated with electronic support systems should be covered in training, and this topic is likely to become more relevant in the near future.

Involving workers in change processes

Social work practice has changed significantly across a range of services and the pace of this change is continuing unabated. Several participants expressed their concern that 'top–down' management-led changes that were introduced without adequate consultation with frontline staff hindered rather than improved their capacity to meet the needs of service users.

For human service workers to be comfortable with changes, these need to be explained in terms of impacts and improvements for service users. Transitional accommodations need to be in place to minimize negative impacts on clients. Workers may also be daunted by changes if they lack confidence about being able to carry out any new tasks that may be involved. When that happens, change can negatively affect workers' sense of accomplishment (Acker 2009). NGO workers become disheartened when they have felt proud of services they have helped to establish, only to see those axed when funding is pulled.

It is important to recognize that such pressures are being experienced by all of the helping professions. So when an organization is restructuring, or funding is reduced so that clients' needs are not as well able to be met, this is likely to make an impact on all of the disciplines. Previously cooperative team relationships may become strained when competition over scarce resources increases.

To ease communication problems, Nissly *et al.* (2005) recommend greater involvement of staff in planning for change, and surveying of staff to explore their opinions. Several of the social workers interviewed for this book noted with approval that they were increasingly being asked to participate in developing change proposals relating to service delivery.

Coping with the impact of emotional labour

Dwyer (2007) notes that much emotional work is hidden from others and remains in the psychological world of the practitioner. Yet social workers are in their jobs precisely because they care, and so they can be expected to feel distress at unfortunate outcomes. Whilst they know that they are going to face difficult situations, what makes their work especially hard is the harshness of the way in which they can be criticized if things go wrong, even when that could not have been foreseen or prevented. By contrast, colleagues, supervisors and managers who recognize their efforts help them to build emotional resilience. Phoebe had found a good fit.

> **Phoebe:** It has just been so good to be away from that whole environment and to go to a new place of work and … to actually be told by colleagues and my manager that we do respect you, we do value you, you are a good social worker, the skills that you bring are great. And that has been so good and that has been quite healing.

While it should by now be clear that organizational rather than personal factors are most central to protecting human service workers from stress overload, the research literature does provide some clear directions in terms of additional personal development tools that individuals can use to build resilience to stress.

Cognitive approaches have a good track record in relation to helping workers put potentially stressful situations into a broader perspective (Collins 2008). They can help us to differentiate the things for which we are responsible and that we can control, from the things for which we are not responsible. Techniques such as challenging hindsight bias and addressing tendencies to assume sole or too much responsibility for meeting service users' needs can be fairly quickly learned, although they require diligence to consistently apply. Self-help books provide basic recommendations and some are included in the additional resources listed at the end of this chapter (Branch and Willson 2007; Knaus 2008; Stahl and Goldstein 2010). If, however, your patterns of self-talk are ingrained or you are significantly distressed, you may like to consider a course of counselling or psychotherapy.

Several participants in my interviews used cognitive restructuring (reframing) techniques – even if they did not identify these by name.

> **Val:** I learned to externalize it. Previously I had internalized everything and now I became able to externalize. So that's made a huge difference for me, is recognizing that what people are reacting to, what people aren't happy about, is very seldom me. It might be that they are insulting or nasty to me, but it's not because of me.
>
> **Steve:** I think that you need to have the belief that you've done what you have to do, what you need to do, and then that's it. You're not responsible for people's decisions. ... And it's not a seven day a week job, you should not have to worry about clients outside of work hours.

More recently, there has been a marked surge in interest in mindfulness-based approaches to coping with workplace stress. The concept of mindfulness may be of help to social workers seeking to attune with their clients and themselves. The three tenets of mindfulness are *intention, attention* and *attitude*. The intention refers to a purposeful focus on a personal goal or vision, which may be the reduction of anxiety. Attention should be on the here and now. The ideal attitude is non-judgmental, including of one's own thoughts and feelings (Turner 2009). This acceptance-based approach contrasts with cognitive interventions, which tend to be more challenging of our thinking patterns, but there is an emerging interest in integrating these approaches (Sherman and Siporin 2008). One participant was currently doing mindfulness training, and another was practising Buddhist meditation.

> **Margaret:** I go swimming and I am doing mindfulness training at the moment. I must be pretty mindful anyway because I do take pleasure in watching the moon, and enjoying the view as I am driving. I am not on autopilot, I am taking in the beauty and the fact that I am driving past the river and it looks really beautiful.

Suggested benefits of mindfulness-based approaches to stress include improved self-attunement and affect regulation that then enable greater openness and empathy in encounters with service users and colleagues (Turner 2009). This suggests mindfulness may deepen social workers' reflective capacity without exposing them to stress overload. However, mindfulness practices can bring into focus some unexpected thoughts, feelings and experiences and this may lead some people to decompensate if they have been keeping control via suppressing or repressing these. It is important to be aware of that potential. There is no 'right way' to begin to practise mindfulness. Simply remembering to be present in the moment, to be conscious of a service user as a human being, and to ground oneself before a session or meeting with the intention of remaining conscious of whatever emerges, is a good start.

For those keen to explore mindfulness training further, courses are relatively readily available and some positive evaluations of results are emerging. Poulin *et al.* (2008) found mindfulness training can help with stress and burnout experienced in human services and appears to improve immune functioning. They provided four 30-minute training sessions to nurses, who were also asked to practise the methods they had learned for 15 to 20 minutes per day. The researchers used the Maslach Burnout Inventory to examine the three dimensions of burnout – emotional exhaustion, depersonalization, and reduced personal accomplishment (Maslach and Jackson 1986). They also applied a Satisfaction with Life Scale (Diener *et al.* 1985) and the Smith Relaxation Disposition Inventory (Smith 2001). Mindfulness training reduced emotional exhaustion in the intervention group so that it became the same as that in a control group of nurses.

Similar results were found with student teachers. Whilst the researchers recognize that burnout tends to be more related to organizational factors than to personal factors in workers, they note that mindful human service workers can use these techniques to enhance awareness of organizational issues and work on the transformation of those broader systems (Poulin *et al.* 2008).

Finally, also in relation to self-care, participants in the book interviews talked about eating healthily, playing sport, listening to music, dancing and praying. The subject of maintaining a healthy work–life balance is expanded in the next chapter.

Continuing your stocktake

The stocktake of demands, resources and supports for your work that you started in Chapter 1 can now be refined:

- Does your organization use appropriately weighted workload measurement tools? Are workloads actively managed? Are they reviewed on a regular basis? Is there a workforce planning mechanism in place? What will happen if one or more staff members become ill for a time?

- Do you have a robust induction programme that is adhered to, even in the busiest of times? Is your in-service training timely and responsive to the needs of workers, or might it lead to further overload?

- Do you have access to externally provided continuing education opportunities?

- Do you have regular supervision? Is your supervisor attentive and supportive? Are your learning and communication styles well matched? Does your supervisor encourage and help you to take a goal-oriented approach to your responsibilities? Is there opportunity for reflection? If not, what are the processes in place to help you address your needs?

- Is there a good atmosphere in your team? Are you having fun together? If not, what can be done to facilitate this?

- Do you have sufficient resources to help your clients, or are these limited and unstable?

- Is change well managed? This means affected staff members are consulted and understand the positive outcomes that are expected, and training in new systems is provided before implementation.

- Are you able to get involved in decision-making in relation to your organization's goals now and into the future? Are your concerns and ideas for improving service delivery solicited and followed through?

- Importantly, remember why you are doing this work and what inspires you, and be kind to yourself in thoughts and actions. If you lack support, you are entitled to be assisted to find it.

You are also entitled to have the energy to enjoy your life outside of work. We take a closer look at that in Chapter 3.

Additional resources

Stress reduction: Self-help

Branch, R. and Willson, R. (2007) *Cognitive Behavioural Therapy Workbook for Dummies*. Chichester, Sussex: John Wiley & Sons.

Knaus, W. J. (2008) *The Cognitive Behavioral Workbook for Anxiety: A Step-by-Step Program*. Oakland, CA: New Harbinger Publications.

Stahl, B. and Goldstein, E. (2010) *A Mindfulness Based Stress Reduction Workbook*. Oaklands, CA: New Harbinger Publications.

Stress reduction: Textbook

Lehrer, P. M., Woolfolk, R. L. and Sime, W. E. (eds) (2007) *Principles and Practice of Stress Management*, 3rd edn. New York: Guilford Press.

Management and supervision

Coulshed, V., Mullender, A., Jones, D. and Thompson, N. (2006) *Management in Social Work*, 3rd edn. Basingstoke, Hampshire: Palgrave Macmillan.

Shohet, R. (ed) (2006) *Passionate Supervision*. London: Jessica Kingsley Publishers.

Website of the National Network for Social Work Managers: www.socialworkmanager.org

Chapter 3

Stress in Your Personal and Professional Life

Introduction

This chapter addresses the way that demands in our personal and professional lives intersect in complex ways that are unique to each of us, and how we can continue to practice effectively and ethically when faced with challenging personal circumstances. Personal backgrounds impact on motivations, beliefs, perspectives, and relationships with colleagues, supervisors and clients.

Difficult experiences are not uncommon amongst human service workers, and these can lead to valuable insights and the building of resilience, provided they have been appropriately processed. Topics covered in the chapter include: Reconnecting with your reasons for pursuing social work or another human service career; being aware of the potential for retraumatization when engaged in reflection; dilemmas and ethics of disclosure; seeking help as and when necessary; valuing strengths achieved through adversity; and maintaining work–life balance.

If you have been, or plan to be, in social work for a time, it is likely that at some stage (and usually on a number of occasions) personal life events will affect your professional capacity. These events might include the birth of children, marriage, an illness or disability experienced by yourself or by a member of your family, a bereavement or separation. Advice is given on how to manage the impacts of such difficult personal events at work, and examples are drawn from the participants' and my own experiences to illustrate how decisions may be made about disclosure or non-disclosure. It is not always possible to control or choose whether to disclose personal matters. Self-care, support from colleagues and family, and organizational provisions are again central considerations.

Personal backgrounds: How did you get here?

Do you remember what first brought you to social work? Who were your role models? What were your experiences? If I look back on my own journey, I do seem to fit the profile of a 'parentified child' (Lackie 1983). When I was 13, the oldest child in a family of six children, I lost my mother after a protracted illness and quickly stepped into a caretaking role. Many human service professionals will be able to imagine what this might entail from personal experience rather than bookish learning, as it has been found that backgrounds of socioeconomic hardship, parental loss, family mental illness, or other trauma are common (Buchbinder 2007; Stevens and Higgins 2002). However, it remains unclear whether this incidence is higher than in the general population or amongst the professions. It is possible that social workers are more alert to the potential relevance of traumatic backgrounds, and they may be more likely to credit stories of abuse, which will increase the likelihood that they will report such backgrounds. They are also more likely to be familiar with diagnostic criteria, and therefore more likely to identify problems such as mental illnesses (Olson and Royse 2006).

There are debates in the literature about the impacts of traumatic backgrounds in terms of their costs and benefits to social workers. It seems that those who are drawn to social work and have faced personal difficulties are better able to empathize with service users. However, that capacity comes at a price. In an Australian study, Stevens and Higgins (2002) explored the impact of experiences of childhood trauma on child protection workers who worked with abused and neglected children. They found that despite employing coping strategies, child protection workers with histories of childhood trauma were more likely to experience vicarious trauma. They were not, however, more likely to experience burnout. Along with other researchers, the authors noted that survivors are frequently resilient.

Over time, age, experience and social connectedness overcome any appreciable difference in the traumatic responses of workers (Adams,

Matto and Harrington 2001; Baker 2003). Without early support, however, human service workers with personal histories of trauma may leave the profession.

Before, during and following social work education and practice, social workers continue to process their life experiences and integrate those into practice wisdom. Although they recognize significant stressors in their backgrounds and generally identify those as underpinning their choice of a social work career, they do not stay stuck. Instead, when they consider their personal family background, they narrate stories that involve developing resilience and a special empathy towards others who experience personal difficulties. They reflect on a quest for meaning that is resolved via a commitment to justice (Buchbinder 2007).

> **“** Social workers' insights into their motivation for entering the profession are important. Knowing and implementing one's own 'fundamental project' is a difficult and demanding process, requiring one to face and transform family-of-origin experiences from the past into a more constructive present. On the path of self-discovery, finding answers gives rise to new personal questions throughout the life project of becoming a social worker. (Buchbinder 2007, p.172) **”**

This then, should be a source of pride and contribute to a sense of self-efficacy. Regrettably, that is not always the outcome. Social workers are encouraged to reflectively and critically consider the influence of their personal backgrounds, beliefs and values on their interactions and decision-making in practice. It is important to reiterate that there are dangers in the concept of reflection when this is indiscriminately applied. Overly frequently, social workers self-reflect only to find fault or failure. Supervisors may encourage this, and on occasion the process can become detrimental. When social workers reflect on experiences of abuse or trauma in a context where the power imbalance is significantly unequal and they are judged for those experiences, they may be retraumatized rather than supported.

Educators and supervisors may be inadequately trained to deal with the outcomes of these exercises in self-examination, and they may be unaware of the distress they cause or even congratulate themselves on having uncovered personal 'problems'. Yip (2006) suggests that when workers are in stress overload due to heavy or difficult caseloads, the requirement to be self-reflective just adds extra demands. A key message emerging from this discussion is that reflection should ideally be strengths-based.

When self-help is not enough

Sometimes, the experiences revealed by clients do bring to the surface emotions or thoughts in relation to personal issues we had thought resolved, or they bring to the fore hitherto overlooked but important aspects of these. Educators and employers should perhaps be more up front with those embarking on a social work career: No matter where you become employed, it is unlikely that you will be able to avoid working with people with mental illnesses or people who have been abused. If you are worried about coping with these issues for yourself, you cannot hope to hide away from your worries by avoiding service users with these problems.

People who have experienced trauma, mental illness or other challenges may become more resilient through having faced these adversities. Just because your personal issues may still occasionally resurface does not mean you are not resilient. Over time, being alert to signals such as over- or under-identification with clients can help you to more quickly identify triggers. When issues are largely resolved, doubts may still arise from time to time, but self-help or a supportive debrief with a supervisor may then be sufficient.

So, in the first place, having chosen to work with people in challenging circumstances will mean your fragilities will be tested. However, what you also need to remember is that we all have those. We attempt to help service users deal with the stigma of abuse or mental illness, and to find pride in survivorship, whilst we may at the same time try to hide any evidence of struggles in our own lives lest we be judged. Apart from the damage this does to our capacity to cope with the day ahead, we end up feeling somewhat fraudulent or less than authentic. This can continue, years after we have recovered from our troubles, and by hiding the good news of that recovery, we deny our knowledge that our clients, like us, may be more resilient than others will suspect. One of the participants had this to say:

Participant: I mean it was an abusive relationship, and I actually went through quite a lot of guilt because of staying with his father and putting my son through domestic violence. I mean, I know now that if CYFS [Child Youth and Family Services] had been contacted they probably would've taken him off me. ... I found the strength from somewhere to get his father out of our lives and my son blossomed. **"**

Ideally, we resolve personal difficulties before engaging in social work. Sometimes, however, this has not been possible because we were not sufficiently aware, or issues resurface in the context of our work. Self-help and reassurance may then not be enough, and you may need to seek counselling or psychotherapeutic assistance. Psychotherapists may have been originally trained as psychologists, psychiatrists, psychiatric nurses or social workers. If they are members of a psychotherapy association, they will have been required to undertake personal psychotherapy, so they are familiar with exploring personal issues as clients whilst pursuing a professional career. In my experience that means most have a very positive and strengths-based perspective on helpers who seek to heal themselves. You may want to get help first, and then tell your supervisor, or tell your supervisor first.

It is important that you protect yourself and service users from harm and you should not work if you are unsafe, nor try to cover up the possibility of that. The truth is that you are in the majority if your stress levels are high, but you are rather more unusual for seeking assistance. Being affected by stress or trauma does not make you a bad social worker, but you may more keenly resonate and that can hurt. You do owe it to yourself to enjoy your career.

Hidden selves

Although recommended everywhere, in reality many students and social workers do not inform educators or supervisors about significant levels of distress they suffer. There are a number of possible reasons for this. Social workers with traumatic personal histories or current personal difficulties may feel embarrassed or ashamed. They may be acutely sensitive to the possibility of being devalued, not only by fellow workers and supervisors, but by lawyers and the public should this knowledge become available to them. They may fear they will be considered to be at risk of blurring boundaries by over-identifying with service users. Sometimes they just don't want to burden others with their troubles (Stevens and Higgins 2002).

Insistence on frank disclosure may ignore the reality that most people have a range of 'true' accounts of their life stories, and bring out those that are socially appropriate at any one time. For some stories, the time is frequently not right, due to dominant cultural perspectives on suitable personal backgrounds for social workers, or on what constitutes normative behaviour. The idea that there can be social competence in and around stories of abuse, for example, still challenges widely held beliefs (Christie and Weeks 1998).

Along with depression and anxiety, alcohol and other substance abuse are associated with high stress levels and are relatively prevalent in helping professions, including social work (McCormick 2003; Siebert 2001). Yet social workers tend not to seek help for substance abuse problems, again probably due to the stigma that is attached to drug abuse and dependence, and for fear of repercussions. When she worked in child protection, Phoebe had noticed a lot of substance use amongst her colleagues: 'People smoking heaps, drinking lots of coffee. I don't know what they were like in their prior life, but just heavy drinking, smoking dope.'

Overall, with perhaps the exception of medical assistance for depression, social workers are disinclined to seek professional help for mental health problems or stress overload and burnout, even when these impact on their capacity to work. They may fear that confidentiality will be breached, or that having sought help they will be required to disclose it to their employer. It may also be the case that admitting that one needs help, creates an uneasy discrepancy or dissonance with one's professional image of oneself as a helper. It has been found that having a prominent professional caregiver role decreases the chances that a worker will seek help (Siebert and Siebert 2007).

Even if they have sought medical or specialist psychological assistance, researchers have found that few workers will inform supervisors that they have been diagnosed with depression or other mental health problems, even though anti-discrimination laws should afford them some protection. The reason for this is that they fear that they will be judged to be personally inadequate, and that they will be stigmatized. They fear this, although in most cases they only develop their depression after they start their social work careers, and in two thirds of cases they attribute their depression to workplace demands such as high workloads, aggression from clients and lack of supervisory support (Collins 2008; Moriarty and Murray 2007; Stanley, Manthorpe and White 2007).

When personal problems are hidden, all forms of support for one's struggles are less available, including resilience building social support. The perceived need to prevent others from discovering what is going on can be an added pressure and may lead to withdrawal and isolation.

However, other matters that are routinely hidden, are not personal troubles, but personal–professional 'differences' and insights that are not safe to reveal due to a persisting chasm between strengths-based anti-oppressive talk, and the realities of workplace discrimination.

Trotter *et al.* (2009) are five women, some of whom are lesbian and others heterosexual, who reflect on how openness is advocated in social work, and yet they have never before discussed their sexuality in public. The sexuality of workers remains outside discussions, including in supervision, in particular when one's orientation is gay, lesbian or bisexual. The authors reflect on what it is like to keep a big part of oneself secret, and not be able to discuss the impact of that secrecy in supervision because this does not feel safe. Being honest about sexuality may not have to mean talking about it, but at least not having to be fearful about being 'found out' and expending energy in covering up (Trotter *et al.* 2009).

Teina knew that she had important cultural knowledge, but she carefully managed her expression of this.

> **Teina:** I'm not a confrontational person in terms of teaching anything Māori, I mean I try and make it a fun thing. … You have to do it in a way to encourage people. I mean, part of me thinks, 'Huh, they *should* be doing it!' But the other part of me [thinks], 'Take the opportunity, teach them, if they want to pick it up they will, if they don't – [then so be it].' And there's all these standards that social workers should have, cultural standards, and when it comes to the crunch, if someone came up to me that hadn't been kind of participating and said, 'Oh Teina, I need a signature,' I'll be saying, 'Sorry, find someone else.' Yeah.

Interest in spirituality has grown in social work, in part because of increasing understanding of diversity and the importance of spiritual beliefs to some service users. Outside of the ethnicity-related cultural arena, however, social workers are still often cautious about discussing the place of their spiritual beliefs, especially more theistic religious beliefs (Hodge 2002), including how these help them to deal with stress.

> **Anthony:** The things that I do are slightly odd, and I don't tell many people this but I have a deep connection with the faith of my childhood which was Anglican ... and I think I can go in [that church] and I think I sometimes feel like some indigenous people on their turangawaewae [home ground]. That's where I went when I was five ... [and] those kinds of memories are very very rich. And I have a strong kind of discomfort with organized religion at the same time, so what I tend to do is just read the old scriptures and the texts that mean something to me. Often I read them in the King James version because that's what I remember as a child. So I have this spiritual connection and I don't know how better to describe it and it is just that it is very very deep and it goes all the way back.

If, by contrast to the above examples, our identities and forms of knowing are part of the dominant perspective, we usually have to give little thought to how these are displayed and conveyed.

When personal challenges impact on work

Along the way, human service workers are bound to encounter new personal experiences that impact on their working lives. If you have been in practice for some years it will not be difficult for you to think of your own examples of this.

When I was diagnosed with breast cancer in the late 1990s, I was never in doubt about my survival although that may have been somewhat unrealistic, having full regard to the facts, as the cancer had spread. Nevertheless, that is how I felt, and still feel to this day. I was completing my PhD and in private practice as a psychotherapist. Chemotherapy rendered me bald, but it could be scheduled for a Friday so that I would have a long weekend to recover from each round. Consistency and empathic attunement with clients was paramount. I donned a wig and carried on. With the involvement of excellent supervisory and collegial support, I worked out 'what-if' plans A, B, and C for my clinical practice. Neither my partner Charles nor my academic advisor ever showed any doubt that I would complete my thesis as planned. I cried a little, but when the chips are down, I have a propensity for telling very bad 'black humour' jokes. The use of humour in coping is noted to be common amongst human service professionals, and it may be used to deal with emotion, help communicate meaning, retain social connectedness and affirm a shared identity (Tracy, Myers and Scott 2006).

Still bald under my wig, I took up a position as an academic in 1999. I felt it was necessary to remind my bosses that I might be a poor (dead) investment and was reassured that this was not a consideration in their decision-making. Equally, when, later that year, I unexpectedly fell pregnant and next had two children in quick succession, parental leave provisions that were ahead of the legislative requirements in New Zealand at that time, helped me balance my career and family life.

However, when the youngest of our children was diagnosed with stage IV neuroblastoma, my approach of 'business as usual' did not fit the context in which we now found ourselves. While I had earlier donned a wig myself, I could not thus conceal a 16-month-old child, nor could I, for example, avoid chance encounters with social work students on placement in the hospital – a nasogastric tube is a telltale sign. When I abandoned a lecture in midstream, following an urgent telephone call from the hospital, my shock and concern were impossible to hide. That first year of her treatment, I didn't teach my loss and grief class. The next year, however, I determined that if loss and grief were part of life and also part of social work, I should figure out how to continue to teach it, or concede defeat and cease.

My daughter survived and her hair grew back. Some years later, when asked to design her passport for a classroom exercise, she proudly noted her unique identifying characteristic to be 'I had cancer and survived'. When next my partner became ill with leukaemia, the 'juggling act' had to be largely managed without his support, and would have been nigh impossible had it not been for the fact that I was on sabbatical. The post bone-marrow transplant ravages impacted on his outward appearance, and by now the question of disclosure had become moot. We had probably become so adept at negotiating the boundaries of discussions in various contexts that we barely noticed the efforts that were previously entailed in deciding what should remain private and what must be made public, and when.

While the details of this story are particular, it is not uncommon for private events to become public knowledge in the workplace, for example when family members are admitted to the general or psychiatric hospitals in which social workers are employed. When already in personal distress over such an event, the public exposure can add to one's vulnerability and normalizing peer and supervisory support is an important coping resource.

Behind the scenes of this personal story of coping are the things that made a vital difference. A chief motivator for me was the desire to continue to be involved in meaningful social activities and work. By the time my child and partner were ill I was also a sole income earner which provided additional impetus for managing multiple demands in order to financially survive. It was helpful to retain a perspective that we had choices, however limited those might have seemed. I earned enough to hire a nanny, and we had family who lived nearby or flew to Christchurch to help. Our freezer overflowed with meals prepared by colleagues and friends. Crucial to negotiating our existence around work, home, and hospital rooms was the flexibility I was afforded in my workplace. When I had cancer I was self-employed and I could schedule my chemotherapy. As an academic, I burned midnight oil at my computer, or used the facilities in the isolation ward. But what of the working conditions of the average human service worker? At a time when supportive and instrumental resources are badly needed, workplaces are not always immediately forthcoming.

Well before I developed cancer, an acquaintance who knew I had faced some significant losses in my life, wondered how long she should mourn her husband's death. Her manager had been very compassionate for the first few weeks. That was considered generous, going beyond a standard three days bereavement leave. But now the manager's patience was growing thin. 'Jane' was at work, but not as quick, she could not see as many service users in a day, and felt more impacted upon by work as she was more keenly tuned in to the multiple losses of the people she worked with in the health sector. Everywhere she turned were reminders of her loss. She knew what she needed to hear; that it was normal for her to feel like this, and that is why she sought me out.

Next Jane devised a workable plan for managing her day, involving adjustments to time spent front and backstage, which she presented to her manager. This plan did not just involve some adjustments to her caseload in relation to taking on new clients, but to the pace and ordering of various tasks. In fact, she found that once she had permission to implement her plan, she had a better sense of control, and felt more capable of handling problems and achieving solutions at work. That sense of competency slowly generalized.

Under stress, our personal style can come through more strongly. I now think I was somewhat desperate to press on as I did when I was being treated for cancer, but that is part of who I am. I was also determined to have a career left in the likely event that I would live. My going running to 'stay fit' only to trip and slide down a stony hillside whilst neutropenic (immunocompromized) was going beyond reasonable expectations of myself. It may be beneficial to attune to such peculiarities. They may need some moderation. For example, Jane tended to be shy and she felt even less comfortable making her needs met under stress. Knowing that, she could give herself an extra 'push', and make a special effort to speak out as she eventually did with her manager.

Flexible work arrangements

When we experience family crises and other challenges to our work–life balance, responsible supervisors and managers will be open to discussing and considering our needs, and initiate inquiries about these. In terms of instrumental support, workers report that flexible work arrangements are of most benefit. When organizations are open to flexible work arrangements, the outcomes are most often rated positively by all parties (Department of Labour 2008). Legislation can assist workers to make their cases. For example, in the UK, the Work and Families Act (2006) became effective in April 2007, followed soon after in New Zealand, by the Employment Relations (Flexible Working Arrangements) Amendment Act (2007), which came into force in July 2008. In Australia the right to request flexible working arrangements was instituted with the Fair Work Act (2009). These laws give workers with caring responsibilities a legal right to make a case for flexible work arrangements, including flexible hours, days and locations for that work, or leave without pay. Government websites in each country provide information about the legislation for workers and employers, with fact sheets and case-study examples of how one might approach an employer with a request.

Although flexible work legislation was by then in place, Anthony took a while to tell his manager that he was becoming unable to balance demands on him as a caregiver with work and was becoming depressed. He had not expected as compassionate a response as he received. He talked about the difference it made to be able to look after his ill family member at home.

> **Anthony:** So my work allows me to be able to attend to what I suppose for many of us, maybe most of us, is most important, which is family. And yes, my boss is great and it is not just her, it is the [organization] in that [they] have agreed that there is no reason why I shouldn't do the hours of contact with [service users] which I do every day during the day, and do my admin work [at home in the evenings]. That's I think terrific. That's been going now for a month and a half and I just feel so different. I was nearly falling over, I was actually having dizzy spells – I was just so exhausted from trying to do it all. My work is extraordinarily rewarding, so when it can be fitted into my home life it is very much a counterbalance.

Anthony did not have the care of children, but as the social work workforce ages, more workers find themselves part of the 'sandwich-generation', juggling demanding midlife careers as well as the needs of their children and ageing parents (Petrovich 2008).

Several participants noted that family circumstances had caused them to reduce their hours of work to become part time. Family needs were usually prioritized over work needs if financial commitments and workplace expectations allowed it. When workers are not afforded flexibility, personal issues or career and family caregiving responsibilities can become a cause of overwhelming stress. This has been noted to impact particularly severely on female managers (Narayan 2005).

> **Ella:** I work full time now. Yeah, I mean that is obviously, currently that's my biggest sort of stress. But I suppose that is an issue of career progression, because if you want to get a management or want to get a better paid job, to get that you have to be prepared to work full time. Which I think is wrong really, but you know under the current law you've only got a right to *ask* to work flexibly haven't you. ... But yeah, I think that is certainly something that employers should look at.

Dilemmas over disclosure

In using my own story for this book, I have chosen to depart from my usual approach in which I tend not to disclose my private life. A key aspect of this decision is that here I am engaged in a conversation with colleagues about reflection upon the use of self. In addition, I retired as a psychotherapist and no longer have a caseload.

Social workers working in child protection and criminal justice settings are particularly cautious about revealing their family circumstance for fear that this knowledge may be used, possibly even to threaten them. When revelations of even the most everyday circumstances are unavoidable, this can be sufficiently stressful to prompt a job change.

> **Joy:** I one day walked out into the waiting room to meet a client and I realized that I also saw him at Nicola's school, and I knew in a flash that I had to leave [the agency] because I never ever wanted Nicola to have a kid say to her, or for a family to recognize or know that I was the [social worker] and knew about … their lives. And the mixing of those two – I never wanted that. So that was a boundary and a line in the sand I drew, because I saw that potentially as very stressful for the family if Nicola was to be bullied because 'Your mum is making my father go to drug and alcohol' or whatever it was because of that statutory responsibility.

In counselling settings, couple and family therapists may be more likely to consider self-disclosure than are clinical social workers who work with individuals (Jeffrey and Austin 2007). At times self-disclosure is a powerful instrument facilitating professional and personal growth in self and others.

> **Teina:** I often had to give talks to nurses on all sorts of cultural things and one in particular would be around death and dying. And I would talk about him and the process that we went through at the hospital and how good the staff was. But there were some things that weren't quite right, and I'm not just talking culturally, just keeping me up with what was happening with him. But how we got together about a month later, the doctors and nurses, and we used it as a learning thing, you know, 'If this happens again, this is what we need to do.' And so I use him as an example because I know that's what he would want me to do.

In many ways, growth is reciprocal. If we have experienced the serious illness and death of a partner or child, we will probably be less afraid to journey alongside clients who are facing such crises. But we will also have to process our strong memories and feelings so that we can be open to their needs, which may be very different from our own (Black 2007). Most often, when service users inadvertently discover something about our lives, we are made aware that they do care about us (Alexander and Charles 2009). Our work offers many opportunities to grow via reflections on our lives and on our work with service users. Indeed, human service workers are often inspired to make changes in their work and in their personal lives through their encounters with service users who have been able to live positively with mental or physical ill health or who overcame other adversities (Arnd-Caddigan and Pozzuto 2008; Kahn and Harkavy-Friedman 1997).

Pause for reflection

Self-disclosure with service users is considered differently across different practice modalities, but most, if not all, would caution against unburdening oneself with service users, no matter how 'natural' it seems in the moment. Don't rush into self-disclosure, especially when you feel compelled. If it seems like a good idea, check it out first. Ask yourself:

- What purpose does it serve, who is helped by this?

- Will disclosure interfere rather than assist with a service user's learning opportunities?

- Does it fit with my practice framework and if not, why am I feeling compelled to depart from that at this time?

These are important questions, and supportive supervisors should help you to explore them. Unfortunately, social workers report that after the initial impact of a personal crisis, follow-up by supervisors is frequently lacking.

Having a life away from work

Most of the social workers I interviewed tried to keep their work and home lives separate, and found this was an important way of managing stress. To achieve this separation they walked or biked home, or visualized leaving work behind whilst concentrating on the changing landscape through which they drove. They tended not to socialize with colleagues outside of work, avoided taking work home or talking about work at home, and avoided places where their service users might congregate. When thoughts about work did intrude after hours this was usually taken as a sign that demands were becoming too high, or that a case might require extra attention.

> **Steve:** I am very clear, if I am thinking about work away from work, immediately my stress levels are up. So I very rarely think about work when I'm not at work except when I'm talking to colleagues or run into people I know. And I've tried to consciously ... keep that separation from, yeah, from your work environment. ... I really don't like talking about work.
>
> **Joe:** I think planned ignoring at home is probably quite something that I use as a strategy.
>
> **Teina:** Usually now, and it's been like that for many years, if I can't let it go it's probably because I'm not meant to and I am actually meant to think it through. Other than that I'm pretty good.

Maintaining a boundary between work and private lives poses special challenges for those whose partners are also employed in the human services. It is also more difficult and can cause social isolation for rural social workers (Green and Lonne 2005).

> **Rachel:** My work and my home life are very separate. I don't have, I don't mix with people outside work. Some people do and that works for them, I keep them quite separate. That may have developed from working in a smaller community as well, where you couldn't go down to the pub on a Friday night and have a drink.

At home participants enjoyed listening to music, reading, and gardening. Most kept active with exercise by going to a gym or dance classes, walking with friends or engaging in other active outdoor pursuits.

When work was particularly stressful, however, partners and friends offered important support.

> **Teina:** I think he's got a good understanding. He doesn't ask a lot of questions but he usually knows when I'm a bit stressed about something.

Cathy: I've got a partner and it has been a learning experience for him over the years too in terms of, I think kind of feeling quite concerned and quite helpless at times when I've been really really stressed at work. And I guess when I look back to the beginning of our relationship and where we are at now, I feel like I'm able to share a lot more with him about when I am stressed about things than I might have done earlier on kind of thing. I was always really aware of keeping work totally separate and although I am not talking about any personal details with him [now], [I am] talking with him about when I am stressed and stuff. And he is able to support me a lot more than how it was in the early days of our relationship. **"**

In later chapters we will see that when workplace situations become very difficult and traumatic, family tends to emerge as social workers' strongest supporters (Shamai 2005). However, whilst family support is necessary and helpful, it does not particularly prevent workers from leaving a stressful workplace (Nissly *et al.* 2005). In fact, it is quite common for supportive families to encourage workers to leave when they are extremely stressed by their work: As they see it, wellbeing takes precedence over a job. Doubtless this encouragement is also in part due to the fact that the worker's distress can badly disrupt the enjoyment of life of their loved ones.

Building the work–life balance toolkit

In this chapter we have considered how personal and professional circumstances interact to increase or alleviate workplace stress. Although it is not clear that human service workers are any more likely to carry histories of personal trauma than other workers, they are required to function well when working with service users who are facing difficult circumstances. Because of this it is most helpful if they have built resilience, and a sense of self-efficacy. Social workers who have survived hardship and developed a sense of self-efficacy are less likely to feel despair or hopelessness in the face of challenges and can model thriving. Unfortunately, many continue to hide the strengths they have developed, along with the occasional struggles in which they may continue to engage, because they fear being judged by their colleagues.

Supportive supervisors who encourage positive self-talk rather than withdrawal or shame, can help workers to identify their competencies and take a positive approach to self and client care. Occasionally workers will need to take time out, and sometimes they will need to seek counselling or psychotherapy to help them deal with past trauma or with new personal challenges that arise.

The impacts of present day home and work demands may be compounding. We saw that when organizations accommodate workers' needs for flexibility, so that they are able to attend to issues at home, this is of mutual benefit. Most employers, once they make a commitment to helping staff to maintain work–life balance, find that the benefits outweigh any costs since workers' health and productivity are enhanced. When employers assist workers with their difficult situations at home, a reciprocal loyalty develops.

Supervisors and managers can build their toolkit of resources for assisting workers who are in stress overload due to combined personal and workplace pressures, by ensuring they are fully aware of the relevant local legal provisions. They can also use their skills to assist workers to make strong cases for flexible work arrangements and to encourage organizations to better adapt their policies to support workers.

In all, collegial support buffers against emotional exhaustion, and supervisory support helps build a sense of self-confidence. While support at home is important, social support at work is a better buffer against intentions to leave work than support from home (Nissly *et al.* 2005).

In the first few chapters you were encouraged to undertake a stocktake of the resources available for you to meet workplace demands. At the end of this chapter, we can draw together questions and ideas to help better balance our work and our home lives.

- Do you recall what brought you to social work or human service work? Where do you stand now in relation to those motivations? If you have lost touch, consider whether your motivations and values have shifted, or whether you want to reconnect and rediscover these. Doing so may lead you to think about the direction in which your work is moving you, and whether you want to continue and strengthen that movement or make changes.

- Are you respected for who you are or do you feel you have to hide your true self at work, even from your supervisor and colleagues? Do you fear being 'found out'? Your fears may be realistic, but an appropriate mentor may help you negotiate your way around this, and help ensure that you can still find ways to celebrate being you and draw on your insights.

- Do you have supervision and other support to ensure that you can safely process times when work situations trigger personal feelings, or when personal difficulties get in the way of your being able to work easily? The ideal time to consider what help you would seek and from whom is now, preferably before a crisis occurs.

- The participants in the book interviews talked about the signs that told them the balance between their home and working lives was out of kilter. How can you tell when this happens for you? The participants also talked about strategies they used to readdress this balance. Flexible work arrangements, drawing boundaries around work to create a separate home sphere, spirituality, and taking time out were important to them. Are there any of these tools that you could put into your toolkit to help restore balance?

- Consider your home environment and the effect that your distress or need for support may have on your family. What can you do to mitigate this? Discuss this with your family members.

- If you are a supervisor or manager, ensure that you are alert to the importance of work–life balance for yourself and your staff, rather than dismissing the relevance of this. Educate yourself, if you are not already aware, about the resources that are available, or might be created to help your staff develop and maintain this balance. Model self-care and remember that when you work long hours and send emails at night, your staff may believe this means that is the expected thing to do.

Additional resources

Work–life balance

Department of Labour (2008) *Work–life Balance and Flexibility in New Zealand: A Snapshot of Employee and Employer Attitudes and Experiences in 2008.* Wellington, NZ: DoL. Accessed on 17 December 2010 at: www.dol.govt.nz/publication-view.asp?ID=267

Hein, C. (2005) *Reconciling Work and Family Responsibilities: Practical Ideas from Global Experience.* Geneva: International Labour Organization. Accessed on 17 December 2010 at: www.ilo.org/public/libdoc/ilo/2005/105B09_142_engl.pdf

Part 2

Thriving in a Social Work Career

Chapter 4

Stress in Frontline Practice

Introduction

This chapter will discuss the stressful situations that social workers encounter when working in frontline practice, in child protection, criminal justice, mental health, and health services. Sources of stress include the expectations of service users and the wider public, scarce resources, working with service users who do not appear to be making progress, and worries over the safety of vulnerable clients. Practitioners' stress levels are also affected by the types of settings in which their work takes place, which may be in statutory organizations or non-governmental organizations (NGOs), institutions or the community, private practices, urban or rural areas.

Social workers work with people who may not welcome their involvement, for example when they need to investigate potential child abuse or arrange an involuntary psychiatric admission. They are required to make decisions that significantly impact on people's lives, often in a context of uncertainty where outcomes depend on many factors outside the worker's control. If clients do voluntarily seek social work assistance, for example during a health crisis, they are often distressed and usually wish they were not in a position to need such help. They may be traumatized and reactive as a consequence. Social work can seem like a thankless job at times, as people lash out at us when they are wounded, and are quick to forget us and move on with their lives when they recover.

To protect workers from stress overload it is important to ensure that there are not just limits on their overall workload, but that they are able to engage in a variety of work that is neither too continuously taxing, nor under-stimulating. Tailored education, for example around legal issues or strategies for resolving ethical dilemmas, may be especially helpful in some organizations where workers experience moral distress over dealing with difficult dilemmas. Robust support from colleagues, supervisors and managers is critical in maintaining a sense that we are engaged in meaningful work.

Beyond the individual and organizational level, ensuring that social workers and other human service workers have adequate resources to enable them to undertake work of a satisfactory standard requires governments and communities to invest in social welfare.

Readers will recognize their own experiences and those of their colleagues in the stories related in this chapter. Some of the stressors encountered in frontline practice, such as the impact of working with trauma, being subjected to workplace violence, or facing complaints about one's practice, will be covered in later chapters and are therefore not focused on here.

The emotional impact of frontline practice

In Chapter 2, I introduced the idea that human service workers are under most pressure when they are unable to provide adequately for the needs of service users, or are unable to meet the expectations of service users. Lack of resources, staff shortages and turnover, funding crises and restructuring, all potentially affect service delivery. Changes in policies and structures are made more manageable when frontline staff feel consulted. They don't necessarily want to be consulted on every detail, but they do want to be involved when there is a likely impact on service users.

When social workers respond to people in need, they are often required to execute a complex balancing act between care and control wherein they try to assist clients to achieve self-determination, but also prevent them from certain choices if those will cause harm. Equally delicate is the balance between helping clients to adapt to their environment, and working for changes in systems that oppress and disenfranchise people. Furthermore, and perhaps most challenging of all, social workers are themselves increasingly constrained from questioning the strict agency guidelines and protocols that define their roles and tasks (Dickens 2006). Workers fresh out of training can be surprised at the extent to which working for social change is difficult under such circumstances.

On a day-to-day basis, with limited resources and bound by legal, policy and ethical rules, frontline workers give advice and endeavour to make good decisions based on their judgments. Because they care about people, this weight of responsibility for the lives of others takes an emotional toll. This is especially so when there are children or otherwise vulnerable people involved who are disadvantaged in relation to being able to defend their rights, for example because they have a major mental illness. If social workers' actions lead to poor outcomes, or outcomes that are unwanted by at least some of the parties involved, this will not only distress the worker, but they may also face severe criticism. Social workers require supervision that recognizes the deeply emotionally taxing nature of their work (Woodward 2009).

With support and encouragement, human service workers are more likely to continue to remain empathically engaged with the troubles faced by service users. They can experience satisfaction in helping others to make even small life-enhancing gains. Compassion *satisfaction* may be derived from considering work as a calling, which may be expressed as the belief that whilst our work is difficult, this is what we are meant to do. It is more likely to be achieved if we are able to have confidence in our ability to do the job because of the inner and outer resources available to us. Important amongst those resources are supportive relationships with colleagues. Studies suggest that even when workers experience compassion fatigue, they do not need to reach burnout if timely support and relief are provided (Conrad and Kellar-Guenther 2006).

Pressures in child protection social work

Several participants in the book interviews had been employed in child protection services and they tended to count this as their most stressful work experience. Their most intense distress was over the plight of children in need of care. They worried that the alternatives they were able to offer these children were not necessarily much better than the situations from which they were uplifted.

Anthony and Joy had each worked in statutory child protection services for over ten years and between them, they had more than

25 years experience in the field. Both encountered ex-clients from time to time and they said:

>> **Anthony:** But they will talk about, and they will confirm what I suspected when I was working there, [which] is that alternative care, even sometimes alternative care with extended family members, can be horrible. And not just horrible because you are separated from your parents or the home that you are used to, but also because people can be actively horrible and classify you as a less kind of a citizen of that household just because you are an outsider. And that happens in all countries in my experience. And I never enjoyed the thought that I couldn't offer them something, and I wanted to take all of them home. And I never did even indicate that to them, although I think sometimes they felt that. They knew that we were really really concerned about how there was nowhere for them. So that is the hardest thing I remember, and it wasn't easy to live with that forever. So I don't think people should work [in child protection] for more than ten years.

> **Joy:** When I recognize children who've been in care, and kids that I've had an involvement with, or I know colleagues have had an involvement with, and they're known, that you just think, you know, the state was your parent and how we've failed you, often would be what I come away with. >>

The distress expressed by Anthony and Joy shows how the pain and suffering of children powerfully impacts on those who care for them (Conrad and Kellar-Guenther 2006). Along with Anthony and Joy, Ella thought there were insufficient alternative care resources, with shortages of quality foster placements and residential facilities. Because parallel planning was either lacking or not well managed, children could remain without stable arrangements for extended periods of time.

>> **Ella:** In New Zealand I think quite a source of stress … is that you feel like you can't do a good enough job because there isn't the resources … There's loads of community resources, there's loads of NGOs, but basic resources like foster placements, like choices of foster placements, good quality foster placements, residential places for children with a range of needs, there is nothing and that, you know, it's a systems failure basically … So you start feeling like you can't do a good enough job, and I've certainly felt like that working in [child protection]. I've thought, you can

deal with difficult stuff if you feel like you're making a difference, but if you feel like this is just not good enough, then –. And of course you see the harm that the system is doing to children, and you don't want to remove children into a situation that's not any better. So I think that's a really big one here. **"**

Rewa worried that a new focus on achieving permanency did not take into account that positive change could take a long time to achieve. This made her question the purpose of her job. She said, 'You can work really really hard and make some really positive movements and then legislation like that will just whip the families away, and then I wonder, what's the purpose?'

Child protection workers handle difficult situations and make decisions that impact on children, young persons and their families in far reaching ways. It is not surprising then that they find their work psychologically and emotionally demanding (Tham and Meagher 2009). Aware that they were choosing between imperfect alternatives, participants worried a great deal about the decisions they made, and they were keenly aware of the uncertain circumstances in which they made those decisions. The greatest potential cost of making a decision that worked out badly was that, 'I could be ruining this kid's life, I could be ruining this family,' and there was a strong sense that this burden of responsibility is ultimately carried alone. A sense of pervasive loneliness echoed throughout the stories of participants such as Phoebe who had worked in child protection services: 'You used to share it with your supervisor, sure, but for the most part it is just little old you out there having to just do the whole thing.'

This distressing situation is not peculiar to New Zealand, and is felt keenly by supervisors and managers as well as frontline workers. It is, however, a story that is somewhat obscured from view as workers feel constrained from speaking out, either for fear of repercussions from their employers or because they do not think it helpful to draw further negative attention to already difficult jobs.

Robert Yin (2004) writes, 'As a countywide CPS [Child Protection Service] supervisor in New Mexico, I shared the pain of one caseworker who experienced daily stress, knowing that her sibling set of three young children had been moved 13 times within two years' (Yin 2004 p.605). He notes that he only felt comfortable writing an article about this once he had left the agency. He emphasizes a range of interventions that centre on supporting workers, such as 90-minute supervision sessions that start with a half hour for validation and support without advice giving; team support sessions; three-monthly resilience building full-day sessions; fitness sessions; and providing more time for actual casework rather than having capacity only for emergency driven responses.

What also emerges from the above is that there is a need to ensure that social workers feel they can talk about inadequacies in services as these occur. It should not be the case that their only recourse is to publish academic writing, or to take part in anonymous interviews in the aftermath. They should be listened to in their place of practice, and their ideas responded to with action plans.

However, talking about uncertainty and worries about making decisions with potentially harmful outcomes is made additionally stressful because social workers carry a fear of being found lacking in competence. This fear is especially prominent in relation to risk assessments in child protection (Littlechild 2008). Chapter 8 focuses on the impact of the pressures that the drive to achieve certainty in assessing risk places on frontline workers, managers and child protection agencies.

The participants in the book project had learned to take care in documenting their decisions and actions, but not to go overboard in regard to this. It seemed that overall, outcomes for children and their families were their main concern. Worries over risk and blame were narrated as taking place in a wider context, where the lives of service users are beset with lack of resources, and social workers are undervalued and unsupported. Writing careful reports was not in itself a burden if it might lead to good outcomes for service users, and most participants were able to strike a balance in terms of what to include and exclude in reporting. They were cognizant that their notes would be the vehicle via which their practice might be examined. Positive pragmatic backup from managers in the face of challenges to practices and unreasonable expectations helped to keep workers' fears in check.

The loneliness felt by workers in child protection agencies warrants closer inspection. Participants felt isolated in their relationships with other professionals such as teachers, who did not appear to understand the nature of their work, and who seemed glad to pass on responsibility for making decision about children at risk. Relationships with lawyers could also be difficult due to a mutual lack of understanding of respective roles.

> **Phoebe:** A lot of the stress that you feel throughout your job does come from other professionals, whether it is counsel for child or the other services, child mental health or whatever. Or teachers saying, 'Why aren't you doing this?' or 'Why haven't you taken [the child] into care?' or 'Why haven't you done something yet?' or 'I'm telling you, so now it is up to you. It is your responsibility from now on.'
>
> **Ella:** Court work for child protection, obviously that's really, really stressful, giving evidence in court. I think social workers are usually pretty unprepared because they don't understand how lawyers think. The lawyer's job is to advocate only for their client's perspective and they will wipe the floor with the social worker if they get the chance. So I think for what social workers get paid, not many people in the course of their job have to give evidence in court ... so I think that's something really difficult.

In the British context, Dickens (2006) notes that managers are aware of social workers leaving their jobs because of the stress of court proceedings. At the same time, lawyers may feel they are asked to be emotionally supportive when they do not think this is part of their job, but that of social workers' supervisors or managers. Especially less experienced social workers may be keen for any assistance they can get from lawyers, but legal advice is an expensive resource.

In the USA, Vandervort, Gonzalez and Faller (2008) also comment that legal ethics increase stress for child welfare workers. They advocate that social workers and lawyers should be taught about one another's duties so as to better understand and be able to respect them. Ella thought she had been lucky to have had access to a combination of training and mentoring to help her prepare for court-related work when she started out in child protection. She worried that more recently qualified social workers may not receive such thorough coaching.

When participants reflected on their experiences in other fields by contrast to child protection, they noted the positive benefits of being able to discuss their work and share responsibilities with practitioners from other disciplines on a day-to-day basis. In New Zealand as in other countries, interagency and multidisciplinary network approaches to child protection have been developed and greatly strengthened over recent years.

However, one participant reflected that in New Zealand, the legal emphasis placed on a social worker having 'formed a belief' that a child is in need of care and protection for a case to proceed to a Family Group Conference, places significant pressure on social workers: 'I think in terms of stress for the social worker that is quite an onus just on that professional judgment isn't it, rather than, you know, collective [decision-making].' By contrast, social workers from other jurisdictions reflect on their frustration that when they do form a belief, this may then be negated in legal processes.

To an extent, frustrations and doubts cannot be avoided and even when decisions are shared, lack of communication may still lead to a sense of isolation. An emphasis on risk avoidance rather than reflective practice is likely to make disciplines more critical of one another. Ways of breaking down meaning and responsibility barriers between professions include the provision of cross-disciplinary education where this is relevant. Overall, teams of mixed disciplinary backgrounds may make more informed decisions. This approach has the added benefit of improving the depth of knowledge that other disciplines have about the work that social workers do.

Other highly distressing experiences for frontline child protection workers include uplifting children from their caregivers. The trauma of this work is discussed more fully in the next chapter. Child protection workers also experience a substantial amount of violence on the job. The pressure violence adds to working lives is the subject of Chapter 6.

Clearly, the participants in my interviews were resilient enough to have been able to continue in child protection work for many years without losing their capacity for compassion or reflection. Nevertheless, most had eventually left and, with hindsight, said that they thought that practice in this field is exceptionally burdensome. They kept in touch with ex-colleagues who told them the work had not become any easier over time. They noted children and adolescents now present with increasingly complex problems of insecure attachment, substance abuse and aggressive behaviours. Notifications of child abuse have increased due to public attention to the problem of family violence. These all require responses, but resources, including funding for frontline and supervisory staff, have not kept pace.

The participants' recommendations for assisting frontline child protection workers are well supported by what other research tells us: Services are more likely to retain workers when they show they care about them and are able and willing to invest in them. Without such investments, this work is increasingly likely to be seen as a low entry level position from which workers depart as soon as they have clocked up sufficient employment hours to find another job (Tham and Meagher 2009).

Participants noted the value of having experienced supervisors who are able to assist workers to continue to think critically and remain reflective under pressure, rather than be oriented only to avoiding the risk of complaints. Few had experienced formal mentoring, but research is emerging to suggest that mentors trained in coaching and knowledge transfer may increase retention rates for public service child protection workers (Strand and Bosco-Ruggiero 2010). Similarly, supervisors and managers require time, training and recognition if they are to best meet workers' needs (Renner, Porter and Preister 2009; Tham and Meagher 2009). Supervisors who are unable to provide open and critical analytic supervision either because they lack training, or because they are too pressured due to their own high caseloads, add to stress rather than ameliorating it (Lietz 2010).

As already discussed in Chapter 2, training for staff at all levels is helpful when it is appropriately targeted. Beyond induction, for example, frontline child protection or child welfare workers seek training that enables them to develop specializations and leads to opportunities for promotion without necessarily needing to move into managerial positions. Other career interventions aimed at retaining staff whilst fostering their development and relieving stress may include enabling them to transfer between positions within the organization, for example from emergency intake teams to adoption-related work (Curry, McCarragher and Dellmann-Jenkins 2005; Westbrook, Ellis and Ellett 2006). Practitioners also favour study leave opportunities and temporary secondments into other organizations (Beddoe 2009). Efforts to tailor jobs to staff (which could include part-time or flexible work arrangements) also convey that an organization cares about its human resources (Ellett 2009).

Investing in staff development will not always lead to the retention of experienced staff, and in fact with their confidence boosted, some may feel better placed to find other jobs. The important thing, however, is not to prevent staff from pursuing a rich and varied career, but to ensure that they are able to retain their engagement and enthusiasm for their work while they are in it. Ideally, people leave to pursue new challenges, rather than to escape intolerable conditions of employment. Indeed, if properly rewarded for their additional experience, people who leave may at a later date be encouraged to return to child protection work, bringing with them learning from other positions (Westbrook *et al.* 2006).

Pause for reflection on key issues in the child protection/ welfare sector

If you are a child protection or child welfare worker this is probably a good place to take a break from reading and make some notes identifying which of the above issues apply to you.

- What tools are available to you to overcome pressures in your workplace? Are these tools fully functioning? If not, identify a number of key issues that need addressing and begin to develop an action plan.

- As an important first step, consider with whom you could begin a discussion about this, perhaps your supervisor, a mentor or a colleague. It is unlikely you are alone in your struggles and you can learn much from the coping attempts of others.

Challenges in the criminal justice field

Many social workers are involved in the field of criminal justice, otherwise known as the correction services. They are not always employed under the title of social worker, but may be employed as, for example, probation officers or therapists alongside workers from other backgrounds such as psychology.

Participants who had worked in statutory probation services tended to speak highly of their supervisors and managers and were appreciative of the input of a diverse range of disciplines in the teams in which they worked.

> **Steve:** I was thinking a while ago, when was the last time I had a good manager? And I don't know if I've ever, probably in probation days, I don't feel I've ever had a good manager outside of probation.

Participants did note that there are pressures in working in the field of criminal justice where control is heavily emphasized. However, roles tend to be clearly defined, with courts determining penalties, and there is a fairly tight system of rules determining the bounds within which services are delivered. Job specific training is provided to new staff. Therefore, there is less uncertainty around how risk should be managed and how roles should be performed than there is in the child protection services.

The participants felt respected, and importantly, if they were employed as probation officers, they were paid equal rates for equal work alongside people with other educational backgrounds.

Some social workers find working with involuntary clients is inherently stressful, as they experience an ethical dilemma in imposing compulsion. However, those who find this most challenging will probably choose not to work in this field or leave at an early stage in their careers (Whitehead 1985).

As predicted by the Demand–Control–Support model of occupational stress, however, for some participants the limited amount of control that can be exerted over work roles and tasks in the probation service eventually led them to leave. The structured processes involved in criminogenic risk and needs assessments, and the compliance driven nature of much of the work became stifling.

> **Joy:** I think one of the things in probation that drove me nuts towards the end was that more and more the computer took over the role and you had to forever feed the computer this compliance sort of information.

For social workers in prisons, pressures result from working with increasing numbers of violent and mentally ill offenders, limited access to resources and support systems for prisoners and their families, and prison overcrowding. Negative public perceptions, a significant international swing to more punitive approaches to dealing with offending, and being caught between the demands of the administration and prisoners can be additionally problematic (Brough and Williams 2007). Social workers can feel alone in having a role that involves caring, in a context where the predominant emphasis is on confinement and control. Networking with other social workers and with human service workers and humanitarian prisoners' aid organizations helps to buffer workers against isolation and to maintain a sense of purpose.

Some studies find high rates of burnout for staff from a range of disciplines who work in prisons, but age appears to be a protective factor (Griffin *et al.* 2010; Lambert and Paoline 2008).

Compassion fatigue and burnout are more prevalent for those working in the specialist criminal justice field of sex offending. It has been noted to be particularly problematic for caseworkers who have contact with survivors as well as offenders. When workers have to switch between empathic attunement with survivors and offenders, they can experience a dissonance because the interests of these clients may appear to stand in contradiction. When our minds are unable to deal with situations by adopting relatively simplistically dualistic alignments and perspectives, even if on reflection we try to resist such thinking, this can be difficult to process emotionally.

Workers may also experience feelings of guilt, as if they are being disloyal to survivors of abuse. This is not helped when efforts to provide meaningful assistance to offenders are disparaged by the public and even by other helping professionals. It may then be difficult to talk about one's work outside professional networks, and practitioners can become socially isolated. Being aware of such impacts, limiting numbers of cases, and building supportive relationships with colleagues can help protect workers against burnout (Thorpe, Righthand and Kubik 2001).

A significant source of stress for workers across all of the criminal justice services is their awareness of the lack of resources available to service users and their families. Human service workers are all too aware that most of the people who are caught up in the criminal justice system have backgrounds of socioeconomic deprivation to which they are simply returned upon release. The rates of poverty and mental ill health in this population are woefully high. When social workers are able to engage in activities at all levels, including political activities in order to lobby for improved conditions for service users, this provides them with a sense of more meaningful involvement.

Research tells us that retention of workers in this field is improved by providing opportunities for job variety and specialization. Specialization should be rewarded via opportunities for promotion (Lambert and Paoline 2008). Workers can be encouraged to develop innovative projects that are aligned with their expertise and interests. These can include outdoor pursuits, grief groups, or cultural awareness raising projects.

Involving staff in organizational policy development has also been found to be particularly helpful in relation to lowering job distress in corrections (Lambert and Paoline 2008; Slate and Vogel 1997). In addition, as in other fields of practice, emotional support from supervisors is related to job satisfaction and psychological wellbeing (Lambert, Hogan and Tucker 2009).

Pause for reflection on key issues in the criminal justice sector

If you work in the criminal justice system, or this section has raised issues for you, take a break here to do some further thinking and writing about the pressures of your work.

- Consider the tools available to relieve those pressures and whether they are working. If they are not, what small steps can you take to seek change?

- If you are reading this as a manager, how can you involve workers more fully in decision-making?

- What steps can you take to enhance opportunities for workers to develop expertise?

- How can excellent workers be noticed and rewarded for their contributions?

Frontline work in mental health services

Most human service workers will find that a significant number of their clients suffer mental ill health, even if this is not their presenting issue. Rising pressures in mental health services have been associated with a move to community mental health services, which increase practitioners' responsibilities in relation to assessing risks for suicide, violence toward self or worsening psychosis (Edward 2005; Reid *et al.* 1999).

Some practitioners find it difficult to contain their concerns, and their worries keep them awake, or impel them to provide their private telephone numbers and take calls after hours. They worry not only for their clients but for themselves as increasingly, when service users harm themselves or others, mental health practitioners may be subject to investigations, reviews of their practice, and complaints. This topic is explored more fully in Chapter 8.

Not all workers in this field of practice are living with daily concerns over the safety of their clients in the way that emergency mental health workers do, but as counsellors, therapists or caseworkers they are all engaged in work that demands high levels of emotional empathy. Clients may be victims of multiple traumas and empathizing with their circumstances exposes social workers and other mental health workers to a risk of vicarious trauma (Rabin, Feldman and Kaplan 1999).

Earlier research that I undertook with social workers in private practice highlighted that social workers may lack some of the established skills for processing the impact of client's stories on their professional selves. The training of psychotherapists, for example, emphasizes the possibility that therapists will experience counter-transference reactions to clients' stories. Having a language and framework for dealing with emotional repercussions and reverberations does perhaps help other disciplines to establish better buffers and boundaries against emotional over-involvement.

The clients of mental health social workers or social workers working in the field of addictions may also make slow progress. Supervisors need to model a strengths perspective in relation to the work done by those on the frontline that parallels the positive regard workers ideally show clients. Achievements may need to be actively looked for, and social workers need to be reminded of the valuable role they play (Webster and Hackett 1999).

Messages of positive regard can be undermined by the fact that social workers in mental health care, whether in community or residential care settings, are often paid less for work that is essentially the same or very similar to the work of other professions. This was a source of annoyance for some participants.

Role overlaps with other professions can also give rise to doubts over the unique contribution of social work. Social workers become distressed when role overlaps or differences in perspectives give rise to conflicts in multidisciplinary teams and with agencies with which collaboration is required in order to best meet the needs of clients (Lloyd *et al.* 2005).

Overall, however, mental health social workers express less stress overload than do child protection social workers (Coyle *et al.* 2005). Strong supportive and trusting teams, with members open to mutual debriefing about concerns and a willingness to share worries rather than hide these from supervisors, are helpful in safeguarding workers. The opportunity to see clients make remarkable progress and regain quality of life is made increasingly possible with improved medications and psychotherapeutic interventions. The mental health field enables social workers to be involved in interesting work that brings a high degree of satisfaction. There is much opportunity for training and developing of clinical expertise (Edward 2005).

Internationally, the profile of social work in mental health is strong, and increasingly, the reintroduction of social work clinical advisors plays a part in ensuring social workers have a voice at middle and upper management levels. Management level input and advocacy for the role of social workers can overcome misunderstanding by other professions, as was also noted by Amanda.

> **Amanda:** I mean they have turned the corner when they're putting in the advance executive leadership management programme which is specific for mental health managers. ... There's a hope that there will be ... a lot of social workers in amongst there.

In all, the experienced mental health social work practitioners who participated in my book interviews were secure in their sense that they contributed valuable and valued perspectives that were neither more nor less important than the perspectives of other team members.

Pause for reflection on key issues in the mental health sector

- Interdisciplinary teamwork is critical in mental health work. Is there a good level of understanding amongst the disciplines in your team? How can this be facilitated?

- Managers and supervisors may consider inviting staff to present interdisciplinary seminars.

- Set a target, for example to carry to fruition at least three ideas for stimulating interdisciplinary understanding per year.

Challenges in the health sector

In general health care services, social workers expect to work with distressed and ill clients, some of whom may not recover. Having to give difficult messages to people, such as that their child suffers from a serious illness, or their adolescent son will not walk again following a spinal cord injury is difficult. When I worked in a spinal injuries unit in the 1980s, patients and their families would often need social workers to assist them to process messages given by asking us to repeat information they had not been able to hear when in shock. They would ask us to translate medical terms into plain language, and help them raise their concerns and questions with medics.

Social workers may need to advocate for clients' self-determination, including in terms of people's right not to pursue extreme measures to extend a life that has become burdensome. Patients' wishes not to be treated, and sometimes not to have their children treated, give rise to complex ethical dilemmas and social workers may be required to assist other staff in working through these. Although those situations are painful, they are expected by social workers entering this field, and working with patients and families is most often enormously rewarding.

What is often unexpected and causes much stress to new entrants to the field, however, is the lack of resources afforded for the provision of social care in the general health setting. Here, social workers have an ancillary rather than core role, and they may have little control over client selection. Social workers complain about a lack of job control, and about being relegated to finding accommodation for people. In the words of one participant: 'Pushing old ladies out of their beds to go back home or into rest homes.' The consequent de-skilling can lead to boredom.

As noted in Chapter 2, a change to practice that has added to the progressive de-skilling of social workers is the separating out of needs assessment and service delivery. This is done at least in part in an effort to save on burgeoning health care costs and has become especially common in older persons health services, including in New Zealand. Social workers complain that it interrupts the opportunity to advocate for their clients, which they have been educated to see as a significant part of their role (Martin, Phelps and Katbamna 2004).

Also particularly noticeable in health services for older persons is the lack of voice of some of these service users, which reduces their political power. This makes it more difficult for social workers to lobby for improved resources for them.

> **Kris:** So getting mental health consumers to be activists is easier than some of the older people [with major health issues] who are less likely to speak out for themselves ... they're just too tired. ... And so that puts me in the dilemma where I'm saying things *for* people which is not empowering and we're meant to be encouraging people to speak for themselves, and that creates a bit of a clash.

Resourcing of the social work occupation is improved when social workers have a say in organizational decision-making. Cathy had seen the valuing of social work wax and wane during the '18 odd years' that she had been working in the health sector. She noted the positive difference made by having a social work presence on the management team, and dreaded the possibility that the level of support she had recently received would be removed once again in structural changes that were being mooted for her organization.

> **Cathy:** I'm also aware that since we've had a professional advisor on board, the number of social work hours we've got has increased and the kind of the morale in the team is really quite good. And we've got quite a good standing, we're quite respected, oh not by everyone, but the other disciplines. [Professional advisors] are really a valuable professional kind of thing. When you don't have the leadership there is the danger of that all dissipating again really.

Pause for reflection on key issues in the health sector

- The questions that were raised about interdisciplinary teamwork in mental health services also relate to social work in the general health sector. Visit these questions now if you have not already done so.

- In addition, think about whether the concept of 'de-skilling' applies to you in your job. Is there a good understanding of the relevance of your role and the range of social work services you are able to provide? If not, how might you take advantage of, or create, opportunities to present that information?

- Do senior social workers have input into decision-making about how services are prioritized and resources are allocated? Involvement at managerial level appears to be of critical importance.

The impact of the contexts in which practice takes place

Across the fields of practice I have discussed, the settings in which work takes place also lead to different pressures. Social workers in smaller NGOs frequently receive lower pay than their colleagues in government or quasi-government organizations, and they may have fewer opportunities for professional development. If staff members are on leave, it may be more difficult to arrange cover. Fellow staff may not be professionally educated, and several participants thought this led to frustrating inconsistencies in practice approaches with service users within their agency. In addition, the lack of legal status of NGO workers can make them more reliant on their relationships with statutory social workers. Some participants found this demeaning or insulting as they felt that their expertise was ignored by those statutory social workers.

Many NGOs were traditionally involved in community development work and this type of work has become significantly underfunded. Funding may also be stopped partway through projects. This is not helped by the diminishing attention paid to community development in social work education programmes which reinforces a perspective that this work is of less importance or less 'professional' than casework (van Heugten 2011a).

Despite these identified drawbacks, however, workers in NGOs often find the values and missions of their employing organization closely match their own, and they may forego substantial remunerative benefits to be able to engage in meaningful work that enables them to avoid moral dissonance.

Social workers in rural areas face more difficulty in maintaining privacy in small communities. They are often isolated from professional colleagues and supervisory support may also be less frequent. For those reasons, whilst we may tend to associate urban work with high risks of violence, social workers in rural areas may feel less safe (Green and Lonne 2005).

Residential workers also have less opportunity to move 'backstage' in their day-to-day work, and have less opportunity to disengage from their clients to gain some physical and emotional distance. They need to be able to take time out to reflect and restore their energies. In addition, good safety measures should be in place, as rates of violence in such settings tend to be higher (Kosny and Eakin 2008).

Pause for reflection on your agency setting

- What stressors are associated with the setting in which your work takes place? Don't minimize these here. Allow yourself to articulate them fully.

- Little niggles can add up to major pressures and yet once these are articulated, plans may be able to be put in place fairly simply to afford great relief.

Dealing with stress in frontline practice: Tools for wellbeing and resilience

The above discussion has highlighted challenges faced by frontline social workers. Some of these are common across the fields of practice, while others are more specific.

It is difficult to see how any amount of quality pre-service education or on the job training can reduce high stress levels in child protection services, unless a stop is first put on workers carrying impossibly high complex workloads. Managers and supervisors also require adequate training for their specialist functions and they need time allocated to enable them to look after staff needs. These are problems that can only be solved via investment decisions made by the wider community and the state. They cannot be fixed by social workers stretching themselves more thinly.

Social workers in criminal justice, mental health and health services appear to be less often overloaded, although this can still be a problem if the service is an NGO. Supervisory support is also more often adequate to workers' needs. However, in some organizations, technocratic rather than reflective practice approaches wherein social workers find themselves having to '... forever feed the computer' lead to dissatisfaction about being under-utilized and result in boredom. The ancillary status of social workers in health teams can result in their being deprived of real work and relegated to bed emptying. They may not be invited to take part in decision-making about policies, or their advice may be ignored. Where managers are genuine in their efforts to consult, this significantly improves satisfaction levels of staff.

In addition to tools already identified in previous chapters, the following are likely to build wellbeing and resilience in frontline practice. These are first discussed in some detail before being briefly summarized at the end of the chapter in the toolkit.

Critical reflection on practice

It appears that when risks of negative outcomes are perceived to be great, organizations tend to emphasize guidelines and rules. These are undoubtedly important, but reflective practice allows for a balancing of boundaries, impressions and the concerns of clients, workers, agencies and the community. This is especially helpful when decisions have to be made in a context of uncertainty or when situations are complex or novel (Lymbery 2003).

In reflective practice, the worker's impressions, thoughts and feelings should ideally not be judged but approached mindfully. Shepherd (2006) advocates the use of a reflective journal. Reflective journalling is a technique also used in fieldwork training and in research by qualitative researchers, and can be carried through into practice. He recommends journalling descriptively and as objectively as possible and then asking six questions:

- How do I feel about this?

- What do I think about this?

- What have I learned from this?

- What action will I take as a result of my lessons learned?

- What have I learned from what I've done?

- What have I done with what I've learned? (Shepherd 2006, p.336).

Reflective practice involves more than merely becoming conscious of information and feedback deriving from service users and people and things in their environment, plus our own impressions. It involves challenging that information and the ideas that flow from it with theories and models of practice. It involves finding new and up to date evidence *as required*, always remaining aware that this is culture-bound, using all of the means at our disposal. Reflective practice and the use of technology are therefore not mutually exclusive.

From the concerns raised about data entry in frontline practice, it appears that *inputs* (items of information that can be used to build a picture; behaviours aimed at achieving a goal) have become confused with *outputs* (results of steps taken towards achieving a goal). If we remain clear about the functions of inputs and that these are not ends in themselves, the use of computers and other tools can aid rigorous reflective practice.

For supervisors and mentors there is a reciprocal requirement to be mindful, reflective and authentic about one's own experiences and development, in order to achieve insight into the development of others. Supervisors and mentors can also helpfully extend workers' conceptualization of reflective practice by recognizing the realities of uncertainty *and* the potential helpfulness of evidence such as is derived from practice research. Frontline workers may need assistance to identify any knowledge gaps that prevent them effectively using all of the steps in reflective practice.

Deepening reflection

Have you been thinking that reflective practice is too non-specific for social work in the twenty-first century evidence-based social work? Is it time to think again?

In-depth reflection is not always necessary – we don't need to reinvent the wheel in every instance. However, in complex or new situations where reflective practice is required, you need to be able to identify gaps in knowledge relatively quickly and how those might be filled. This requires you and your supervisor to be comfortable with introspection as well as to have the skills required to identify relevant evidence-based knowledge. You may need assistance to help you build confidence in undertaking all of the steps in reflection.

Education and training that is timely and targeted

Social workers are cynical about training that seems primarily aimed at achieving compliance with their employer's ever-changing input or audit-oriented requirements. They are, however, keen to develop relevant expertise and learn how to apply this in an appropriately flexible way in the service of clients.

In addition, there are some generic capacities that could be developed in more depth to assist workers to cope with workplace distress. One example of such a capacity is the resolving of ethical dilemmas.

Students in social work courses tend to be presented with rule-bound codes of ethics, and technical models for ethical decision-making, such as the ETHIC Decision-Making Model (Congress 2000). Whilst these can be helpful in relatively straightforward situations, social workers often deal with situations where codes of ethics and rules about practice do not offer clear guidance. There may be no right answers, only choices between less than ideal options (Gray and Gibbons 2007).

This can lead to struggles with conscience and result in moral distress and burnout (Gustafsson *et al.* 2010). We saw how participants worried about not having enough time to spend with clients, or not being able to offer children adequate care because of a lack of resources. Social workers also typically struggle with questions about the right to self-determination of clients when those clients may make decisions that lead to self-harm (Saxon, Jacinto and Dziegielewski 2006). Rather than trying to escape from a heavy conscience, viewing one's conscience as a guide and an asset appears to be more helpful in avoiding burnout (Gustafsson *et al.* 2010).

The increasing diversity of social workers' client groups challenges the concept of universal values and the idea that there can be one-size-fits-all ethical rules. In reality, research has shown that experienced social work practitioners rarely consult ethical codes, but engage in context-dependent considerations of caring ways of working, in which the nuances of people's lives are taken into account.

I am not advocating that we should ignore ethical codes, but it does seem helpful to acknowledge the challenges posed by complex and diverse life-worlds. Social workers' capacities to engage with ethics could be significantly enhanced via a broader understanding of disciplines such as moral philosophy and ethical politics. This is more likely to prepare social workers for the realities of practice, than training that demands adherence to coded rules as if these are uncomplicated facts (Banks 2008).

Also with relevance to education and training, participants high-lighted difficulties when workers from other disciplinary backgrounds did not understand the roles and concerns of social workers. Regrettably, perhaps in an effort to claim professional or academic independence and status, social workers have over recent decades tended to create educational silos wherein students are increasingly isolated from those pursuing other careers in health and social sciences. This has, however, ultimately done little to improve social work's standing amongst the professions or in academia (van Heugten 2011a). A more mixed model, in which at least some courses are taken alongside students in other professions and academic traditions, could improve mutual understanding. This approach is already utilized in some organizations such as the health sector to enhance interdisciplinary collaboration.

Identifying educational opportunities

When you consider the educational opportunities available to you, it is helpful to focus on your developmental goals. If necessary, a mentor may be able to assist you to clarify these. You can then more consciously select options that will assist you to achieve your aims. A targeted plan may also help you to secure agency support in terms of money or time off work.

Opportunities for specialization and advancement

A number of participants stressed the importance of providing opportunities for frontline practitioners to develop specializations so that they could continue to develop and grow. Such specialization would ideally be rewarded, including with senior status and pay increases, without necessitating a move into managerial roles.

Considering specializing

Specialization may bring you in touch with practitioners from other disciplines. Consider actively seeking out such opportunities. This will increase your exposure to new knowledge, and, with little extra effort, it will also enhance your networks, and advertise the capacities of social workers to the wider professional community.

Engagement of social workers in decision-making

It makes good sense to involve frontline workers in making major decision about changes in organizational policies and practices. Frontline workers will understand the likely positive and negative impacts of changes on service users, and what resources will be required to effect a smooth transition. When their input is not sought, workers tend to become disillusioned and their investment in their employing organization tends to diminish over time. Engaging workers into decision-making requires a genuine interest in their views. These can be actively solicited by inviting membership on committees, and establishing focus groups or working parties to share in project planning. In addition to improving the likely success of a project, these methods also assist with team building and fostering collaborative work processes. By working together, colleagues experience a sense of involvement, empowerment and organizational citizenship (Turner and Shera 2005).

As NGOs have become increasingly dependent on targeted government funding, the characteristic democratic approaches to governance in such organizations have begun to diminish and it is important to be aware of this so that safeguards similar to those mentioned above can be employed (Hardina 2005).

In interdisciplinary health and mental health services, clinical or professional social work advisors with input into senior management are seen to strengthen the status of the profession and improve its resourcing.

Becoming involved in decision-making

Identify opportunities for engagement in decision-making. Put your name forward, or nominate people who you think will strengthen the democratic profile of the organization.

Ending collusion with unfair and unduly stressful workplace expectations

Whilst reflection can help us to challenge dominant voices, it does not necessarily provide us with tools to overcome structural injustices. Action taking may require us to identify how we are continuing to collude with unhealthy practices by accepting overly high workloads, unplanned change and so on. Assertive team responses and the involvement of professional bodies are needed to deal with these matters and to draw a line in the sand (Morley 2004).

Ending collusion with unfair workplace expectations

Becoming more pro-active in overcoming structural workplace problems requires a team approach. Coaching and mentoring by experienced practitioners can also be invaluable. If there is nobody within the agency, consider the possibility of accessing external mentors. Look for mentors with good work–life balance. Confidentiality is critical, and you will need to ensure that your assistance seeking meets the requirements for safeguarding information as set out in your employment contract or agency policies.

Finding a good fit

Finally, in this chapter we considered a range of fields of practice, and found that the Person–Environment Fit model applied in as far as types of work preferred by one social worker may not suit another, and this may change over time. For example, occasionally working through the night to complete an exciting project may be stimulating when we are single, but be impossible to entertain when we have young children. Employers and employees are becoming more aware that a good fit is essential. It is better to face the truth about a position and one's disposition in the appointments process, rather than to obscure these realities, and have a poor fit emerge later (Turner and Shera 2005).

Across fields of service internationally, dissatisfaction with the amount of paperwork or computer entry work is a significant contributor to job dissatisfaction or lack of fit, and warrants closer investigation (McGowan, Auerbach and Strolin-Goltzman 2009).

Providing technical training and training in time management can provide some assistance. Increasing administrative assistance may also free up valuable time for core social work. However, most practitioners complain of unnecessary and duplicated administrative tasks that need to be identified and removed.

Improving P–E Fit

Don't hesitate to ask questions in interviews. If you are already in a job, meet supervisors or managers to consider if your work can be better shaped to fit, or look out for other positions. You may not have to leave the occupation of social work to achieve a better accommodation.

The frontline practice toolkit summarized

- Critical reflection continues to be a key capacity for working with uncertainty. Enlist support to develop a deeper understanding of critical reflection in practice.

- Source education and training that is timely and targeted to your goals, so that it nourishes rather than further depletes you.

- Seek out opportunities for specialization and advancement to enable you to continue to develop professionally. Identify how you will be meaningfully rewarded for doing this. Meaningful rewards will help sustain your commitment to professional development.

- Pursue involvement in decision-making to ensure that social workers influence key organizational trends that impact on service delivery.

- End collusion with unduly stressful and unfair workplace expectations. Endeavour to model self-care.

- Strive to find a good Person–Environment Fit in relation to your occupation and the organization in which you work.

Safety is another key issue in frontline work, and is a broad concept referring to psychological and physical protection from harm. Over the following chapters, we enter into a discussion about major threats to the safety of social workers and other human service workers, including those posed by working with trauma, experiencing violence directed at workers, and facing complaints.

Additional resources
Stress in frontline practice

Davies, R. (ed.) (1998) *Stress in Social Work.* London: Jessica Kingsley Publishers.

Donnellan, H. and Jack, G. (2010) *The Survival Guide for Newly Qualified Child and Family Social Workers: Hitting the Ground Running.* London: Jessica Kingsley Publishers.

Chapter 5

The Stress of Working with Trauma

Introduction

On 4 September 2010, my family and I along with most of the citizens of Christchurch, New Zealand, were rocked awake by an earthquake measuring 7.1 on the Richter Scale. Although smaller earthquakes are relatively common in New Zealand, most of us had never encountered an earthquake of such magnitude. In fact, we had tended to think we were safe from such an event as local belief was that the next 'Big One' would be likely to strike the capital city of Wellington, which sits on several known fault lines.

Within minutes, people began receiving text messages from worried relatives and friends overseas. Fortunately, the timing of the quake, at 4.35 a.m., and the fact that most buildings complied with strict earthquake regulations, meant that there was no loss of life and few injuries directly attributable to the quake. Civil defence, police and other emergency services acted quickly to cordon unsafe inner city streets, prevent looting, begin to restore power and assist people as necessary. When dawn broke, the extent of damage to houses and businesses was revealed. Some areas appeared largely unaffected, whereas others were uninhabitable and people had no option but to abandon their homes and possessions.

The government put in place emergency measures, for example to ensure that employees of small businesses that were unable to continue to employ their staff would have access to an emergency benefit of NZ$350 a week. Nevertheless, people with limited financial resources were stretched. Social services reported an increased need for food parcels.

Questions arose over a lack of democratic processes in relation to emergency laws passed by government, and about decisions made by the city council. There were concerns over possible discriminatory treatment, for example when a Māori family was evicted from an emergency shelter for allegedly intimidating other residents. Residents in a council social housing estate complained that their flats were boarded up without notice after a re-evaluation found them to be unsafe and community workers noted these residents were members of a vulnerable population who lacked resources to advocate for their rights. Several weeks on, tempers were fraying as streets remained without functioning sewerage systems and tour buses were reported to be conveying picture snapping tourists around some of the most devastated suburban quarters.

For many people also, initial relief at having survived a major natural disaster, gave way to weariness caused by lack of sleep and an underlying persistent anxiety provoked by the hundreds of felt quakes amongst the thousands of aftershocks that stretched out over months (Earthquake Commission and GNS Science 2010). Some people were very anxious. Many commented that, whilst they were overtly becoming accustomed to the changes that had taken place, their minds remained fuzzy, and they experienced problems with concentration and focus.

Within days of the main quake, the Salvation Army had flown in counsellors from Australia; the Save the Children Fund had organized workshops for parents and teachers wanting to understand how to help traumatized children; and the government promised to provide several million dollars in funding for counselling. I noticed this influx of trauma counselling experts from outside the quake region with some initial concern. Christchurch general medical practitioners and the Royal New Zealand Association of Medical Practitioners warned that premature or inappropriate psychological interventions can do more harm than good, citing Cochrane reviews of post-disaster interventions such as debriefing (Rose *et al.* 2002; *Press* 2010a).

It was heartening, however, to find that providers emphasized social support and education. The most frequently repeated message in relation to the psychological effects of the earthquake was that it is normal to be feeling anxious, slowed down, sleepless, confused or irritable. This message quickly became part of a normal daily discourse, in which people comforted and reassured one another, thereby normalizing such effects and minimizing the likelihood that affected community members would feel ashamed and isolated.

The fact that there was no large-scale loss of life or long-term devastation of most of the infrastructure, community facilities, and educational and recreational resources, were helpful factors. Although for a while it seemed as if the aftershocks would never end, the reality was that most people could expect to recover fairly well from their ordeals. A poll of 378 residents of Christchurch and affected surrounding districts taken between 23 and 26 September showed that whilst nearly 80 per cent suffered stress, 65 per cent expected to recover within a year, and only 3 per cent did not expect to ever recover (*Press* 2010b).

Whilst traumatic stress responses are common following natural disasters of this kind, these effects normally begin to wane within about a month. Post-traumatic stress disorder (PTSD) is not a likely consequence of encounters with traumatic experiences. Even for those people who encounter a natural disaster that involves the death of close family or friends, or a threat to their own existence, the likelihood of developing post-traumatic stress disorder is approximately 20–30 per cent (Breslau 2009; Cairo *et al.* 2010; Erdoğan *et al.* 2006; Lai *et al.* 2004; Mari *et al.* 2009).

Education, normalization, and social support are the most helpful interventions in the immediate aftermath of trauma. During this time, the brain needs to heal and memories should be allowed to fade. Forced debriefing can instead reinforce trauma response pathways and traumatic recollections. Those most at risk of developing psychiatric symptoms include people who are isolated, already suffer mental health issues such as PTSD, have small children, and lack economic and other resources.

In Christchurch, where the frequency of powerful aftershocks came as an unpleasant surprise, some affected residents were too frightened to undress, shower, or move from under tables or out of doorways for extended periods of time. They needed active support from people who reached out and offered comfort. Some had to leave town. For others, cognitive behavioural interventions to deal with anxiety were most effective.

Amongst the 80 per cent of citizens who were distressed (*Press* 2010b), there were people working in human service-oriented occupations such as social workers, elder care providers, nurses and doctors, search and rescue workers, ambulance drivers, psychologists, psychotherapists, police and teachers. Many returned to work while the extent of damage to their own homes was still unclear and their families were worried and frightened. For some this was a welcome distraction from their own troubles, whilst for others the burden of witnessing the distress of others was difficult to bear.

Again, it was heartening to see an emphasis put on 'caring for the caregivers', whereby most organizations made clear efforts to offer support to staff so that they would be in a comfortable and secure enough state of mind to be able to undertake work with others. This was not always fully the case, however, as one participant found out when she decided her family needed her, and she was put under pressure to come into work.

> **Participant:** I got called and I said no. And having, I guess, having burned [out previously], there's some disciplines you learn from that – you know what is of value anyway. So I said, 'No, I can't,' and they said, 'Well, you know people need us.'

Although major natural or human caused disasters may be becoming more common, these are fortunately still relatively rare events that the majority of social workers will not encounter in their working lives. By contrast, in the course of their working lives most social workers will see enormous deprivation in the homes of clients, and listen to stories of anger, trauma and loss. They may have to remove children from parents, be party to decisions to compulsorily admit people under mental health legislation, or help people process the news that they have a life-threatening illness. As we have seen in previous chapters, workers may be haunted by the thought that their interventions may not necessarily lead to better outcomes. They are often forced to work with a lack of resources and that means their clients do not always get the services they need. They feel responsible and may be blamed when things go wrong.

In a survey by Horwitz (2006) in New England, USA, the vicarious witnessing of trauma had more negative effects on workers than being attacked verbally or even physically. The author suggested that this might be so because workers feel they have more control over encounters with violence than with trauma, which is often an inescapable consequence of working in the human services. Horwitz

(2006) also found that supervisors were traumatized by listening to the reports of their supervisees. This impact is often overlooked, and highlights the fact that supervisors also need support.

For many human service workers, traumatic impacts are transient and manageable. However, if one is forced to suffer in silence or in ignorance that these impacts are normal, then this may diminish confidence in coping. For example, beginning workers need to know it is normal, after hearing stories of abuse, to look at the world through different eyes at least for a while. It may seem as if abuse is everywhere in the news. You may feel uneasy about images that pop into your mind when your partner has a child on his or her knee or you may not want to have sex. You may be jumpy and not like people coming up from behind, have sleepless nights or frightening dreams. You may be thinking about situations at work to such an extent that you are not quite engaged with your own moment to moment life.

Normalizing such effects may prevent depersonalization and social withdrawal. Nevertheless, normalizing effects should not be taken to suggest that it is helpful to force workers to discuss imagery or experiences in detail. As already noted, it is now thought that 'debriefing' from trauma, especially in the early days following traumatic experiences, whether encountered vicariously or otherwise, risks solidifying the traumatic response pathways that, without such interventions, will likely fade over time. The brain takes a while to accommodate new shocking information, and it is normal to feel disoriented whilst it adapts. Indeed, workers may need to be protected from trauma overload and be provided respite in alternative work experiences. By contrast to formal debriefing interventions, informal support amongst peers is frequently of benefit.

In a similar way to how traumatic stress was normalized for the population of Christchurch, we need to become more forthright about the likelihood that human service work will lead to encounters with trauma and that these encounters will have expectable distressing impacts. Unfortunately, education about this aspect of our work is often still lacking, perhaps because educators fear that they will frighten students. Instead, however, education can help workers to prepare for normal but unsettling effects, and provide them with tools for coping. This chapter aims to do just that.

Vicarious trauma or secondary traumatic stress

As mentioned in Chapter 1, the terms vicarious trauma (McCann and Pearlman 1990) and secondary traumatic stress (Figley 1995) are used to refer to the impact of working with, listening to and observing trauma experienced by others, and absorbing this trauma into one's own psyche via a pathway created by empathy.

Full-blown vicarious trauma is much like PTSD in its manifestations, although these are usually experienced at a lower intensity. You may have intense emotional reactions to traumatic experiences that you have heard a client describing. As a consequence, you may have difficulty undertaking work that requires you to empathically engage with other clients who describe similar trauma. You may also be hypervigilant and easily startled, especially in circumstances that mirror those in which clients have, for example, been assaulted, such as in a car park at night. Vicarious trauma can lead to changes in cognitions, so that workers change their beliefs and values in relation to safety, intimacy and trust. This can be lastingly problematic, resulting in altered worldviews. There is more risk of that happening if workers have insufficient support. The onset of vicarious trauma can be quite sudden and it does not require multiple exposures (Phelps *et al.* 2009). It is important for new social workers and their supervisors to be aware of this.

Another important aspect to note, however, is that not everyone is equally badly affected, and attempts are being made to learn why that is so in order to provide better assistance to workers. It does appear that less experienced workers, less supported workers, and those with high workloads (and presumably less time for processing) are worse affected. Past trauma may be reactivated and prior PTSD does appear to predispose workers to developing symptoms (Evans *et al.* 2009).

People who are not engaged in human service work may not realize the traumatic impact of removing babies from distressed mothers soon after birth, reading reports about sexual abuse or working with perpetrators of abuse (Hesse 2002). Researchers have noted that child protection work more often impacts negatively on workers' emotional wellbeing at home than other types of social work (Tham and Meagher 2009).

Whilst such work gives rise to the possibility of developing vicarious trauma, there are ways in which social workers can be protected from developing these symptoms or heal if they do develop them. This chapter draws on recent evidence of how social and organizational support, hope, meaning making and spirituality can help build workers' resilience.

Community disasters and vicarious trauma

After the earthquake in Christchurch, some human service organizations were unable to continue to work from their inner city offices and had to relocate. They regrouped to provide essential services, made telephone calls to clients, and endeavoured to ensure the safety of workers and students on placements.

Unlike the Christchurch earthquake, most large-scale community disasters involve loss of life and serious injuries. First responders include utility workers who restore essential services such as power, water and sewerage; police, fire, search and rescue, and ambulance staff; and health professionals in hospitals and emergency relief centres. Social workers are called upon to support displaced persons and grieving families. They may have to make decisions about needs and priorities in conditions where resources are scarce, which may give rise to ethical dilemmas (Linzer, Sweifach and Heft-LaPorte 2008), and anger being directed at them. This would be stressful under any circumstances, but these decisions now have to be made at a time when workers themselves may be impacted by the community crisis, and they are perhaps frightened, exhausted, and concerned about the wellbeing of their own families.

In the aftermath of the flooding of New Orleans that followed Hurricane Katrina in August 2005, 80 per cent of first responders were without homes and faced multiple personal losses. Local first responders experienced conflicts between their responsibilities to their own families and their work duties. In order to enable emergency responders to carry out their work, it is therefore essential to recognize the impact of trauma on their personal wellbeing, ensure that they take adequate time out, and have opportunities to engage in non-trauma related activities (Osofsky 2008).

When disasters are deliberately caused by humans, the initial impact may be similar to that of a natural disaster, but the stress-related consequences may last longer (Eidelson, D'Alessio and Eidelson 2003; Gregerson 2007).

On 11 September, 2001, more than 3000 people died when two passenger planes were deliberately flown into the World Trade Center in New York, another into the Pentagon in Washington DC, and a fourth was forced to crash into a field in Shanksville, Pennsylvania. Since these attacks took place in an affluent country with a well-developed research culture and mental health system, many quantitative and qualitative studies have been undertaken about the psychosocial impacts of these attacks. Amongst these are studies of the vicarious impact working with survivors had on counsellors, social workers, psychologists and other human service workers.

Researchers have found that most New York social workers providing counselling services to trauma victims following the September 11 attacks experienced some symptoms of traumatic stress (Boscarino, Figley and Adams 2004), especially increased anxiety levels. If they had personally witnessed the attack, or lived less than ten miles away from the World Trade Center, knew someone who died or knew a recovery worker, this increased the chances of symptoms occurring. This impact was not caused by providing more general social work services, but by listening to stories that detailed trauma (Colarossi, Heyman and Phillips 2005). Disaster relief workers who have a prior diagnosis of PTSD or psychiatric illness have been found to be more likely to experience secondary traumatization in the wake of a disaster (Evans et al. 2009).

People's tendency following an emergency such as this is to first reach out to family, especially children and older people, and to friends. Since the September 11 attacks occurred during the day, social workers with children went to schools to collect them. Other initial reactions included going to the site of the disaster, going to hospitals, and volunteering services to Red Cross or blood banks. Social workers expressed sadness for people they knew directly such as clients, for affected populations including Muslim Americans, and for the nation as a whole. For some, a coping strategy was to return to work. Others found this very hard as multiple health problems, tiredness or depression combined with the stress of listening to clients' stories. Managers might have the care of staff and service users and not get much attention themselves (Matthieu et al. 2007).

Especially for workers close to the centre, even if they were able to stay in the same site, increased security measures changed the context in which work took place. I recall meeting New York social workers later that year, who talked of the retraumatizing impact of travelling to work in the vicinity of 'ground zero', where constant reminders were unavoidable. The amount and pace of work increased, with more clients needing attention, and increased levels of anxiety and drug and alcohol use. However, social workers also commented about feeling their work was valuable and meaningful as never before (Matthieu *et al.* 2007). For some, worldviews changed, and patriotic feelings ran high. I was shocked to hear a social worker express hatred toward a Muslim family member. Later, shame emerged as the world to some extent began to turn against the global impact of the 'war on terror', and visiting social workers hastened to note that not all Americans were of like minds.

Research shows that social workers in Israel also express high levels of patriotism, and derive a strong sense of meaning from their work. There, social workers have clearly defined roles in the aftermath of bombings. They visit families of the injured or dead, and they work in general hospital settings where victims are treated. They accompany families into morgues where maimed bodies are waiting to be identified. These social work interventions are highly regarded by service users and the public, and are favourably reported in the media (Dekel *et al.* 2007; Landau 1997).

Despite the trauma they encounter, Israeli social workers experience fewer psychiatric symptoms including lower levels of PTSD than the general population, although levels of anxiety are equal to those in the general population and levels of phobias are higher. Being able to actively contribute rather than passively stand by in the face of terror may provide a sense of control and accomplishment. It appears that high levels of social support, adequate resources, and being able to make meaning in terms of the importance of their work are important buffers against developing PTSD (Dekel *et al.* 2007; Shamai and Ron 2009).

By contrast, there is a lack of published research about the impact of working with trauma on Palestinian social workers. This is at least in part due to there being few social work and social care practitioners, and even fewer social work researchers in the area. Researchers who have explored the impact of working in a war zone on social workers in Palestine, have found that the Intifada makes a significant negative impact.

Ramon *et al.* (2006) found that Palestinian social workers live in constant fear and experience high levels of emotional stress due to concerns for their own safety, and for the safety of their families and service users. Difficulties that workers in such situations encounter include getting to and from work. Being stopped at checkpoints causes feelings of humiliation, and leads to delays or inability to keep appointments. Many see themselves as survivor-helpers (Ramon *et al.* 2006). A survey of West Bank social workers also found that 20 per cent experience high levels of burnout, and many experience low self-esteem. Older, more experienced social workers experience less burnout than younger, less experienced workers (Abdallah 2009).

There is also a developing body of research that explores the impact of working in the context of pandemics or threatened pandemics.

The HIV/AIDS epidemic in South Africa shows no sign of decline. In 2006, approximately one in every three or four patients admitted to a general hospital was infected with HIV, and its prevalence in pregnant women was 29.5 per cent. Health care workers, including nurses, doctors, social workers and counsellors, as well as teachers, some from the same communities as their patients, experience bereavement overload due to the overwhelming numbers of deaths amongst young people, and the orphaning of children. Entire communities are devastated. Resources are so scarce that not only antiretroviral drugs are lacking, but adequate nutrition is unavailable to impoverished families. Human service workers feel distress and hopelessness over government inactivity and conflicting policies (van Dyk 2007).

In 2008, the replacement of a controversial Minister of Health who advised that garlic, onions and lemons would offer protection against HIV/AIDS, offered hope (Kapp 2009). However, working in this field carries a high level of stigma that will take a long time to overcome. Misinformation about infection risks leads to social ostracizing of workers. In addition, as many as 20 per cent of younger health workers are themselves living with HIV and a majority hide this fact for fear of consequences (van Dyk 2007).

Pandemics can give rise to serious moral distress that has to date received relatively little consideration in the human services literature. Moral distress may arise over conflicts between safeguarding one's own health whilst caring for service users. Human service workers may also have to make decisions about access to scarce resources, including scarce essential medications and other necessities of life, as well as access to psychosocial care.

For example, in 2003, during the worldwide scare over an outbreak of severe acute respiratory syndrome (SARS), just over 100 Taiwanese hospital workers, almost one-third of those reported to have been infected with SARS, had come into contact with the virus as part of their work. Those infected included nurses, doctors and allied staff in general hospitals. Staff in quarantined hospitals experienced conflicts between their fears for their own health and their duties to patients (Lee *et al*. 2005).

In Canada also, workers exposed to SARS developed symptoms of PTSD and were in need of psychosocial care. Again, questions arose over whether nurses should have to show up for work. Social work ethics do not clarify whether one's duty of care means one is required to continue to care for service users when one's own family or one's own health is at risk (Rosoff 2008).

Disaster relief plans tend to focus on medical interventions and the availability of assistance, including essential resources that can be brought in from outside the immediate region. In a widespread influenza epidemic such help may not be available in time. Care will need to be rationed, and there is a high likelihood that many people will die. Mass cremations may be necessary and will challenge cultural norms of care for the dead. These are scenarios for which we still do not adequately prepare prospective social workers, and yet they will be amongst workers in essential services when disaster strikes (Rosoff 2008).

Tosone (2007) suggests that 'shared trauma' is a better concept than vicarious trauma for situations such as those described above. In situations of shared trauma, in order to be able to put aside their own emotions to respond to those of others, social workers need first to know that their own families are safe. In the Taiwanese outbreak of SARS, video cell phones helped workers stay in touch with families in ways that were mutually reassuring as they were able to see each other in good health, and clothed in protective gear (Lee *et al*. 2005).

Workers also need to know that their organization supports them and that in addition to having access to resources for service users, they will receive backup and have access to professional support for themselves. Where trauma is likely to be encountered in home visits, it is important for this work to be carried out in teams so that there is opportunity for mutual support. After completing a particularly traumatic task, workers may need to take time out, including by not answering the phone or not going in to work the next day (Landau 1997).

Social workers also deal with disasters that occur outside their native territories, and they are active participants in international humanitarian work. There again, they witness violence and offer psychosocial support to survivors of appalling atrocities.

Cronin, Ryan and Brier (2007) note that most humanitarian disaster workers experience mild forms of stress, and when properly supported, such work can lead to personal growth and resilience building. However, approximately one-third at some time experience severe stress. Given that the pathway to traumatization is via empathy, this is expected, since disaster workers tend to be driven by compassion and altruism. They often have difficulty limiting their caring, and putting boundaries around their responsiveness. Cronin et al. (2007) suggest that when support is provided in the field, this is most effectively done by mental health workers or trained peers who work alongside disaster workers and who are therefore viewed as having an understanding of the nature of the work.

After humanitarian workers return home, they may experience difficulties reintegrating back into their home communities. Social support is vital, but when workers return home, their experiences may be at odds with those of almost everyone around them and they may withdraw as a result. Traumatic responses that have been delayed during their deployment may now emerge unobserved and untended. Humanitarian organizations are becoming more aware of the need to ensure people have access to informed peer supporters after the return home. Matching workers with buddies is a means of providing this (Eriksson et al. 2001).

Social workers are well-equipped to lead the development of support programmes for disaster workers, because they understand the importance of ecological and strengths-based approaches such as building positive social networks. There is a persuasive argument to be made that schools of social work should include education about disaster relief work in their curricula, as this is becoming a more relevant aspect of social work internationally (Cronin et al. 2007). Moving into the second decade of the twenty-first century, the topic is becoming more frequently taught as well as being addressed at international conferences.

More widespread education around disaster relief and responding would also mean that the burden of work would not need to fall on a few 'specialist' workers. If we are living in a world where encounters with ecological, viral, or human caused disasters have become more likely, then we need to know how to help people live against this background of uncertainty and threat (Eidelson *et al.* 2003).

A critical aspect of our learning will need to be around developing our understanding about how worldviews change in the wake of disasters. Frequently, negative views about 'outsiders' to the dominant culture become more extreme. This has been seen in relation to responses to minority Muslim populations. Social workers are also vulnerable to impacts on their values, and knowledge about how such changes may be mitigated is critical.

Helpful interventions include social support from those familiar with the depth of moral distress workers may experience. Cognitive approaches that include non-confrontational challenging of distortions, and behavioural interventions that enhance self-efficacy can assist with the rebuilding of resilience.

Some of the creative therapies, such as journalling and drawing that have been found helpful with PTSD may also be helpful if vicarious trauma does develop (Gregerson 2007). Other methods that have shown positive results include Eye Movement Desensitization and Reprogramming (EMDR) (Lehrer, Woolfolk and Sime 2007). Significant progress has been made in relation to our understanding of helpful psychological interventions, but these do need to be carried out by people who are trained in their use.

It is important to remember that despite the likelihood of initial traumatic distress, post-traumatic growth is the most likely outcome of work in community disasters. Working in the context of community disasters can engender an enhanced sense of one's capacity for coping and the meaningfulness of one's work.

Working with trauma behind closed doors

While earthquakes, wars and pandemics are large-scale events leading to 'public' trauma, much of the trauma encountered by social workers is of a more private nature. The devastating consequences of disfiguring accidents, painful deaths due to cancer, suicides, child abuse, and the anguish of sex offenders as they develop insight into their crimes, are kept out of public view, being considered too painful or unpalatable to share. This can obscure the impact of such trauma on individual workers, teams and organizations.

Day-to-day hospital work can be distressing for social workers, perhaps especially for beginning social workers. Working with critically injured and ill patients and their families takes an emotional toll. Team support is critical, and may need to be actively sought and provided, as social workers are usually in a minority in interdisciplinary teams (Dane and Chachkes 2001). Sometimes also, other members of the team will see social workers as psychosocial experts, who, by virtue of that expertise, will not need emotional support.

To some extent at least, the social work profession has projected a stoic image of itself. For example, whilst there is a significant body of research that considers the impact of working with cancer patients on nurses, there is still very little written about this in relation to social workers. Nevertheless, social workers also witness the physical ravages that accompany advanced cancer or cancer treatments. As they empathically engage in interactions with patients facing death or possible death, they too are likely to question the meaning of life, their identity, spirituality and worldviews.

I recall my own early experience of hospital social work, when I was assigned to visit a small number of patients in a surgical ward. In that setting, there were also several people who were being operated on for advanced melanoma. Their cancers had spread, and yet they were very optimistic about their prognosis. They were not assigned to me, but I noticed that nobody appeared to be attempting to correct their belief that their surgeries would be curative. No-one seemed able to adequately answer my questions about what, if anything, should be done. Seeing these people daily as I went about my other work and yet feeling unable to intervene, led me to experience what I now recognize as guilt and moral distress.

Social workers today continue to struggle when working with people who remain optimistic despite poor prognoses. They feel particularly distressed when they lack access to resources to support ill service users and their families, and have insufficient time to spend with them or to adequately attend to complex workloads (Simon *et al.* 2005). Workers may develop survivor's guilt for not having suffered like the patient or for having withdrawn some of their emotional energy as a coping mechanism (Dane and Chachkes 2001).

Education about such expected distresses, and the provision of peer and supervisory support are of vital importance (Dane and Chachkes 2001). When support is good, work that one might tend to expect to be especially traumatizing may in fact be less so. An example of this is working in a palliative care hospice where there is strong collegial support (Kootte 2001).

Normalizing emotional reactions is important in order to reduce the stigma of experiencing distress when encountering painful situations, especially for inexperienced workers. Time out can be helpful with respect to absorbing shocks, but workers should not be abandoned and should be given opportunities to talk if they wish. Helpful interventions that can reduce early hyper-arousal include increased support from peers and supervisors who express caring, practical attention to material needs, and positive feedback about work. A little extra time spent on such basic cares can potentially reduce significant costs later (Halpern *et al.* 2009).

Teina recounted how, after the unexpected death of a patient that evoked personal memories for her, she valued the support of her close knit team.

> **Teina:** At work, the team, we're a really tight little bunch ... plus our supervisor ... he's used to dealing with trauma. We all work together really well. ... He's learning from us, we learn from him, we learn from each other. And yeah, over that week after that patient died, every now and then one of the others would just look at me [and ask], 'Are you okay Teina?' And that's good and we do it to each other.

One of the most traumatizing experiences encountered by practitioners is the suicide or attempted suicide of service users, especially when we have been working closely with them. Joe and Steve knew how overwhelming worries about suicide could be, especially in one's early career. With training and experience they had learned to put boundaries around their sense of responsibility. Joe reflected that social workers may spend much time with high-risk clients, get to know and like them, and feel much grief when they take their own lives. When that happens, there are private as well as collegial and public reviews of what might have been done to prevent this from happening. Hindsight bias can cloud our judgment of what is reasonable to expect of ourselves and our colleagues.

> 66 **Joe:** The other thing that I think is impossible about that is that you look back after having an incident, you know, somebody might commit suicide or something major might happen at work and you look back and you think, oh I should have done this or I should have done that, but you can't actually do that for everybody because the workload is too high. So I think that is difficult. 99

It can be difficult to talk about these things with other people in one's life. Joe said, 'I generally don't talk a lot about my work with other people, one because it's probably traumatizing for other people and also it's probably something quite removed from their lives.'

Ting, Jacobson and Sanders (2008) suggest that between 28 and 33 per cent of mental health workers have experienced fatal suicide attempts by clients, and over 50 per cent have experienced non-fatal suicidal behaviours by clients. When a client suicides, it is entirely normal to feel sadness, anger, depression or irritability, and it is likely that you will experience at least some temporary loss of self-confidence. Thoughts of failure and self-blame are common. Other reactions include avoidance and isolation, and sometimes attempts at justification of actions. Workers engage in less self-blame and experience less isolation when there is clear agency support and a collegial, rather than fault-finding, approach to reviewing the events leading up to the suicide (Ting *et al.* 2008). Unfortunately, however, as some participants in the book interviews commented, supervisors and organizations sometimes seem more concerned with avoiding liability than supporting their workers.

The most effective means of coping in the aftermath of professional bereavement by suicide include talking with colleagues and a supervisor, and accepting the possibility of suicide as an outcome. Your family and friends may also be supportive, but they tend to expect effects of the bereavement to pass before they realistically can (Ting *et al.* 2008).

Perhaps less commonly expected, certainly by the public, is that child protection workers experience trauma when removing children from their caregivers. These interactions may be especially impactful for workers who have children and empathize deeply with the distress of children and parents.

> **Phoebe:** When I was pregnant, like, you know, out like this, you are still expected to go out. ... Sometimes if you had a case, there would be the old school kind of thing that would be there, where they'd say, 'Well you should be able to separate this baby from your baby and go out' and ... I didn't want to deal with it anymore, eh.
>
> **Margaret:** I've seen lots of this happening and lots of different emotional responses that need to be processed, and not just me but for the rest of the workers who are exposed to some of that trauma. And whether you agree or don't agree with the decisions, it's still got to be dealt with otherwise it just continues to build until you feel like every family is going to be like that, and everyone who comes through is always going to have that outcome. And that is how you sort of think, or, 'I don't want to do this job, it is too hard, too hard to think of babies being taken away, children being harmed.' It is just very difficult stuff.

In addition, child protection workers with personal experiences of childhood abuse may be more at risk of experiencing vicarious traumatization (Nelson-Gardell and Harris 2003). However, on a more encouraging note, workers who feel they have resolved their earlier traumatic experiences suffer less stress when dealing with situations of family violence (Bell 2003).

Trauma is encountered in many social work settings including statutory, NGO and private practice settings. Over recent decades, a significant body of research has built up about the impact of counselling survivors and perpetrators of trauma. Relatively well-researched topics include working with survivors of family violence (Ben-Porat and Itzhaky 2009); childhood physical and sexual abuse survivors (Brady *et al.* 1999; Chouliara, Hutchison and Karatzias 2009; Steed and Bicknell 2001; Van Deusen and Way 2006; Young 1999); perpetrators of sexual abuse (Carmel and Friedlander 2009; Crabtree 2002; Cunningham 1999; Ennis and Horne 2003; Hatcher and Noakes 2010; Moulden and Firestone 2007); and victims of crime (Salston and Figley 2003; Shubs 2008).

Self-care measures include the setting of clear boundaries around home and work lives, limiting exposure to trauma generally, and having supportive networks of colleagues and friends. It is important to nurture one's own body by keeping fit or at least remaining physically active and eating healthily. Restoring meaning via connecting with spirituality, and making a point of noticing beauty, kindness and positive actions in the world are also often found to be helpful (Hunter and Schofield 2006). In earlier research that I undertook with social workers who had entered private practice, counsellors also noted the importance of screening clients for their suitability for the private practice setting, and not feeling one has to accept all referrals (van Heugten 1999).

Counsellors and psychotherapists use devices such as breathing techniques to remain grounded and calm in sessions. This enables them to observe and be mindful in the moment, and engaged without emotional over-involvement. Psychotherapists spend considerable time during their training in developing the capacity to shift between empathic attunement with clients and observational self-awareness. This may be a skill set that social workers could helpfully develop to avoid emotional contagion (Rothschild and Rand 2006). The practice of ensuring there is transition time between clients is part of the way psychotherapists' and counsellors' days are structured and note-writing also fulfils a reflective function. Weekly loads and holidays are structured to support balance, and four day weeks are relatively common.

Beyond attention to nurturing themselves in their immediate contact with traumatized clients, many therapists, counsellors and caseworkers also advocate for social justice. Taking action in relation to the broader sociopolitical issues impacting on service users' lives helps workers avoid feelings of helplessness and hopelessness.

Social workers with psychotherapy or counselling training more frequently use personal therapy than do social workers without that additional training. Although social workers dealing with trauma are at an elevated risk for substance abuse, few seek professional help for these problems (McCormick 2003; Siebert 2001). Supportive and developmental supervision are highly valued (Hunter and Schofield 2006).

Generic considerations for coping with trauma

From the information presented above it should be clear that Critical Incident Debriefing has largely fallen out of favour, at least in the form that it was initially applied, whereby workers experiencing traumatic incidents were advised to recount the details of these in a psychological interview that took place within 72 hours. Research questioning the efficacy of debriefing has been available since the early years of the twenty-first century, and it is dismaying that participation may still be required in organizations today. Perhaps Joe's comments point to possible explanations for that.

66 **Joe:** I don't believe in debriefs, I don't really like debriefs and I don't think there's good research behind it. Organizations insist on doing it and ours is one that does. … It's very trendy, and also like for protecting, litigation stuff, it's really useful. I mean, I think if you know you're gonna go to the coroner's court, everyone getting together and talking about the incident afterwards is really good in preparing your statement. So I mean, organizations from that point of view will like it, but also too if they end up in the employment court with somebody who says, 'I'm burned out, I can't do this job anymore,' they can say, 'Well, the day after that incident happened we provided you with a debrief.' You know, it looks good on paper. It might have no clinical evidence that it's good, but that's not an issue in an employment court. Also I think generally too, not all management's intentions are bad. I think they generally do do that in a way of trying to sort of support people. And it is something you can actually do, because the other things involve you doing nothing really don't they, a lot of them. Which is probably a bit uncomfortable for people. 99

The suggestions outlined in this chapter provide options for alternative courses of action. Emphasis is placed on taking an openly educative approach that normalizes consequences of trauma on workers. Well-informed peer groups ensure support is more widely available, and help to prevent isolation even if workers need to temporarily withdraw from certain kinds of work. Supervision should be grounding, ensuring material needs are met and that workers are reminded of what they do well. To facilitate this requires supervisors who know and understand the complexity of the work that is being undertaken.

In the context of community disasters, workers also need to be supported to attend to the needs of their own families, and if they are out on work assignments they need to know they can call on backup support from their organization and that this will be available when required. This includes knowing that every attempt will be made to extricate them from dangerous situations. If deployed internationally, post-deployment support for reintegration is essential.

Workers can be encouraged to apply positive self-care by having fun, keeping fit, relaxing, or journalling.

Several participants managed stress by spending time without people contact, or with people who had little knowledge of their work. They made conscious efforts not to think about work and service users outside the workplace. Over time they had learned to recognize personal signals indicating that they were at risk of losing their balance. Those signals included loss of sleep, becoming irritable, being unable to focus on the moment, and being unable to get work out of their minds.

It may be helpful to consider encounters with major trauma as involving experiences akin to loss (loss of certainty, loss of innocence). From research into normal processes following major losses such as bereavement, we find that oscillating between approach and avoidance of feelings and thoughts in relation to that loss is a healthy aspect of adaptation to a changed world.

The model that has become well-known for encapsulating this oscillation is the Dual Process Model (Stroebe and Schut 1999). According to this model, people move between mourning and processing of loss (the loss orientation), and putting those feelings aside to deal with pragmatic matters at hand (the restoration orientation). It is only when they are overly fixed in either distressing feelings or denial of feelings, and unable to move between these orientations as circumstances demand, that there are problems in adaptation.

If we integrate this model with an ecological perspective, we can see that, in relation to working with trauma, problems in adaptation may be due to environmental factors (such as workplaces that do not allow sufficient time out) or issues that have arisen for the individual (such as a recurrence of post-traumatic stress). Supervisory, or if necessary therapeutic, interventions can be targeted at overcoming an imbalance. For example, empathic supervision facilitates emotional expression, strengths-based cognitive approaches are helpful in assisting workers to reconnect with their competencies, and active behavioural approaches may encourage workers to break out of withdrawal and isolation.

The setting of emotional boundaries is an issue that also deserves specific consideration. There is a debate in the literature around whether workers should be taught to restrict their empathy, or whether instead the concept of 'deep empathy' is one that has merit in terms of enabling people to resound to extreme emotions without being overwhelmed or vicariously traumatized. Certainly, in emergency situations the capacity to set aside emotions can help us to take the immediate actions that are required. However, because our work normally takes place in relationship, a significant degree of empathic attunement to emotion is usually important (Dill 2007).

The capacity to *modulate* our emersion in our emotional responses is especially important. It appears that when we are able to be empathically engaged whilst yet remaining able to emotionally separate or differentiate ourselves from our clients, we may be best protected from vicarious traumatization. These skills are ideally learned in training or early in one's career (Badger, Royse and Craig 2008; Phelps *et al.* 2009).

Mindfulness-based approaches of various kinds may assist in the capacity to achieve this kind of state in which we are empathically attuned and yet differentiated from the other person.

Berceli and Napoli (2006) proposed a mindfulness-based trauma prevention programme for social workers. Three simple steps constitute the programme. The first of these involves breathing and body scanning whereby you focus on being aware of the energy in each part of your body. Next you recollect a traumatic event, and this is finally followed by a repeat of the breathing and body scan. The approach involves a 'here and now'-based noticing of bodily experiences, patience and understanding, and adopting a 'beginner's mind'. With a beginner's mind, one considers every emotion and thought with a fresh and open attitude, as if for the first time, and without judgment. This meditative practice decreases rumination (dwelling) and has been found to have a positive impact on emotional exhaustion.

In addition, being able to make positive meaning in difficult circumstances has been found to contribute to wellbeing and build resilience to trauma. For some this involves a religious or spiritual component (Gall *et al.* 2005; McKay 2007; Phelps *et al.* 2009). The making of meaning assisted my participants in the setting of emotional boundaries. They believed that one person's small contribution plays an important part in achieving a greater good, and that to continue to do their part they needed to stay well enough to enjoy their work.

Tools for coping with trauma

This chapter has considered how human service workers can be protected from developing vicarious trauma or secondary traumatic stress, despite the fact that they will inevitably witness much human tragedy.

Special attention was paid to environmental and human caused community disasters, which are still relatively neglected as part of social work education. Such disasters may become more common and social workers have much to offer because of their capacity to understand systems and mobilize networks of support. To make the most of this capacity, social work education, and human service education more broadly, need to include learning about the human impact of disasters. This would require increasing the community development component of most programmes.

In addition, there is a need for more extensive education about the impacts of trauma work, and about ways of protecting oneself and one's workers against these impacts translating to vicarious trauma. A number of important protective mechanisms have been discussed above and these are now gathered into a generic trauma, and a community disaster toolkit.

The 'generic' trauma toolkit

- It is vital that we educate students and practitioners about expectable responses to vicariously witnessed trauma so that these are normalized rather than pathologized. Remember that post-traumatic type symptoms are not indicative of a disorder until at least a month after an encounter with trauma.

- Consider the use of assessment tools to identify anxiety and depression, but remember that a good understanding of signs and symptoms is often sufficient.

- Some workers will require specialist psychological assistance, but for many peer and supervisory support are best accepted and most helpful.

- Supportive supervision continues to be important. Pay special attention to reassuring workers about common symptoms. Do reinforce competencies. This does not, however, mean that you should overlook real concerns and signs of ill health.

- Ensure that workers have an opportunity to take time out after encounters with trauma, but don't isolate them from colleagues. Provide opportunities to talk but don't force debriefing on workers. Information may need to be obtained for legal and risk management purposes. If this is the case, be careful to protect the worker from unnecessary rumination on trauma.

- Social support is vital in building resilience to trauma. Foster social connections in teams via fun activities, and encourage workers to spend quality time with family and friends.

- Meaning making is a buffer against traumatization. Pay attention to meaning making, including by cognitively reinforcing the value of the role played by the worker *and* the importance of self-care.

- Develop the ability to empathically attune without emotional contagion. Relevant skills can be developed via mindfulness-based approaches. Other helpful suggestions include deliberately stopping mirroring a client to differentiate yourself from them once empathic understanding has been achieved (Rothschild and Rand 2006).

- Self-care includes fitness, healthy eating, getting enough sleep, and spending time having fun.

The community disaster toolkit

- As a worker in a human service organization, or as a manager of staff, you need a clear disaster management plan. Civil defence information for your local area is a good start. As a social worker or human service worker you are also well-equipped to use an ecological model to help you map out a plan for your agency and its service users, from micro through to macro levels.

  o Consider, for example, whether workers in your agency have access to emergency kits in the event of being trapped at work. I got my emergency kit delivered to my third floor office *after* the 4 September Christchurch earthquake, having been too 'busy' to collect it when it was made available earlier that year.

  ○ If office computer and paper-based records are lost, will you still have access to essential records?

  ○ Who will be your most vulnerable service users and how are they likely to react? What would be the most effective avenues for helping them?

• In addition to seeking out local information on disasters, check out international web-based resources such as those included in the resources listed below.

• Families are extremely important to us all, and in the event of a civil emergency, workers will want to ensure that their families are safe. Expect that some members of staff will not be able to turn up for work, or may refuse to come to work as they will prioritize their families' needs. Avoid penalizing them for that.

• Pace staff members' engagement in trauma work. This may require active intervention as caring staff may find it difficult to take breaks in the face of human needs. Check in regularly to reassure them about your availability and support.

• Ensure that there is sufficient office-based backup for staff out on calls. Do not leave staff out in the field if there is insufficient backup.

• If workers are based outside of their home locale, be aware of their re-integration needs. Support from peers with similar experiences may be especially helpful.

• Disaster relief work can be enormously rewarding. Caring for and supporting workers helps ensure that they are able to continue and find personal satisfaction in this work.

The following chapter continues the theme of trauma, as it looks at violence toward workers from service users.

Additional resources

Compassion fatigue and vicarious trauma

Rothschild, B. and Rand, M. L. (2006) *Help for the Helper: The Psychophysiology of Compassion Fatigue and Vicarious Trauma*. New York: W.W. Norton.

Websites with information for disaster relief workers

The Headington Institute: www.headington-institute.org

The International Strategy for Disaster Risk Reduction: www.unisdr.org

Chapter 6

Working with Aggressive or Violent Service Users

Introduction

Alongside increasing awareness of other types of violence, workplace violence became an issue of international concern during the 1970s. It has been noted to be particularly prevalent in social and health care fields (Gately and Stabb 2005; Littlechild 2005b). Violence may come from service users and their families as well as from colleagues. Violence from colleagues is the subject of the next chapter, so here we will focus on service user violence. This chapter will look at protective measures, as well as remedies for dealing with the consequences of violence if this does take place.

Specific attention to social workers has been somewhat lacking in the more general literature on workplace violence. The research that has been done has been primarily based in the UK and USA (Koritsas, Coles and Boyle 2010). Violence includes verbal aggression, and intimidation, property damage and theft, physical assault, stalking, sexual harassment and sexual assault. Although findings vary from one study to another, in part because different definitions of violence and different time spans are used, it is clear that at least half if not most social workers experience significant violence from service users during their career (Lowe and Korr 2007; Spencer and Munch 2003).

Overall, verbal abuse and intimidation are the most common types of violence. Men appear more likely to experience physical assaults and damage to property than women, whereas younger and inexperienced female workers experience more sexual harassment than other workers. Child protection workers and workers in institutional settings most often experience violence of all types (Jayaratne, Croxton and Mattison 2004; Macdonald and Sirotich 2005; Newhill and Wexler 1997; Winstanley and Hales 2008). Although fortunately infrequent, human service workers, including social workers, are also killed in the line of duty (Littlechild 2005b; Pollack 2010).

Research, including survey research, suggests that experiences of violence are becoming more common. A number of factors are likely to account for this. Deinstitutionalization of mental health service users has led to more people with severe mental health issues being seen in community settings. Drug and alcohol abuse is more prevalent; and youth violence is increasing (Jayaratne *et al.* 2004; Winstanley and Hales 2008).

Impacts of threats of violence towards workers may include immediate feelings of fear or anger, and fight or flight type responses. Often those reactions are suppressed and replaced by trained responses. If de-escalation is not able to be effectively employed, shame and loss of confidence may result in the aftermath, and post-traumatic stress disorder (PTSD) is a possible outcome. However, the impact of violence is not simply relative to the level of that violence. Much depends on the meaning making that occurs around violent incidents, and the extent to which workers feel supported by their organizations.

Despite increasing attention being paid to the problem of workplace violence, and improving attitudes toward victims of violence more generally, about a quarter of social workers and human service workers do not report incidents of violence (Jayaratne *et al.* 2004; Macdonald and Sirotich 2001). As a consequence, the true prevalence of violence remains obscured, and many workers do not gain access to social and practical support. When organizations are not provided with accurate reports, it becomes more difficult to institute appropriate policies and mitigate organizational risk factors.

Lack of reporting may be due to the fact that there continues to be some stigma, whereby workers may be more likely to blame themselves or one another for assaults than to blame the perpetrators. The notion here is that social workers who fall victim to violence have somehow provoked this. Another explanation may be that social workers are sometimes concerned that reporting will lead to already disadvantaged service users being penalized for expressing their frustrations about unmet needs, albeit in unacceptable ways (Kosny and Eakin 2008;

Macdonald and Sirotich 2005). They may also worry that their relationships with service users will be disrupted if they report them for their aggression. However, for workers to be able to be better protected, violence does need to be reported, and followed up by active anti-violence and support measures.

Violence and its impacts

Several participants in the book interviews were yelled at, some were threatened with weapons, and one worker continued to fear dogs due to having been attacked by one.

> **Ella:** A number of times people have threatened violence to me, so I've had to have a plan, a safety plan for me in terms of getting in and out of the office and that kind of thing. I've had people threatening to hit me when I've been in court so I've had to go into court through the judge's chambers to ensure I was safe.
>
> **Rachel:** I think though, when I think about the things that scared me or used to cause me the most distress, and I still, to this day if I'm walking up a strange garden path to a house I don't know, I can still feel my adrenalin rise, because I have been bitten by dogs, I have had clothing torn by dogs, I've had a guy appear at the door with a shotgun, I've been yelled at, and that's still, that's still there. That's the bit I hate.

Probably even more worrying than threats against social workers themselves are threats against their children. These can cause them to leave their employment, and even their homes as did Phoebe, because they decide that work is not worth the risk of their children being harmed.

> **Phoebe:** It was just too much, because I became fearful for my own family because they said that they were going to find out personal details. So that was quite a stressful time. ... I took some leave for a month because we moved. I thought I can't live in my home anymore because they know where we are. ... I had one child at that stage, and of course every time I dropped her off at day care I was going, 'Oh God, are they watching, do they know where she goes?' And my husband for the first time was really

worried too. They did give us a police contact to talk to and things like that. But it wasn't very nice. **,,**

Frontline workers are most at risk and tend to feel least safe (Macdonald and Sirotich 2005). This is understandable because the more direct client contact that workers have, the more likely they are to encounter aggressive service users and their associates. However, while frontline workers have more direct encounters with aggression, supervisors feel distressed when they are unable to protect workers (Spencer and Munch 2003).

In rural areas, human service workers have more social contacts with service users as part of their day-to-day lives in the community. This can make it more difficult to implement strict protection guidelines and zero tolerance policies. In rural communities there are few options but to use community facilities that are also frequented by service users, or to withdraw and live as a virtual recluse.

,, **Val:** You know, X is a small town, and so you'd be in the supermarket getting your groceries and you'd bump into somebody whose kids you'd removed two days before. And you had to be able to get over it and get past it. **,,**

But if service users are unable to 'get past it', rural social workers may be intimidated, subjected to gossip, excluded and become socially isolated. This ostracizing can be extended to their families as well.

Although there is less research into violence directed against community development workers than against caseworkers, they too are likely to be at risk in the community (Spencer and Munch 2003). They may be amongst workers least likely to want to report such violence, because they are concerned that reporting will lead to community members being further disadvantaged, or community projects being imperiled.

The impacts of workplace violence from service users are wide ranging. Workplace violence has been linked to physical symptoms of distress such as migraines, digestive problems, and vomiting. Psychological health problems include depression and anxiety. Quality of work may deteriorate, and workers may avoid working in fields of practice where the risk of violence is perceived to be greater. If workers become burned out as a consequence of ongoing exposure to a threat of violence, they may begin to withdraw from active engagement with service users, and depersonalize clients more generally (Lowe and Korr 2007).

It has also been suggested that fears for their own safety may prevent social workers from intervening assertively, for example in situations of suspected child abuse. They may fail to fully follow up or report on concerns, and fail to network effectively with other agencies (Goddard and Stanley 2002; Littlechild 2002).

Brian Littlechild (2005b, p.66) uses the term 'developing violent scenarios' to describe how social workers can be progressively intimidated and made more vulnerable to increasingly serious abuse over time. He notes that, at the outset, verbal abuse may not be perceived as violence until it escalates. Workers may keep these interchanges secret from others for fear of making matters worse or because they feel embarrassed. Intimidation may also be so subtle that it is difficult to prove that it is taking place.

At this early stage in the development of a 'violent scenario', any prevention or intervention plan will need to be made with full awareness that workers are likely to worry about whether they will be supported and kept safe if they disclose emerging concerns that they may be at risk of violence. Workers are likely to fear that reporting will leave them at increased risk of further violence if, for example, threats they have received are not taken adequately seriously. Workers may also fear that if they report intimidation or other violence they may be retaliated against with complaints. The investigation of complaints can leave them further victimized and under scrutiny when they are already feeling vulnerable.

Without support, if the social worker continues with the case, they are at significant risk of being subjected to escalating violence. In such an unsupported context, their fear and anxiety can generalize to other service users, and even extend outside of work to the home sphere. This may be particularly so if boundaries are crossed by the service user, for example by stalking or intrusive telephone calls (Littlechild 2005b).

As happens with other types of trauma, worldviews may change whereby a social worker's trust in other people becomes diminished. Interpersonal relationships with their colleagues, clients and family members may become negatively affected, to the extent that these parties become secondary victims of the violence toward the worker (Spencer and Munch 2003). The impact of violence toward social workers and other human service workers clearly reaches far beyond individual workers to their families, other service users, colleagues, and the organization.

An important impact of violence that has been relatively overlooked is the intense fear and terror that workers may experience. Fear is infrequently mentioned in social work literature and leaves students feeling uncomfortable when it is raised. Fear of being assaulted is amongst the most distressing recalled experiences at work (Dwyer 2007; Smith and Nursten 1998). Yet fear, as well as being an impact, is also a warning sign telling us that a situation is unsafe. It is therefore important to more clearly identify, even highlight, the experience of fear so that workers will be more likely to heed it.

Pause to reflect on feelings of fear

Fear has physical, cognitive and emotional effects. Physical signs of fear may be felt in the stomach, or result in a rapidly beating heart, quickening of breathing, or a dry mouth. It may be so intense that we lose control over bodily functions. Thoughts may seem to rush, and we may not be able to remember what we have learned, or conversely, our thinking may seem crystal clear. Time may appear to slow down. We may feel emotionally overwhelmed, with a sense of losing our boundaries (Smith, Nursten and McMahon 2004).

If you are unable to identify fear, or habitually push the feeling aside, this can put you at increased risk because you may be ignoring warning signs that you are in danger. If instead you frequently experience fear, this suggests there are significant problems that need to be addressed. It is also likely that you are at risk of being traumatized.

Causes of workplace violence

Before we begin to think about how to protect human service workers from the distress and anxiety of workplace violence, it is helpful to consider what they perceive to be the causes of this violence. It was clear from my discussions with participants that their analyses of those causes were complex. Participants were sensitive to the difficulties faced by service users, whom they did not want to see further penalized by actions taken in response. This needs to be taken into account in any measures for prevention and intervention.

Those working in human services are charged with assisting people to meet their needs and achieve their goals, and yet are also in real or perceived positions of control over how resources are distributed, and whether people will retain the right to self-determination. The desperation service users feel when their aims are frustrated, is a significant factor in the violence directed toward human service professionals such as social workers, nurses, and psychiatrists.

Coupled with this desperation, there may be a lack of capacity for modulating affect (self-soothing of feelings). This may cause service users to feel intense shame at being asked to reveal private information. They may also have difficulty communicating their feelings. Mental health issues including schizophrenia, bipolar disorder, and personality disorders, as well as substance use problems and brain disorders may further compound these difficulties in coping with feelings.

People's desperation can reach critical proportions when they fear their children will be removed from their care. In such circumstances mothers are more likely to attack in a reactive way in immediate situations such as at family group conferences or in court, whereas male service users and their acquaintances may be more likely to use premeditated intimidation and violence. Access to weapons and histories of violence further increase risk (Jayaratne *et al.* 2004; Littlechild 2005a; Lowe and Korr 2007; Pollack 2010; Shields and Kiser 2003).

Some attempts have been made to identify particular types of aggressive patterns, in the hope that if such patterns can be identified, this will then provide guidance on helpful preventive measures. For example, if a service user is prone to over-arousal, it may be helpful to ensure that interactions are kept calm and undemanding. Likewise, if clients are impulsive, predatory, or instrumental in their use of aggression, workers who are alert to the relevance of such information will be able to approach encounters in a more tailored fashion (Gately and Stabb 2005).

While typologies of clients and risk assessments are frequently used in some statutory organizations, for example in criminal justice settings, these approaches may cause considerable unease for workers who are sensitive to the contexts of their clients. Talking about her time in statutory child protection work, Val said, 'It was hard to have people spit at you and call you all sorts of names.' At the same time she also noted:

> **Val:** It has made all the difference to recognize that what people don't like is what you're doing, especially when people, as I said, nobody sets out to be a bad parent. So when someone knocks on your door and says, 'Look, you're not doing a [good job], things aren't going well for your child,' I can't imagine how awful that could be. Well, I can *imagine* how awful that would be, but I can *only* imagine. It must be incredibly difficult.

In community-based non-governmental organizations (NGOs), workers may believe violence, especially verbal violence, results from clients' frustrations with a disempowering system, and they may also be less inclined to take this personally. Sometimes they reframe verbal aggression as occurring because service users trust the helper enough to feel they can vent these frustrations.

> **Rewa:** So I called the way he speaks 'colourful language'. … I said, 'It's like this, it's all part of the job.' … Because, why is it that we expect our clients to say to us, 'Look how lovely it is you've come to take my children away today'? It's just, you know, and I say, 'They want to swear and abuse us because they do not want us social workers in their face.' So when he swears at me, I say, 'He's allowed to, it's his right, it's his way of expressing.' Regardless of whether I think he's right or wrong, it's all part of the work.

Kosny and Eakin (2008) undertook research in three community-based non-profit organizations in Canada and found that human service workers were less likely to report incidents of violence when they perceived that their clients could be disadvantaged or judged when they did so. They were inclined to think that violence was an inherent risk of the job, and they thought statutory workers were more fearful and less committed to a mission of supporting clients. Sometimes workers put themselves in dangerous situations as a result of this discourse and their adherence to these views. Not only frontline workers, but also managers appeared to believe that providing a risk-free environment for workers would have a negative impact on work with clients. The organization might be thought to belong to the clients rather than the workers (Kosny and Eakin 2008).

If social workers are less likely to report incidents of violence when they believe their clients may be disadvantaged or judged if they do so, this needs to be taken into account when designing workplace anti-violence policies.

Interventions

The acknowledgement that human service workers are at risk of workplace violence from service users is an important starting place for any prevention and intervention attempts. Until recently, attention to issues of violence toward social workers was lacking in curricula and textbooks. There was a relatively widespread lack of knowledge amongst social workers about whether and what safety procedures were in place in their agencies (Beddoe, Appleton and Maher 1998; Spencer and Munch 2003). New social work graduates in New Zealand also complained of a lack of attention paid to safety-related training during their induction into agency practice by comparison to their colleagues from other professions such as nursing (van Heugten and Rathgen 2003).

More recently, the level of awareness about the need for safety procedures for social workers has improved (Shields and Kiser 2003), and there is less expectation that social workers will put up with verbal and other harassment, although in practice, out in the community, social workers may still be at risk.

> **Rachel:** I don't think anyone should have to deal with it, so, you know, there is much more acceptance of [saying], 'Look I'm not going to continue this conversation and I'm going to hang up,' and that's the end of it. But if you're in someone's house you don't get that opportunity.

Training in de-escalation has become mandatory in many statutory organizations and NGOs.

> **Joe:** They have yearly mandatory training on what they call de-escalation where they teach you how to break away from people that might grab you and things like that. Yeah, and also in the same training they talk to you about the basics of de-escalating people. ... Those things I think are probably quite positive.

Amanda noted that even with careful assessments and safety plans in place, a degree of uncertainty about the risk of violence remains. As a manager, she worried about the wellbeing of her staff, and did not feel fully at ease in the evenings unless she knew they had returned safely from visits.

> **Amanda:** And we have good measures to check, prior, all the practicalities around any of the safety issues, but there's that unknown. It's like [wanting to know], 'What time are you going to be finishing work and will you be back here in that car and that car be parked up nice and everything fine?' – so that as a manager you are having a restful evening.

Recommendations to improve staff protection from violence abound, but recommendations are only effective when they are followed. Furthermore, when violence does occur, it is important that there is follow-up support for staff, and that there are appropriate consequences for perpetrators.

Some of the most common recommendations relate to home visits and include carrying cell phones set up to call for assistance, not visiting alone when there is a risk of violence, and ensuring someone knows where you are and when you are expected back in the office (Jayaratne *et al.* 2004).

In office settings, the organization of the physical work environment and the way in which service users are treated within those settings are important factors in reducing the risk of service user aggression and violence. For example, reducing waiting times and providing reading materials lead to service users feeling calmer and more respected. Waiting areas and offices should not contain furniture or fittings that can be easily used as weapons, and should have exit routes and alarms. Most organizations have policies that prohibit working alone in the agency, especially after hours (Lowe and Korr 2007).

Staff should be trained about risks of violence, and have the skills to recognize early warning signs, including signs that violent scenarios are developing (Littlechild 2005b) or that aggression may be imminent such as may be indicated by staring, shouting, muttering, pacing and other signs of increased agitation (Pollack 2010).

Means of defusing anger include verbal skills such as apologizing without taking on blame, and not interrupting clients or arguing with angry clients. When working with potentially aggressive people, general safety measures may include keeping one's physical distance, perhaps by remaining behind a desk, and when a client becomes angry, avoiding eye contact and not turning one's back. Where weapons are involved, personal safety is paramount and it is normally wisest to leave immediately, or if that is not possible, to call for help. If neither of these options is available, remaining calm and obeying the aggressor's instructions are important. It is also essential to have good relationships with law enforcement organizations (Lowe and Korr 2007; Pollack 2010).

As de-escalation training and safety training become more available, there is a risk that social workers may believe that they should be able to manage and avert violence in all situations. Seasoned practitioners in particular, may develop false confidence (Spencer and Munch 2003). It is important, therefore, to emphasize that when we feel afraid it is often wise to trust our instincts, which may be to leave first and analyze the situation later.

Physical or pharmacological restraint may be required, but should only be used when workers have received adequate training in techniques, and about the circumstances in which restraint may be used. The use of restraint is often distressing for both parties. When a worker has used restraint, this may be legally challenged as the restraint needs to be the least restrictive necessary to achieve safety of self or others. In heated situations, there is always a risk that restraint may be overused (Fish and Culshaw 2005; Pollack 2010).

Joe continued to feel traumatized by an incident he had observed many years ago.

    Joe: And this particular police officer went into the back of the car and smashed him across the face to get him to stop spitting at people, and I still think about that as quite traumatizing. And I guess it wasn't me directly involved in the situation, but I sort of felt that it was reasonably traumatizing. I actually went with the client to the police station so he didn't actually get hit again.

With increasing experience, workers do come to feel more confident in dealing with angry and aggressive clients. They learn to recognize phases in the development of aggression, including triggering, escalation, crisis, recovery, and post-crisis depression phases. Each of these offers unique challenges as well as opportunities for intervention (Gately and Stabb 2005). Active training that involves enacting scenarios, and building response plans around 'what if' examples is helpful (Spencer and Munch 2003). Passive learning alone is not enough.

In the aftermath of a violent incident, social workers and service users may all need support (Gately and Stabb 2005). Possible outcomes for service users and workers need to be carefully considered, and in some contexts, mediation and restorative responses may be possible and valuable (Spencer and Munch 2003). At other times, it will be unwise or impossible for the worker to continue to engage with the client. Being alert to post-crisis phases will assist everyone involved to understand that this can be experienced as a loss for both parties, and to respond with compassion.

There is a tension between the need for workers to process the traumatic impact of violent incidents at their own pace, in keeping with the recommendations presented in Chapter 5, and the contrasting need for reports to be completed as soon as possible after a violent incident. Care needs to be taken in explaining and structuring the reporting requirements. In addition, for incident reports to be truly beneficial, the information that emerges from them needs to be used to prevent further events, including by warning other workers about dangers. This step in responding to violence is still too often missing (Lowe and Korr 2007).

It is critical that the aftermath of reporting is well-handled with a balance between under and over-reacting. If reports are neglected there is a significant risk that staff will fail to report in the future and safety will deteriorate. Compassion fatigue may result, and lead to staff becoming helpless or moving into denial in the face of service users' violence and perhaps failing to heed warning signs or making full assessments (Spencer and Munch 2003). On the other hand, workers may experience over-reactions by supervisors and managers as depowering, and then may worry about negative consequences on the aggressor, or all service users if more extensive risk management measures are instituted (Smith *et al.* 2004).

Supportive peers and supervisors can offer empathic as well as practical support. Practical support includes assisting with cancelling appointments if there is a need to take time out, taking a distressed colleague home, and helping with the transfer of clients if necessary (Spencer and Munch 2003).

Supervisors should receive sufficient training and management support for addressing concerns. Without these, supervisors may ignore issues due to lack of knowledge, pressures of time and worries about reactions from their superiors (Littlechild 2005b).

By contrast to colleagues and supervisors, senior managers are often less accessible and they may appear to express more concern with liability-related matters than with the practitioner. They may also use formal approaches when problems might potentially still be able to be resolved at a lower level (Smith *et al.* 2004). In a survey of former and current social work supervisors in mental health services in the USA, researchers found that some supervisors think that organizational managers tend to be insufficiently supportive of anti-violence measures, and yet will blame supervisors if their workers get hurt (Lowe and Korr 2007).

Although workers may express misgivings about the engagement of managers around issues of workplace violence, it is crucial that they are involved. Managers can attend to violence as a workplace rather than an individual issue. In the immediate situation, line managers are organizationally best placed to support workers by ensuring they have access to adequate legal advice (Spencer and Munch 2003). In the longer term, managers are in a position to encourage a holistic review of patterns around the antecedents of violence, leading to identification of workplace measures that better prevent recurrence (Pollack 2010). They play an important role in setting expectations of civil behaviour, and model by their example that aggression is an issue worthy of attention. When managers actively engage supervisors and workers in the development of policies and practices, they help foster a workplace culture wherein support is made available and concerns about under and over-reactions are heeded.

Workplace 'zero tolerance' policies are generally advocated (Jayaratne *et al.* 2004), but it is not always clear what 'zero tolerance' means in practice. As we have already seen, such policies may in fact reduce reporting if human service workers believe their clients will be unfairly disadvantaged. The definition of violence also poses difficulties. As was clear from participants' comments, swearing at a worker may be perceived as legitimate venting by some practitioners whilst others regard this as abusive.

Whilst a blanket approach is an impossible goal, overt discussion of these complexities is vital. What is clear, is that for workers to be comfortable about reporting aggression there needs to be more consideration of how their client service values will be weighed into the balance when reports are dealt with. They are likely to want to retain some control over that.

Macdonald and Sirotich (2005) also note that social workers may find it difficult to talk about service user violence because they may feel this would be disloyal to clients who are already oppressed. They suggest that future research could explore the impact of ideology and values and how these may contribute to minimizing of client violence and victim blaming. They also suggest that the male–female imbalance of managers and frontline workers may play a part in the ongoing minimizing of violence, when male managers fail to listen or respond to women's fears. They recommend that information about predicting violence and managing violence should be integrated into educational curricula and in-service training.

In many countries, including the UK, the USA, New Zealand and Australia, organizational policies are situated in a background of legislation, in particular labour laws that have made violence and aggression a health and safety workplace issue. In keeping with such legislation, codes of conduct, practice and ethics also require that staff and clients are kept safe from violence. In the UK, for example, the General Social Care Council (2010a, 2010b) stipulates that social care workers, including social workers, must keep themselves and others safe from violence and abuse, and report abuse when it occurs. Employers are exhorted to support staff to achieve safety in practice and to notify clients that threats and violence are unacceptable.

The workplace violence toolkit

The discussion above covered major issues that need to be taken into consideration when dealing with workplace violence from service users. These are summarized below. The importance of education and training is emphasized because inexperienced workers are most at risk. The period of induction into an agency also offers opportunities for establishing good practices and emphasizing team support.

Individual considerations

- Do you feel safe at work today? If you are a supervisor or manager, do you believe your workers are safe? Pay attention to your gut feelings and if you do not feel safe, and instead feel fear, consider what needs to happen to change this. Living with a significant worry that you or your workers will be harmed is not something that should be tolerated on an ongoing basis.

- Do you take shortcuts in relation to your safety, for example do you avoid asking for support because your team-mates are busy, even when you know your agency protocol recommends that you do? You may get away without incident many times, but just one event of violence can lead to major repercussions for you, your clients and your agency.

- If you need to report a lack of safety, you need to be able to do so in the secure knowledge that this will be more likely to improve rather than deteriorate the situation. Most often you will meet with organizational support, but not always. Workers who have reported on workplace health and safety risks have sometimes needed to use whistleblower legislation to do so safely. It may be wise for you to determine your rights as a worker, to ensure your reporting will not put you at further risk, either from client violence or from organizational responses. You may want to seek advice from your supervisor or from your union depending on your circumstances.

- Do you have particular vulnerabilities, disabilities, or training needs? Discuss these with your supervisor so that you can plan for how your needs may be met.

Organizational considerations

- If you provide social work education, does your programme overtly address the fact that violence from service users is a real risk for those engaged in human service work? Are students provided with training in relation to dealing with potential violence prior to their involvement in fieldwork with service users? It may be difficult for a generic programme to adequately provide for this, and if so, there needs to be an articulation of how essential education and practical training will be provided in the induction of students into fieldwork agencies.

- In agency practice, the safety needs of workers need to be prioritized alongside the mission and values of the organization. Any seeming conflicts between the interests of service users and workers need to be identified and overcome.

- Policies should be known, readily accessible, and regularly reviewed. They should be developed with the input of staff. Some organizations establish a violence management team including members from various levels of the organization. Service user representatives or advocates may also be involved. This ensures that the issue of violence is kept to the fore. New information about best practice and legal developments is fed into the team's work.

- Risk management to prevent or deal with incidents should be ongoing:

  o Practical steps include attending to such things as safety of the office environment, and safety of workers undertaking work in the community. Workers need to be adequately resourced with equipment, such as cell phones, and staffing levels to allow for team backup.

  o Reporting of workplace aggression from service users should be routine, and these reports should be used as active tools for improving workplace safety. This means that the information that is collected needs to help identify antecedents to incidents of violence. Feedback is also required about what worked in terms of responses, and what did not work so well. The factual information in reports should be used to adequately protect other workers.

  o Plans must be in compliance with local legal requirements around health and safety of workers. They should also be compliant with legal requirements and codes of ethics around service users' rights.

- Outside of immediate incidents, input can be sought from staff about suggestions for improvements that may help protect workers from workplace violence. Near misses can provide especially constructive insights in this regard.

- Good relationships with external organizations such as the police are essential, as is adequate access to legal advice and confidential counselling services.

- Ongoing practical training and refresher training are helpful for frontline staff but it is important not to overlook the needs of supervisors and managers. We know from research that even the best policy documents are of little use if supervisors and managers are unclear about how they can supportively implement these.

Finally, remember that it is your right to be safe from violence at work, and your employers have a legal duty to protect your safety. This includes keeping you safe from violence perpetrated by colleagues, which is the topic covered in the next chapter.

Additional resources
Fear in social work
Smith, M. (2005) *Surviving Fears in Health and Social Care: The Terrors of Night and the Arrows of Day.* London: Jessica Kingsley Publishers.

Workplace violence
International Labour Organization, International Council of Nurses, World Health Organization and Public Services International (2005) *Framework Guidelines for Addressing Workplace Violence in the Health Sector: The Training Manual.* www.ilo.org/public/english/dialogue/sector/publ/health/manual.pdf

To find further information, access the website of your country's ministry or department of labour. These sites provide links to current occupational health and safety legislation, research reports, and recommendations for safety measures. Your union or social work association may also be able to support you or direct you to further assistance.

Chapter 7

Rudeness, Bullying and Violence in the Workplace

Introduction

The problem of workplace violence from service users that was covered in the last chapter has only relatively recently begun to be addressed. Yet attention to that issue still far outstrips the extent to which we address workplace violence from colleagues. Aggression directed by workers to one another has the potential to cause more stress and trauma than any other workplace issue. It strikes at the heart of social workers' belief in the integrity of their own profession. While the profession purports to stand for justice and fair play, this is hardly the experience of those who are at the receiving end of violence from colleagues.

My interest in violence between colleagues in the workplace was sparked some years ago when I received a University of Canterbury grant to research service user violence against social workers. I undertook a literature review and found that there was already a reasonable amount of information about violence from service users, but a lack of consideration of collegial violence amongst social workers. This was curious given it had been, by contrast, recognized to be a serious problem amongst nurses. Because of this, and because of my own and others' anecdotal experiences I thought it likely that violence amongst social workers would be just as common.

I therefore revised my research project to enable me to investigate workplace violence from colleagues, and in 2004 I undertook semi-structured interviews with social workers to find out more about their experiences (van Heugten 2010). It transpired that all of the

17 participants for that research talked about psychological violence of the kind we commonly call bullying.

It is interesting to speculate why there was no-one amongst the participants whose account centred on sexual harassment. Several did note that the person who had bullied them also crossed sexual boundaries with other team members and that this behaviour impacted on team allegiances. The absence of accounts of sexual harassment may be in part due to this being a rarer form of workplace violence. In many countries, sexual harassment has been outlawed since the late 1970s and most workplaces have strongly prohibitive policies although implementation of these may not always be adequate. It is also possible, however, that sexual harassment remains a significantly shaming experience and that workers are less likely to speak about it than about other forms of violence.

In any case, when considering workplace violence, it is important to remember that this concept covers a spectrum from rudeness to serious physical assault. Workplace violence perpetuated by colleagues may take the form of sexual harassment, gender, race, age or disability-related discrimination, or psychological bullying or mobbing. It only rarely escalates to physical violence.

The related concept of organizational violence is complex. Whilst organizational practices and policies may negatively impact on workers' levels of stress, the term violence is reserved for situations where the pursuit of organizational goals overrides workers' needs. Stressful impacts on workers are treated with reckless disregard, as if these are irrelevant (Parzefall and Salin 2010). Bullying and organizational violence may be linked in complex ways. One of the ways organizational goals may be achieved may be by allowing bullying to persist.

In this chapter I discuss forms of violence perpetrated by colleagues, the distress these cause, and what we know to date about what works in dealing with these relatively common problems. The models introduced in Chapter 1 continue to be applicable, and in particular the Demand–Control–Support model's message that loss of control coupled with lack of support increase workplace stress is borne out. The discussion about bullying and the related toolkit recommendations draw on the findings from my workplace bullying research. All of the quotes in this chapter are from participants in that earlier research.

Sexual harassment
Legal definitions of sexual harassment

The concept of sexual harassment first emerged in the literature in the 1970s when there was a growing awareness that women were made uncomfortable and left places of employment because of the sexualized behaviour of men toward them. American lawyer Catharine MacKinnon has been credited with defining sexual harassment as sex discrimination which brought it under the purview of human rights-related legislation, specifically 'the right to work' (Baker 2007).

The topic received considerable attention until the late 1990s, but over the last decade little new research or literature has emerged (Hunt *et al.* 2010). In terms of the social work literature, there has been almost no attention to the subject of sexual harassment in the twenty-first century to date.

Legislation continues to be refined. In the UK, the Sex Discrimination Act 1975 (Amendment) Regulations (2008) prohibit sexual harassment in the workplace. The regulations broadly define sexual harassment as unwanted conduct related to a person's sex. Employers may be liable for prosecution if they fail to protect their employees from sexual harassment or sexual discrimination in the workplace, whether this harassment or discrimination is from other workers or service users. Whilst the complainant must establish a prima facie case, the burden of providing an adequate explanation thereafter falls to the employer.

In New Zealand, sexual harassment is prohibited under the Employment Relations Act (2000), and people who are sexually harassed in the workplace may also make a complaint to the Human Rights Commission.

Two types of sexual harassment are commonly identified. The first is quid pro quo harassment, which usually involves an implication that 'I'll do this for you if you do that sexual something for me'. The second is 'hostile environment' harassment where sexualized demands or behaviours, including jokes and innuendo which may not necessarily be aimed at the complainant, create an intimidating or hostile or offensive work environment (O'Donohue *et al.* 2006).

Disclosures and impacts of sexual harassment

It is difficult to find out the true extent of workplace sexual harassment. Despite awareness, improved legislation, and workplace policies and support, it is still often difficult for people who have been sexually harassed to disclose this.

Impediments to disclosure include shame and self-doubt, and the stigma of being judged negatively for raising concern over inappropriate sexualized behaviours (Fitzgerald, Swan and Fischer 1995). Victims may also fear, not without justification, that their past and present personal lives, including, for example, prior childhood sexual abuse may be used to try to cast doubts on their reliability, despite the fact that such attempts have no credibility (Fitzgerald *et al.* 1999; Stockdale *et al.* 2002). Women who are sexually harassed, whether they do or do not report this, are often labelled negatively, and fear being judged to be less trustworthy by their colleagues (Marin and Guadagno 1999).

A recent survey conducted in the UK found that only one in every 100 workers declared they had experienced sexual harassment during the last two years, although four in every 100 declared they were aware of someone else having been harassed during that time. The researchers note that this points to difficulties in undertaking research into a subject on which people are reluctant to disclose personal information (Grainger and Fitzner 2007). Even in anonymous surveys, women will under-report sexual harassment. A meta-analysis of survey research undertaken in the USA found that if people are asked directly whether they have ever been sexually harassed, only about a quarter of female workers will disclose this, whereas just over half will acknowledge that they have been subjected to particular behaviours that are harassing (Ilies *et al.* 2003).

There appears to be more sexual harassment in larger hierarchically structured organizations (Ilies *et al.* 2003). In particular where there is a power imbalance between the sexes, the more dominant sex will extend their power across personal as well as professional boundaries (Hunt *et al.* 2010). This would suggest that in human services there is an increased risk that male workers will be harassed, and there is some evidence that this is the case. For example, in social work education, male students have been found to be proportionally more likely to be harassed by female students (Risley-Curtiss and Hudson 1998).

Shame and stigma about having been subjected to sexual harassment may be even more intense for men. When they report their experiences, these may also be minimized by others who fail to conceive of men as potential victims (Risley-Curtiss and Hudson 1998). Reporting has also been found to be more difficult for women from collectivist or patriarchal cultures who find it more difficult to seek assistance following such attacks on their dignity (van Heugten 2004; Wasti and Cortina 2002).

Some of the significant publications on sexual harassment in the field of social work have emerged in the educational arena. Students typically find it difficult to interpret inappropriate behaviours from academic and field instructors, or to know how to deal with them when they happen (Strom-Gottfried 2000). Although educators may express a belief that sexual relationships with students are unethical, their behaviours sometimes belie this (Congress 2001).

Sexual boundary crossing by people in positions of power over students tends to make completion of study more difficult. Such boundary crossing by educators also models poor practice. If students do eventually graduate and enter practice, it has been found that those who have been subjected to such behaviours are subsequently more likely to cross professional boundaries with clients (Congress 2001; Pope and Feldman-Summers 1992).

For practising social workers, sexual harassment is not only against the law, but it is against their codes of ethics. Codes of ethics of social work professional associations typically began to incorporate statements in relation to sexual boundary crossing with clients, supervisees and colleagues from the 1990s (Reamer 1998; Risley-Curtiss and Hudson 1998). However, while codes of ethics provide some relatively clear guidelines, parties involved in relationships that contravene these codes may not agree that a problem exists. It may not be until conflicts of interest arise when a relationship deteriorates and there are consequences to employment or education that concerns are expressed (Pope and Feldman-Summers 1992; Robinson 2006; van Heugten 2004; van Heugten and Jones 2007).

The impacts of experiencing sexual harassment include distress, depression, low self-esteem, fear of more unwanted sexualized encounters, isolation, work withdrawal and absenteeism, problems with sleeping, difficulties in sexual functioning in intimate relationships, and substance abuse (Hanrahan 1997; O'Donohue *et al*. 2006; Risley-Curtiss and Hudson 1998). Some authors suggest that sexual harassment may be so traumatizing that victims develop symptoms consistent with a diagnosis of PTSD. Traumatization may result not only from the actual harassment, but from the gossip, isolation, retaliation and financial losses that may accompany it. When victims make complaints, their private lives may be exposed and this loss of privacy is also traumatic (O'Donohue *et al*. 2006).

Seemingly low level but frequent harassment, such as sexual jokes, may have just as negative an impact on personal and professional confidence and wellbeing as one-off high level incidents, such as sexual coercion (Schneider, Swan and Fitzgerald 1997).

Reflecting on sexual harassment

Is there a problem with sexual harassment in your workplace? Have you noticed inappropriate remarks, jokes, requests or touching that makes you or your colleagues feel uncomfortable? Does your organization have a clear sexual harassment policy and are there identified persons with whom you can talk about your concerns?

Dealing with sexual harassment in the workplace

While sexual harassment continues to be surrounded by stigma, reporting rates are likely to remain low. Attempts to prevent or deal with harassment will then naturally meet many obstacles. Workers who do report sexual harassment are typically retaliated against, for example via gossip and isolation. Nevertheless, silence in the face of harassment has the most negative consequences on health and self-esteem (Cortina and Magley 2003).

It is generally recognized that prevention via establishing an organizational anti-harassment culture is the best method of dealing with harassment. Since higher levels of sexual harassment have been found in organizations where there are major power differentials between genders, improving power sharing and equity is likely to be of benefit. Providing training in appropriate conduct is generally considered helpful and such training can increase levels of sensitivity to what might constitute inappropriate behaviour. Case studies, role plays and group discussions may be helpful awareness raising techniques.

On their own these techniques are insufficient. What is also necessary are effective policy and intervention mechanisms that send a clear message that harassment will not be tolerated. Consultative approaches to developing policies are most helpful. Organizations that provide a network approach to advice giving with various entry points to support are more likely to receive notifications of harassment than organizations that provide for formal reporting only. Organizations that have higher levels of reporting do not necessarily have higher levels of harassment. They may have better processes in place that encourage staff to raise their concerns (Hunt *et al.* 2010).

Individuals who take a formal route to complaint continue to find that they are not taken seriously, that complaints take a long time to resolve, and that they may be blamed. Complainants have often left their jobs by the time a case comes to a hearing. It is not surprising, therefore, that many people attempt to resolve situations themselves via direct confrontation or perhaps more commonly, avoidance (Hunt *et al.* 2010).

During court proceedings and in their aftermath, informal networks as well as more formal counselling where people can begin to discuss what has occurred are important avenues for support. Outside support may be important in view of the fact that work retaliation has been found to be common, and also because collegial and managerial loyalties may be divided.

Workplace bullying
Defining workplace bullying
The type of workplace aggression that is now termed bullying was first identified as a significant problem in the 1980s by Swedish psychology professor Heinz Leymann who noted the impact of persistent workplace aggression, which he termed mobbing, on victims and their families. He insisted on a relatively rigid definition of mobbing as occurring at least weekly and over an extended period of at least six months (Leymann 1996). Over time, the term mobbing has come to be associated with situations in which a group gangs up, commonly against a colleague

or superior, whereas bullying stands for the psychological harassment of a target, usually but not always by a superior. The most commonly cited current definition of bullying remains Ståle Einarsen *et al.*'s (2003) definition:

66 Bullying at work means harassing, offending, socially excluding someone or negatively affecting someone's work tasks. ... it has to occur repeatedly and regularly (e.g. weekly) and over a period of time (e.g. about six months). Bullying is an escalating process in the course of which the person confronted ends up in an inferior position and becomes the target of systematic negative social acts. A conflict cannot be called bullying if the incident is an isolated event or if two parties of approximately equal 'strength' are in conflict. (Einarsen *et al.* 2003, p.15) 99

In addition it is generally accepted that '[the bullying behaviours] clearly cause humiliation, offence and distress, and ... [they] may interfere with job performance and/or cause an unpleasant working environment' (Einarsen *et al.* 2003, p.6).

There is now a significant international body of literature on workplace bullying and during the first decade of the twenty-first century research into this phenomenon outstripped research into sexual harassment. Whilst the definition above is widely accepted, other aspects, such as whether behaviours must be intentionally perpetrated or deliberately harmful to qualify as bullying continue to be debated (Parzefall and Salin 2010).

The prevalence of workplace bullying is also still unclear although it does appear to be relatively common. Meta reviews of research suggest that, except perhaps in Scandinavian countries where rates may be lower, between 10 per cent and 20 per cent of workers in Europe (including the UK), the USA, Australia and New Zealand are subjected to at least a moderate level of bullying each year (Beale and Hoel 2010; Bentley *et al.* 2009; Høgh *et al.* 2009; Roscigno, Lopez and Hodson 2009). Using more stringent criteria suggests approximately 4 per cent of European workers are exposed to severe bullying at any given point in time (Zapf *et al.* 2011). Bullying has been recognized to be particularly common in hospitality, education, health and social services (Bentley *et al.* 2009; Zapf *et al.* 2011). Between 50 per cent and 80 per cent of the perpetrators are superiors and managers (Beale and Hoel 2010; Høgh *et al.* 2009; Janusz 2010). Other perpetrators include colleagues and subordinates. First line supervisors and middle managers may be bullied by others higher up in the hierarchy, as well as by subordinates, and female managers appear to be at greater risk of being bullied than male managers (Høgh *et al.* 2009; Janusz 2010).

In addition to growing interest from researchers, there is also an increasing interest from government bodies, including ministries/ departments of health and labour, and from unions and large employers. Despite such increasing interest, workers may be sceptical and disbelieve that managers will do more than pay lip service or take effective action against other managers who bully staff. Bullying is most often dealt with via non-specific complaints mechanisms and internal mediation.

Internationally, there are few specific laws against bullying and because of this, people who pursue complaints via the courts have to creatively use other legislation. In the UK, USA, Australia and New Zealand they may use health and safety legislation citing stress, human rights legislation citing discrimination, or harassment or stalking-related legislation. Few cases are upheld, but over time clearer outcomes and frameworks for decision-making are emerging (Beale and Hoel 2010; van Heugten 2007). In the UK, the Employment Act (2008) emphasizes early intervention and mediation in workplace disputes, but it is yet to be seen how helpful this will be in cases of bullying (Beale and Hoel 2010).

It is striking that, despite over a decade of research, there continues to be a lack of specific policies in organizations, and a lack of specific legislative prohibitions. This may be related to concerns that tough or unpopular management styles will be complained against more easily if legislation is put in place. Managers undertake performance appraisals and performance management of staff in a context where restructuring, which often amounts to 'rationalizing' or 'downsizing' of staffing complements, has become ubiquitous. They are frequently under significant pressure from above to implement these measures.

When I invited participants for a grounded study of collegial violence, I had not set out to specifically study bullying (van Heugten 2004), but to investigate the various types of coworker instigated violence encountered by social workers. However, I found that the people I interviewed all spoke of having been subjected to behaviours that fit within the standard definitions of bullying.

The participants were 13 women and four men from five New Zealand cities. Four participants were indigenous Māori and four had emigrated from Europe. Eight of the settings in which the bullying took place were public health organizations, including hospitals, and the rest were NGOs, child protection and criminal justice organizations, plus one private practice. In some other occupations such as nursing, the research suggests that workers who are bullied tend to be younger and less experienced workers (Duncan *et al.* 2001). This was not the case for the group of workers who took part in my research. All bar one were above the age of 35, and they were mostly highly experienced. Eight were in supervisory or middle management positions at the time they were bullied.

Whilst almost half of the participants were themselves in positions of relative authority, most had been bullied by a person at a yet higher level in the organizational hierarchy. In only one case was a manager bullied by a colleague and mobbed by her staff. Whilst 'upward bullying' is a less common occurrence, it may be a particular risk for female managers. It may also be more likely to occur in situations where managers depend on staff who have expertise that they can selectively withhold in order to exert expert power (Branch, Ramsay and Barker 2007).

Bullying behaviours consisted of verbal putdowns and derogatory remarks; interference with professional tasks and roles; and efforts to isolate the worker.

Personal comments included comments on clothing and appearance. Participants were shouted and sworn at and they were called names. More frequently, however, participants were insulted and excessively criticized in relation to their work. They felt they were being micromanaged by their supervisors. Five participants complained that their supervisors failed to attend to their needs, talked mostly about themselves, yelled and swore, or took breaks to smoke cigarettes.

> **Lara:** She kind of hijacked supervision, and she would say, 'No, hang on a minute, don't [talk about that], that's enough,' and, 'This is what we are going to talk about. Now what of this, and what of that?' And she would control it, and I didn't like the feel of it.

A bullying culture developed wherein participants would be prevented from carrying out their roles and tasks effectively. Eleven commented on ways in which they were losing job control. They felt increasingly de-skilled, and their access to clients was more often coming under the control of managers from outside their profession. They were concerned that vital information was withheld from them and they were stopped from participating in decision-making that related to their jobs. They did not necessarily perceive all of the processes via which this happened as bullying, but they narrated a general context in which they were increasingly losing voice.

Participants who were middle managers and supervisors felt distressed when they were deprived of adequate information about the direction in which the organization was moving, and they were unable to effectively plan and support the team for which they were responsible. Others, whilst they did have information, were threatened with disciplinary action if they revealed it.

In human service organizations, team meetings and gatherings are important sites for professional networking and information sharing as well as for making social connections. Participants talked about how they were excluded from meetings by not being told when and where these were being held. Five participants talked about multidisciplinary meetings, most often in public health settings, which had become occasions for being publicly humiliated.

> **Megan:** For example, one of the things which had become a weekly headache for a lot of people was the weekly … meeting. And the reason for the distress was this particular person and the way she responded and worked with some members of the team when they were presenting cases.
>
> **Timothy:** [I was] at times belittled, made to look foolish, or not in control, or not in full possession of the facts when it was implied that I ought to be – those kinds of things.

Ten participants talked about extensive divisions that had arisen in their teams. Bullies caused 'splitting' by forming alliances with some staff while excluding others. They employed friends and occasionally engaged in sexual relationships with staff. Gossip also caused divisions and mistrust in teams. Lara said, 'I was aware that she always had somebody in her sights that she was running down, and she frequently, she talked about everybody behind their back. There wasn't one person that she didn't run down.'

Most participants found that their colleagues remained silent bystanders to public displays of inappropriate behaviours. This led them to feel uncertain and insecure about in whom they could place their trust.

In addition to experiences that impacted on participants in the work environment, bullying also interfered at the interface of work and home. Normal workplace flexibility that was provided for other workers as a matter of course, such as time off to take children to appointments with medical specialists or to attend meetings with teachers, were arbitrarily refused.

'Cyber-bullying' via emails has become more prevalent in recent years, and in my research, emails had been used to threaten or expose workers, for example by responding to private communications by copying multiple parties. The extent of cyber-bullying is probably limited by the fact that this provides targets with concrete evidence of misbehaviour.

Reflecting on workplace bullying

Do you recognize patterns of bulling or incivility in your workplace? Sometimes these become easier to identify once you have a name for the behaviours you have observed. Are you aware of relevant policies in your agency? Are there clearly set out protocols for raising concerns?

Impacts of bullying

Distress caused by bullying is reported to be increasing internationally (Dawood 2010). Participants in my bullying research reported a large range of negative consequences. These included sleeplessness, over and under eating, stomach upsets, muscular tension and skin rashes. They felt distressed and found themselves crying on the way home from work or in bed at night. They became more anxious and stopped enjoying their work. Five had been diagnosed with depression by their general medical practitioner although only two took prescription medication. Just one female participant said she had developed problems with drinking. Fear was frequently mentioned and participants appeared to experience a sense of uncertainty about how far the bully would take their abuse. None had been hit, but they reported that the bully used standover tactics, and in a small number of cases they knew of the bully's violence toward others.

Although only one of the participants noted that her collection of symptoms qualified for a diagnosis of PTSD, others identified similar effects such as being constantly on guard and hypervigilant, avoidant, and yet unable to stop ruminating or obsessively talking about the bullying to family and friends. Participants said they could think of little else and not only their working days but also their family and leisure time were impacted by this. They were irritable and grumpy or simply very unhappy and distracted from the present moment (Einarsen and Mikkelsen 2003; van Heugten 2010).

> **Amy:** I avoid people on the weekend because I'm too stressed and I don't feel like I can communicate well with people. Yeah. I met a friend in the street yesterday and I said, 'hello,' paused for a moment and turned and walked off. That's someone I've known for many years. I just didn't think that I could talk, because it's become like the hugest part of my life – which I never intended for it to be – and because of the way that it's made me feel about myself. I feel very fragile a lot of the time. I feel like I might cry, sometimes.

As workers felt demoralized and undervalued, they were less able to draw on their creative capacities. They withdrew from work projects or extra roles such as supervising students, not only because they had lost self-confidence, but also because they feared that the bully would damage their efforts and cause them to fail.

Interestingly, however, whilst participants lost confidence, they rarely said they lost self-esteem. Their socially supportive connections to at least some colleagues, and in the case of seven participants the support of their external supervisor, probably saved them from that.

Support from colleagues was severely limited, however, and became further reduced over the duration of the bullying. It was particularly the silence of bystanders that led participants to become uncertain about whom they could trust, and nine spoke of the isolation they had felt as a result of that (van Heugten 2010).

Following an initial period of bewilderment and failed attempts to directly approach and achieve a better relationship with the bully, many participants had become angry. The extent of anger and revenge fantasies took them by surprise as they conceived of rude names to call bullies, or how they would like to damage their cars. Other researchers have noted that anger may also develop toward the employing organization because targets perceive that they are being treated unfairly or not helped. They may then retaliate by under-performing at least in some activities (Hershcovis and Barling 2010).

Over time, the meaning of work may change and investment in caring work may be reduced (Gray *et al.* 2010). Participants talked about how disappointed they were in their 'helping' profession. Worldview changes impacted broadly on views of women, managers, or for one immigrant participant, on his view of New Zealand as his adopted home.

> **Phillip:** Having thought that this country was one that gave the women the vote first, I find sexism actually, just as racism, as rampant as I've seen it in the worst other situations I've been in, and um, this is not very welcoming or not very helpful for integration in a society.

The wider literature reports that bullies often stay and may even be promoted while targets eventually leave. This was the case also in my research, where by the time of the interviews, 12 participants had exited the workplace in which bullying took place and all of the others were considering or actively planning to do so (van Heugten 2010).

The distressing impact of being bullied can be so serious that workers begin to feel suicidal (Hanley, Bryant and Buttigieg 2009), and distress tends to continue after they have left the organization in which the bullying took place (Roscigno *et al.* 2009). This may be in part due to long-term consequences such as loss of employment and financial difficulties. Most of my participants found other work because they were well-experienced, they had good connections, and there is a shortage of social workers. Following a recovery period, they emerged more resilient, but eight participants talked about the grief they felt over how they had been treated, and over the loss of a job in which they would have remained, had they not been bullied.

> **Judith:** Yeah, and a sense, I think, of going ... through a grieving process, because it's been a job I really loved, and I felt very at home in. And I think I've always been a very good worker in that particular area, so I know that I have done a good job, but it's almost been, um, quite a lot of sadness to think, 'Yeah it's time to go' because of something that's come from outside of you.

Bullying causes negative impacts not only on targets but also on bystanders, service users and organizations. Witnesses may become desensitized to incivility in the workplace and this may alter the workplace culture. Group cohesion tends to be reduced, and the consequent lack of communication and networking between colleagues is detrimental to service users who do not get access to an adequate range of services as a consequence of this. Bystanders may become ill or decide to leave to escape the unpleasant atmosphere, causing problems with turnover, continuity of services, and maintenance of institutional knowledge. Ultimately, the reputation of the organization may be impacted negatively and recruitment of staff may become more difficult (Heames and Harvey 2006; Janson *et al.* 2009; Janson and Hazler 2004; Mayhew and Chappell 2007; Vartia 2001). As participant Stephanie noted, 'That's the danger, that when the healthy people leave you only have the unhealthy people running it. That's scary.'

Beyond a developing awareness that bullying impacts negatively on bystanders' health and wellbeing, the role of bystanders is as yet under-examined. Yet if we consider bystanders from a strengths perspective, they are a potentially helpful human resource. I will come back to this point a little later in the chapter when I look at what can be done to prevent or overcome bullying. First, however, it is important to look a little closer at the possible causes of workplace bullying and incivility.

Causes of workplace bullying

In the popular literature, bullying encounters are often personalized, with bullies being typecast as power hungry narcissists, and targets as weak and neurotic (van Heugten 2007). More sophisticated analyses tend to point to multiple causes, including organizational ones.

In my bullying research, it was striking that bullying often started soon after a participant's promotion to a more secure or better position. Some had been fixed-term employees who now became permanent employees, and others had recently been promoted. Several participants had been supported to achieve their promotion by the person who soon afterwards began to bully them. Ben noted that at the start of his employment his manager's approach to him was to 'pump' him up as a worker and praise his skills. To his extreme confusion, however, this positive approach was reversed without any apparent cause, and, 'very quickly after that, she basically pulled the rug from beneath me.'

When bullying arose in such circumstances, targets usually came to believe that the bullying was due to envy of their competence on the part of the bully (Vandekerckhove and Commers 2003). However, it seems likely that as the participants' confidence or power had grown, they began to challenge practices and policies. This may have been experienced as a threat by the bully. Some managers and supervisors may experience anxiety in the face of questioning by well-qualified staff, while at the same time they may face pressure from above, including to implement unpopular restructuring. Participants in my bullying research, as well as in the interviews for this book, noted that the training of social work managers is often inadequate for the complexities of their role. The idea that status *anxiety* rather than status envy may lead to bullying has not been widely noted in the literature, but warrants further exploration.

Another cause of bullying that was suggested by seven research participants and which is also echoed in the international literature is that of discrimination in the workplace. Participants thought they had been discriminated against because they were older, or immigrants, or because they projected a more middle-class image, including dressing more formally than their colleagues. Other researchers have also pointed to this propensity for cultural minorities or outsiders to be bullied, and identify gender, ethnicity, sexual orientation, age and disability-related discrimination (Exline and Lobel 1999; Fox and Stallworth 2005; Messinger 2004; Quine 2002; Salin 2003; Zapf *et al.* 2011). Scapegoating of outsiders may increase in workplaces where levels of stress and frustration are high (Einarsen *et al.* 2003).

Noting that there is a relationship between stress and aggression and between stress and change, some researchers have begun to explore whether bullying may be more prevalent in organizations that are being restructured. From the limited research undertaken to date, it appears that bullying increases as organizational change increases, but only if the changes bring about worsening workplace conditions, including higher workloads, more part-time employees, budget cuts and more autocratic audit oriented leadership styles. When changes are accompanied by role conflicts and job insecurity, workers also develop more negative perceptions of relationships with colleagues, supervisors and managers (Baillien and De Witte 2009; Salin and Hoel 2011). These findings suggest that it is not change per se, but the types of changes that are made and the ways in which they are implemented that make the difference in whether bullying is perceived to have increased.

Changes in workplace cultures are not simply internally driven but are situated in the wider socioeconomic and political context. Organizational practices are frequently externally imposed, and both statutory and NGO human services are significantly impacted by increasing government emphasis on rationalization and auditing.

Phillip noted that in his agency, contract negotiations with funding authorities affected managers' attitudes toward staff and service users. He went on to explain that in an effort to gain lucrative contracts, organizational expedience had come to override human service values and ethics. For example, waiting lists for mentally ill patients were manipulated to make funding claims for increases in staffing. He said that service users had died as a result: 'They don't even mind to gamble people's lives when it's for their personal interests. Which, yeah it's, it's sad, but if that's how it is I can't change it easily, I just try to.'

McLean Parks, Ma and Gallagher (2010) refer to organizational expediency as knowingly executing behaviours that '(1) are intended to fulfill organizationally prescribed or sanctioned objectives but that (2) knowingly involve breaking, bending, or stretching organizational rules, directives, or organizationally sanctioned norms' (p.703). When change evokes role and task conflicts, and there is a lack of behavioural integrity on the part of leaders, workers may come to feel that the organization has breached its psychological contract with them and they begin to disassociate themselves from their workplace.

In the light of the realization of the importance of the organizational context for bullying, there has recently been a perceptible shift in the literature. Whereas this was previously dominated by psychological or interpersonal perspectives, the focus has broadened to include analyses of workplace organizational structures, processes and cultures. It is not difficult to imagine, for example, how uncertainty, anxiety and competition may arise in human services with limited resources and where mission and vision are line managed from the top–down. This may foreseeably create a climate in which bullying can thrive.

Increasingly, writers are commenting that theorizing in the field is still under-developed, and they are now also beginning to look more closely at sociological explorations of how the organization of work is influenced by broader sociopolitical forces (Beale and Hoel 2010). Included in these considerations is the possible impact of global neoliberalism, since this political movement has favoured economic expediency over considerations of human welfare.

If explanations for bullying are to be found in broader contexts outside of simplistic ideas about personality clashes, then approaches to prevention and intervention must also attend to the broader context. Within the workplace, this requires buy-in from upper management, but such support is still often lacking and difficult to achieve (Salin 2003).

Preventing and intervening in workplace bullying

In the initial phases of being bullied, most participants in my bullying research simply made efforts to remedy the situation in which they found themselves by working harder, being nicer to the bully or explaining how the bully's behaviour made them feel. Nine participants talked about how long it took for them to begin to apprehend what was happening and how much this was impacting on them.

With hindsight, they wished they had kept a journal record of events, including times, details of behaviours, and witnesses present when incidences occurred. They recommended keeping such a record for a number of purposes, not only to refer to if one decides to make a complaint, but also to be able to reassure oneself of the reality of events and accuracy of memories when doubts are cast on those.

Participants found non-bullying supervisors, especially external supervisors, were extremely helpful in assisting and coaching them to maintain and build self-esteem. However, external supervisors had little power to change practices in the organization. Similarly, family and friends provided important support, but their main advice tended to be to 'get out' and find another job. Internal mediation was of little benefit because this appeared to be heavily biased toward more powerful perpetrators, as has also been noted by other researchers (Einarsen 1999; Lewis 2006).

By contrast, external mediation was again more likely to lead to recommendations to leave the workplace, but could also help secure a negotiated exit package that included positive references and financial compensation. Advice from unions and lawyers was generally appreciated, but formal processes were fraught and difficult, leading to few gains. Most helpful were outside auditing processes, especially when such an audit was instigated by a group of workers who supported one another.

For workers from communitarian cultures, or who work in organizations that reflect a communitarian cultural value base, dealing with bullying from an individualistic complaints base can feel inappropriate or foreign. A Māori participant talked about how Māori principles that emphasize 'mana' (respect) enhancing processes, which endeavour to foster mutual regard rather than shame, had led to her workplace becoming more open and supportive where there had previously been gossip and mistrust. The involvement of cultural elders as consultants had been essential to the success of these processes.

Other researchers also suggest that open communication may be the most effective means of avoiding or overcoming bullying, and that shame reducing processes are most likely to build supportive and resilient organizations (Bentley et al. 2009; Quine 1999). Contrary to popular perceptions, not all bullies are incorrigible. They may not be conscious of the harm caused by their actions and education may assist them to improve their practices (Crawshaw 2007).

In cases of serious bullying impacting on individual workers, a case-by-case approach to dealing with these matters that relies on policies and laws cannot usually be avoided. It is essential to have specific codes of conduct in place, and policies that outline steps to be taken when these are breached. It is important that these codes and policies are developed collaboratively (Dawood 2010). Legal redress is presently still difficult to achieve, but may be more readily available in particular cases. Where, for example, discrimination has occurred, whether in relation to ethnicity or gender, recent employment law changes in the UK (2008) have clarified the responsibilities of employers for ensuring that workers are safe from oppression. In the USA, researchers and advocates continue to lobby for better legal redress for targets of workplace bullying (Namie and Namie 2009). Improvements to laws are likely to continue with increasing international awareness of the financial and psychological costs of bullying.

Rhodes *et al.* (2010) point out that discussions of workplace bullying rarely mention the ethical obligations of organizations to oppose such behaviours, and they suggest that this is neglectful. They argue that if organizational cultures and practices are at least in part responsible for causing problems in relation to workers' wellbeing, then organizations are ethically responsible and could be taken to task if they fail to attend to this. They claim that when discussions about bullying fail to identify the centrality of organizational ethics, there is a danger that violence in organizations will continue to be approached only at an individual level. They warn that ritualized responses such as training courses and zero tolerance policies do not touch organizational processes and may bolster organizational bullying (Rhodes *et al.* 2010).

Several participants in my research noted that bullying would contravene the Code of Ethics of the Aotearoa New Zealand Association of Social Workers (1993, 2008). Internationally, the codes of ethics of social work associations and other relevant professional bodies specify that social workers should relate to colleagues with respect, address unethical behaviours, and strive to improve the functioning of their employing organizations (van Heugten 2011b). In view of the prevalence of bullying in human service organizations, it seems appropriate that these codes should be examined to see if they may be able to be refined to more clearly specify bullying as unethical behaviour.

On the evidence, when dealing with workplace bullying, external mediation may be required earlier rather than later in the process. To prevent targets and those accused of bullying from experiencing the most deleterious effects, early intervention and support are necessary via education, coaching and peer support. For people with moderately severe symptoms, there are a number of therapeutic interventions that can be of help. Tehrani (2011) commends integrated approaches, such as cognitive behavioural therapy combined with mindfulness.

Given that we know that workplace change and instability may provoke stress and incivility or perceptions of incivility, managers require additional assistance in times of restructuring. Managers with human resource responsibilities need support from their human resources department so that they understand the protocols for raising performance issues with staff. Otherwise they may be accused of bullying for doing their job (Dawood 2010).

Most helpful, however, in improving civility in workplaces, averting bullying and building resilience in its aftermath, is social support, including support from peers. Yet my research participants found it difficult to access this, or avoided doing so until they were ready to leave the organization in which they were bullied. Several participants talked about trying to cope by denying the bully's behaviour and its effects.

> **Erica:** Why didn't I meet with [the person who was previously in the position]? Why didn't we just have a phone conversation? And what I worked out was, I was kind of ... in minimized mode. That if I'd met with her [it] would have been difficult for me to keep on minimizing and kind of trying to contain it all and trying to make excuses for it.

In addition, colleagues tended to remain silent and avoided involvement in what was happening until the targeted participants declared their intention to leave. It was at that point that many participants found out that they were victims of serial bullies. Fifteen participants in all had been bullied by people who had previously exhibited similar behaviours toward other staff. Following this revelation, mutual support enabled people to externalize the problem of bullying so that they were able to stop taking blame. By the time of the interviews, almost all had rebuilt their confidence and thought they had grown in resilience as a consequence of their experiences.

> **Judith:** Now I also have support from ex-colleagues, the ones that left. There's about five of us [who] have coffee. Yeah, so, you know, there's a bit of saying, 'How are things going, what're you doing?' ... We meet up once every four months or something.

As I commented earlier, bystanders have tended to be overlooked as a potential resource in dealing with workplace bullying. This is in contrast to how bystanders have been perceived in school bullying, where whole-of-school community approaches that include the education of peers are now a major part of the approach to this problem.

In working with bystanders to change workplace cultures, it is important to understand why bystanders remain silent. Although some bystanders lack empathy and side with the bully, most silent witnesses stay silent because they do not understand what is happening, fear they may be punished for speaking out, or are unsure about what is going on or how they may be able to help (Scully and Rowe 2009; van Heugten 2011b).

66 **Timothy:** I think there were probably three camps: Those who were supportive [of me]; those who weren't; those who didn't want to rock the boat or jeopardize their own position and those who ... were more sitting on the fence, not wanting to be seen to take sides. 99

In seminars I presented, I came to the realization that many bystanders were keen to know how they could be of more assistance. They had often not fully understood that by remaining silent they appeared to approve of the bullying and had left targets isolated. This realization led me to explore the literature on whole-of-organization interventions, such as are applied in school bullying. I found there has been limited development of such models in relation to workplace bullying.

Scully and Rowe (2009) describe and discuss Active Bystander Training, which would appear to have good potential, although evaluations are still lacking at this stage. Active Bystander Training encourages positive esteem building interactions and discourages negative ones, and is therefore in effect strengths-based. People are encouraged to identify supportive collegial behaviours, overtly remark on these, and seek to reward them. In addition, they are taught to identify negative, discriminatory or humiliating behaviours, including by noticing their inner reactions of discomfort. They are then taught, including via role plays, to 'pivot' or turn around such behaviours by actively interrupting them. Interruptions can be made by verbally supporting and identifying the qualities of people who are being excluded or putdown, and actively ensuring they are included and re-engaged. Whole-of-workplace training can be provided without labelling people as bullies or targets (Scully and Rowe 2009; van Heugten in 2011b).

Such approaches may be best taught by trainers from outside an organization. They may be most helpful, and perhaps also most safely applied, when they are used by more than one bystander, for example during team meetings. This may reduce the risk of retaliation which is a significant fear for workers who may already feel insecure in their positions due to restructuring that has led to increased balance of power issues with employers (Roscigno *et al.* 2009).

The above discussion highlights that the problem of workplace bullying cannot be remedied by merely inserting bullying prohibitions into more general conduct-related policies. Active implementation of policies is essential, and if an organization does not actively lend support when breaches of policies occur, organizational attachment of targets and bystanders becomes disrupted. Indeed, it is not sufficient to merely adhere to and follow policy, but to respond promptly and supportively above and beyond the requirements that are set out (Parzefall and Salin 2010). Non-bullying managers do find it difficult to deal with complex situations and they need to be supported with training. In NGOs, the education of members of boards of governors is also important because of the role they play in ensuring these organizations remain true to their values (Dawood 2010).

Bullying has many negative consequences and investigations are expensive and time consuming (Hanley *et al.* 2009). If difficulties can be prevented from escalating by enhancing general levels of civility amongst workgroups, and improving adherence to principles of mutual respect, the positive benefits will far outweigh any costs.

The workplace harassment and bullying toolkit

- At whatever level of the organization you are currently working, investigate whether your agency has specific anti-harassment and *separate* anti-bullying policies and familiarize yourself with those.

- If there are no such policies, identify who is in charge of developing them. You may need to involve yourself in a working party.

- Is there a network of people who can be approached by workers with concerns about workplace conduct?

- Whole-of-workplace approaches to education may be of most benefit. These may start with speaker-led seminars, and progress to workshops that are aimed at increasing workplace civility. Most large cities now have training institutes that specialize in assisting workplaces to develop training packages.

- Training events should not seek to label or shame workers, including people identified by others as 'bullies' but who may not understand that their behaviours are hurtful. You may need to spend time articulating your group or team's expectations about communicating and behaving with respect. In relation to workplace bullying, you may next move on to learning skills such as 'pivoting' conversations to change these from criticizing to esteem building communications.

- Employers have important legal and ethical responsibilities to protect workers from harassment, discrimination and bullying. Managers with human resource responsibilities will require training to support them in implementing anti-harassment, anti-discrimination and anti-bullying policies.

- Restructuring and change increase the risk of workplace bullying. Although the precise mechanisms of the relationship between change and bullying are not yet clear, if you are managing change you will need to be particularly attentive to key stressors such as role conflict, higher workloads, and loss of control over key tasks that can give rise to disputes between workers.

- If you think you may be being bullied, keep a diary record of events, times, and witnesses. Archive or print out emails. Careful record keeping is also important because your memory may be questioned as part of a destabilizing bullying tactic. Meeting times and job assignments may be changed without notice or in contradiction to information you have been given. Be aware that your record may become evidence if you proceed to a formal complaint, and ensure your notes contain only factual information.

- Do seek support from colleagues, supervisors and other relevant people such as human resources staff, union delegates, professional association advisors, and lawyers. It can be difficult to work out in whom you can put your trust once harassment or bullying has been ongoing for a time, but it is essential that you identify key support people. Support is the number one resilience building resource for targets of bullying.

- Whether you are a target or a witnessing bystander, staying silent in the face of bullying or other kinds of harassment is not helpful. Remember that there is likely to be more than one person at the receiving end of this treatment. Carefully consider ways in which you can make your disapproval of these unwanted behaviours more overt and observable.

- If you are a manager and you are bullied by staff, support can be even more difficult to find. You will need peer as well as higher level management support. External support can also be helpful in enabling you to take a step back and consider systemic or organizational issues that may be leading to the problems that are arising.

- It is almost impossible not to take the impacts of workplace bullying or harassment home. Work out with your family how you can continue to engage with them while you are under this amount of pressure.

- Bullying and witnessing of bullying can have major negative effects on your physical as well as psychological health. Health checks and appropriate interventions, whether these involve better eating, exercise plans, counselling or medication, are all part of a comprehensive self-care package.

- Human rights legislation and employment law are helpful in cases of sexual harassment and also in cases of age, gender, ethnic and disability-related discrimination. Laws are also beginning to require employers to pay attention to workplace violence as a health and safety issue. However, what is needed in most cases is a more global shift in workplace culture.

If support is not available in your workplace, and in particular if senior managers are unsupportive, you may need to consider looking for another job before your physical and psychological health and your professional capacities become too damaged. Sadly, the most frequently given advice by the participants in my bullying research was for targets to leave and to find alternative employment.

Despite some of the popular literature promising instant results if you use a particular method, the truth is that we still lack knowledge about how some of the worst cases of workplace bullying can be effectively stopped. The mechanisms that are in place in policies and the law are still often difficult to apply. Formal remedies can be costly in terms of energy, time, reputation and money, and they can have disappointing outcomes. However, it is important to seek union, legal and other opinions as this situation is gradually improving.

The good news is that most of the social workers who participated in my bullying research found much to appreciate in their working lives in the aftermath of bullying. They were able to draw on their networks to obtain new employment in which they could apply their learning about civility, and their confidence was restored.

Today, with information about workplace bullying and harassment of social workers finally out in the open, bystanders and managers are coming forward to seek out learning so that they can stand by their ethical principles of respect, justice and human rights. There is indeed reason for optimism.

Additional resources
Workplace bullying and harassment: Self-help

Namie, G. and Namie, R. (2009) *The Bully at Work: What You Can Do to Stop the Bully and Reclaim Your Dignity on the Job*, 2nd edn. Naperville, IL: Sourcebook Inc.

The Workplace Bullying Institute (USA): www.workplacebullying.org

Workplace bullying and harassment: Textbook

Einarsen, S., Hoel, H., Zapf, D. and Cooper, C. L. (eds) (2011) *Bullying and Harassment in the Workplace: Developments in Theory, Research and Practice*, 2nd edn. London: Taylor and Francis.

Chapter 8

Being Human, Making Mistakes

Introduction

During our working lives, we all make mistakes, worry we have made mistakes, or, with the benefit of hindsight, think we could have done better. This chapter addresses the distress social workers experience when they worry that their work may have had a negative impact on the service users they had intended to help. It also deals with the distressing impact of having a complaint threatened or made against you, and the need for support whilst under investigation. It will help you to consider how to put these painful matters in context, and, if appropriate, to continue to practice safely and ethically in your professional role.

Most of the social workers interviewed for this book talked about the pressure placed on them by the notion that they should avert, minimize or otherwise manage 'risk'. The concept of risk refers to the chance that adverse outcomes will result from an activity in which one engages, or from a process in which one is involved, whether as an active protagonist, a recipient of an intervention, or a bystander.

Participants frequently talked about how the processes that had been put in place in their agencies to manage risk, put considerable strain on them. Their concerns were less often about making actual mistakes that might impact on service users, although they did worry a great deal about how to make balanced decisions with limited resources or in a context of uncertainty. Instead, it seemed that 'risk management' had itself become a prominent drain on workers' time and energy.

Actual complaints were faced by few of the 14 participants in the book interviews. By contrast, eight people who participated in my bullying research that was discussed in the previous chapter had complaints made against them. Six of those complaints were made by people they had accused of bullying, apparently in direct retaliation against their raising of their concerns. At least two more complaints were made by service users, seemingly with prompting from the bully.

The title of this chapter reflects the fact that human service practitioners are likely to practice imperfectly. However, the concept of a 'mistake' is a hazy one. Mistakes in practice are often identified with hindsight. The same practices, whilst perhaps not ideal, may have led to reasonable outcomes on numerous other occasions. On closer examination, practice oversights are frequently due to failures of systems, but currently available processes tend to emphasize individual fault.

Social workers and mistakes

Retrievable errors and near misses are part of every social worker's story.

Early in my career as a social worker, I was delegated to write a court report on a young man who had committed a minor offence by urinating in a public place. Since I came from a village in the south of the Netherlands, where this was commonplace male behaviour outside the central marketplace, I immediately wondered if I was being teased by my colleagues. But my encounter with the earnest, embarrassed and worried service user and his family led me to take my task very seriously, irrespective of the reason for its assignment. I wrote a report recommending a discharge without conviction, after having assessed that the penalty would otherwise far outweigh the 'crime'. I was proud of my first court report and thought it was highly likely that my recommendation would be followed. My mistake was to put the report in the in-tray rather than out-tray. The court officer assumed I had not written a report and did not ask, and, there being no report from the social worker for the judge to take into consideration the youth was convicted. I went to his home and made my first apology as a social worker.

I felt sobered, and learned several things, including that I may overlook important details if I get too excited about my achievements in advance of their delivery. I also realized that the best of efforts on paper will come to nothing if basic practical actions are omitted. Today, almost 30 years later, I still hand deliver or request confirmation of the receipt of important reports whenever possible, especially when they concern someone else's hopes and dreams.

Later in my career, with more responsibilities came more critical assessments, and I did not always sleep easy at night. A wise supervisor advised me that it was appropriate to take into account my anxiety level along with all of the other information available to me when I was trying to determine acceptable risk. I learned to document carefully, to consult, and to be especially wary if I start to believe that I am the only person available to solve a problem or help someone.

The most serious allegations of errors by human service workers arise when there are homicides of children, and killings by, or suicides of, mentally ill service users. Public reactions to such deaths tend to be very strong. Although the ensuing investigations almost always point to errors in networking within and between systems, and failures in responsibility taking by professionals in multiple organizations, individual workers may be vociferously blamed. In the view of one of the participants in the book interviews, who had been working in England at the time of Victoria Climbié's murder in 2000, this happened to the frontline social worker involved in that case to the extent that, 'it was almost as if she'd killed the child'.

Internationally, inquiries into child homicides have identified a number of typically occurring factors that underlie such preventable tragic events. Following the Lambert Inquiry into Victoria's death, the UK's House of Commons Health Committee (2003, p.5) lists those factors as:

- failure of communication between different staff and agencies

- inexperience and lack of skill of individual social workers

- failure to follow established procedures

- inadequate resources to meet demands.

Where there is concern over a social worker's competence, the aspects of their work that are most likely to be closely examined relate to their investigation and assessment of a service user's needs and circumstances. Common criticisms include failure to take into account all of the relevant factors and speak with all of the significant people involved, as well as a lack of basic skills, such as interviewing, networking and referral skills. Other problems that may be identified include a lack of up to date knowledge about problems and their diagnoses. The quality of supervision is also often questioned, as well as the extent to which agency protocols are adequate and have been followed (Munro 1998; Overholser and Fine 1990).

Social work assessments often involve drawing conclusions in relation to hypotheses about levels of risk. Murdach (1994) described errors made in clinical prediction as Type I and Type II errors. A Type I error occurs when a social worker concludes that there is little risk of harm, when in fact there is a significant risk. A Type II error exists when a conclusion is drawn that there is a serious risk, when this is not true. Social workers are most concerned to avoid the Type I error, in which they underestimate the risk of harm, because they are expected to guarantee safety of service users or of other potential victims.

Connolly and Doolan (2007), two former Chief Social Workers for the New Zealand statutory child protection organization Child Youth and Family, have noted that as a consequence of a belief that all such errors should and can be avoided, social workers are often scapegoated when a child dies. Public inquiries may offer temporary solace by holding out a promise that we can avoid future tragedies, but the recommendations that emerge may not ultimately improve systems for the better. Inquiries have tended to focus on finding failings in workers and organizations.

To protect themselves from accusations, workers and organizations may resort to more rigidly applying high-risk protocols and interventions across the spectrum of child welfare and protection services, including with families who might really only need support to improve their functioning. If social workers become overly risk averse, decisions may be made to rescue children by removing them from their families despite statutory requirements to support and keep families together wherever possible. (Connolly and Doolan 2007). Rachel had noticed this effect.

> **Rachel:** I think that's what happened through the nineties with child protection practice. They became sort of squeezed into this really narrow tick box exercise in terms of practice [so] that we've lost a lot of that clinical judgment and what makes sense for this child. ... I do get

really frustrated with the lack of sort of common sense …
that it's almost like people feel safe with being told that …
'You do this, this, and this and if it doesn't fit in that little
line of what to do then you can't do it.' Rather than saying,
'I can do this, but I need to make sure that I've covered off
these bases.' **"**

In Chapter 5 where I discussed the impact of trauma, participants
who worked in the area of mental health discussed how they worried
about the possibility that a client might suicide. In mental health social
work, the most common allegations about incompetence relate to
the completeness of information sought from service users and from
other people in their environment, and the worker's experience and
knowledge of assessment and reassessment criteria. In addition, staff
training and staffing levels are thought to contribute to patient suicide
(Roberts, Monferrari and Yeager 2008).

To protect themselves from allegations, mental health practitioners
pay particular attention to keeping careful notes in relation to actions,
assessments and consultations. It is important to be detailed and
specific in writing care plans, for example clearly noting the resources
that have been made available to clients, and the follow-up that has
been arranged.

Joe and Steve talked about how they attempted to take care in their
documentation without letting their anxieties override common sense
or becoming obsessive about this.

" **Joe:** And you tend to also have a lot of documentation that
you need to keep up with. You're always filling out the risk
forms, you're making sure that you write your progress
notes because you know that that night he might call one
of the emergency services or something might happen. So
there is quite a lot of sort of litigious covering your butt.
… I think when you're in those situations you're always
worrying about whether your documentation is enough,
whether you're doing enough. And there's restraints on
that, because, I mean you could probably document more
than you do but it's a time thing and there's other clients
that you need to see.

Steve: I've got a suicidal client at the moment I've just done
a risk assessment on today. I'm yeah, as confident as one
can be in your assessment, so I've done that assessment
even though I probably didn't consider it was necessary

> because I have confidence he won't do it, kill himself, but I
> still did the paperwork and covered myself in case. **"**

Over recent years, lack of cultural competency has more frequently been identified as a potential source of error. Cultural competency is required with respect to race, ethnicity, national origin, sexuality, and religious and spiritual beliefs. To be culturally competent requires self-awareness on the part of social workers so that they are alert to the risk of imposing value laden worldviews on clients (Allen-Meares 2007; Hodge and Bushfield 2006). A lack of ethnically aware cultural competence was cited in the case of Victoria Climbié and also emerges as a focus of concern in cases involving indigenous Māori children or adult service users in New Zealand. Problems include a lack of knowledge about cross-cultural communication, appropriate protocols and networks of support. Consultation with cultural advisors is essential, but should be undertaken as part of everyday work, not only when problems arise.

Other concerns over social workers' practice relate to ethical conduct more broadly, where social workers may be alleged to have breached standards by placing their own desires ahead of clients' needs, including financial or sexual desires. Social workers may be accused of having breached confidences without adequate justification, or of having failed to seek informed consent for interventions. Allegations of discrimination may arise when service users believe they have been treated in an unfair manner because they belong to a different culture or adhere to a different belief system (Strom-Gottfried 2003).

Ethical codes are sometimes presented as if they are unquestionably correct rather than socially constructed in their presentation and interpretation. The 'right' approach to difficult ethical issues is frequently unclear, however.

This is particularly obvious when questions arise in relation to balancing risk of harm against self-determination. Where suicidal mentally ill service users are clearly incapacitated with respect to decision-making, questions of self-determination may remain in the shadows. But when capacity is uncertain, for example when older persons self-neglect or live in squalor, then dilemmas are more prominent, opinions between professionals are more divergent, and paths to resolution are less clear. When, if ever, are self-neglect and living in squalor risks that require forceful intervention? Are people living in such circumstances almost always impaired in their decision-making capacity? To what extent are these lifestyle choices that should be respected (McDermott 2010)? It is not difficult to imagine a situation in which a complaint is likely to result whatever approach is taken. These dilemmas may become increasingly prominent as age and ethnic demographics become more diverse.

There will be some social workers or human service workers who are unfit for the work they are being asked to do. They may never have been competent or suitable, or they may have become less so over time. They may have pursued social work because it brings them into contact with children and they have paedophile sexual desires, they may be impaired by mental ill health, too severely traumatized to attend to the needs of others, or suffer dementia. Sometimes they continue to practice for years despite problems having been noticed by colleagues. If you are uncertain about how to take adequate action, then talking about this with a supervisor is often a good first step.

However, most often the causes of negative practice outcomes can be found in organizational rather than personal domains. Workers are impacted by the kinds of pressures in the workplace that have been the focus of the preceding chapters. Overly high workloads, lack of induction and training of new staff, and lack of institutional knowledge due to turnover of staff are systems failures rather than individual failures of workers.

Lack of expert or even regular supervision is an identifiable problem that persists in agencies large and small, in contravention of espoused policies and professional requirements. Amanda declared that it is permissible to nag if necessary to receive this absolute entitlement.

> **Amanda:** I had to keep coming back and back and back to it. And it's not really my personality type to nag but it's also not really my personality type to let go, because I think it's a risk [to be without adequate supervision] and a terrible risk if you are working in an organization that can show a somewhat punitive and blaming culture. And if you make the wrong decision no-one is going to support you.

Such deficiencies may in turn be consequences of political decisions to reduce funding for social services.

The impacts of worries about risks, mistakes and complaints

Brian Littlechild (2008) considers how the fear of being found inadequate when undertaking risk assessments can profoundly impact on child protection social workers. He considers that the drive to achieve certainty when assessing risk, places unreasonable expectations on frontline workers, managers and child protection agencies.

While the public, media and government call for perfect application of risk assessment tools, these tools are not exact. The overwhelming demand to achieve certainty against any reasonable expectation that this is possible leads to fear. Individual workers fear being considered personally responsible for not having competently assessed risk. Supervisors fear being held to account for the actions of supervisees who may not have provided them with sufficient information. Agencies fear being publicly named and shamed when children in their care get hurt.

When assessing a situation as 'low risk' creates a risk for the social worker, it becomes understandable that fear inspires a bias toward caution. At the same time, social workers are aware that they may become overly risk averse because to misjudge risk can be so costly for service users and for the worker in financial and personal terms. They try to keep their fears in check.

> **Steve:** I think because I don't have dependants [and] I don't have any real financial – I mean, if I lost my job tomorrow it wouldn't matter particularly. So if the worst came to the worst and I was in front of a court of inquiry and was sacked it wouldn't be the end of the world. So I'm probably a bit more relaxed than some.

Worry about being blamed for unfavourable outcomes may become so overwhelming that it leads workers to leave jobs. Joe noted that several people had recently left his mental health service team, and he thought this was due to their concerns over the high levels of risk of suicide in the client group.

As we saw in earlier chapters, not only frontline workers are impacted by concerns over risk and the possibility of complaints being made about practice. If an agency is implicated, for example, in the death of a child, managers may ultimately be expected to take blame and resign.

When this happens, frontline workers are deprived of the institutional wisdom held by experienced managers (Woodward 2009).

Dealing with mistakes and reducing the risk of errors

Ideally, making mistakes leads to learning. As Munro (1998) has said:

> Making mistakes can be a sign of good practice insofar as recognition of one's fallibility is part of a general approach involving a willingness to be self-critical and to change one's mind. All social workers make many misjudgments because of the complexity of the work but skilled social workers recognize their fallibility and are open to rethinking their assessments and decisions. (Munro 1998, p.806)

I have been fortunate to have been able to learn from my mistakes. But having to openly admit errors brings with it a sense of exposure and shame. Appropriate supervision and collegial support are essential if resilience and thriving are to emerge from the ashes of the intense self-questioning that is involved. Colleagues and supervisors can become a source of distress if their interactions appear to be primarily aimed at risk management (Collings and Murray 1996).

If social workers fear that their mistakes will lead to public shaming, they may, instead of disclosing these, respond to clients and colleagues in inappropriate ways, such as by lying and avoiding. This can lead to a tangled web that ultimately results in more damage to reputation, self-esteem and authority. Hiding oversights leads to more difficulty mending problems, diminished effectiveness, and failure to refer and network as fear of exposure grows with each encounter.

Reamer (2008), in exploring the management of errors by social workers, stresses the importance of having clear protocols for error prevention, and for disclosing of and responding to errors. There should be sound documentation of steps taken in exploring incidents, and response plans should be developed in collaborative teams.

The experienced practitioners and managers I interviewed for this book emphasized the critical importance of management level understanding of the difficult job done by staff. The availability of this understanding and support was variable, and depended at least to some extent on whether there was social work representation at senior management level.

66 **Margaret:** I don't think they understand the level of risk management that I have. And I try to explain some of that and when push comes to shove they do get on board, but again it is me educating them. You have to educate the mangers to do their job to support you, and that's okay but I shouldn't continue to have to educate the same people. 99

If the concept of learning from mistakes and learning from near misses is to gather any real impetus in social work, we will need to develop reporting protocols that protect workers from unfair criticism, as has begun to occur in other parts of the health sector. Until then, the culture of blame is likely to continue to frighten workers and prevent at least some from declaring problems that occur. In developing better systems, it is important to remember that these should not be delivered from the top–down. It is necessary to include workers and service users in the development of policies, procedures and support mechanisms (Littlechild 2008; Reamer 2008).

In an attempt to reduce risk, more health and social service agencies are using computerized Decision Support Systems or Integrated Information Systems. When using such systems, social workers enter data and a computer programme then identifies what decisions are statistically most often made by other social workers in similar circumstances. Where there is a directive to use such systems, researchers in Israel have found that social workers will comply with entering data, but they tend to pay little attention to the recommended actions. This is especially so if the workers consider that a case is straightforward or their minds are already made up. They are more likely to use computerized systems in a reflective way when faced with atypical cases and when they are uncertain about what decisions to make (Monnickendam, Savaya and Waysman 2005; Savaya, Monnickendam and Waysman 2006).

Social workers can experience such structured attempts at managing risk and liability as being overly regulatory or mechanistic. These concerns are understandable, but may be able to be allayed to a considerable degree through training on the integration of the use of these systems into research-informed reflective practice. Tony Stanley (2010), in noting the derision piled upon computer and paper-based approaches to child protection practice, suggests that it is time we consider the place of things in practice from a more sophisticated perspective.

Other attempts to prevent errors and mitigate risk focus on the education of social workers. Liz Beddoe (2009), a New Zealand social work educator, undertook research to discover how social workers viewed an increasing emphasis on lifelong and workplace learning. She found that social workers were sceptical about workplace learning that emphasized compliance-based skills. Such learning was often focused around changes in agency practices and technologies, but these changes were frequently temporary and overturned by new initiatives requiring new learning.

The social workers were also dubious about agency statements that professed a valuing of learning from mistakes, when they believed that in reality they would be chastised and punished for their errors. They further thought that only mistakes that are made by frontline workers are focused upon and investigated, whereas managers escape scrutiny. The participants in Beddoe's research suggested there were opportunities for learning from frontline practitioners, but that in large organizations, managers are not interested in this. Practitioners identified an audit culture wherein they feared showing a lack of understanding or knowledge.

Rather than workplace-based learning, workers favoured sabbaticals to reflect on work away from the workplace. They preferred critical and reflective learning approaches that take account of the complexity and uncertainty of social work practice, and they wanted to learn from good practice examples (Beddoe 2009).

More recently, not only organizations but also governments have stepped in to attempt to prevent 'risk' to service users by controlling social work practitioners. From the 1990s in particular, there were calls for social workers to become registered as a means of holding incompetent workers to account. These calls strengthened following inquiries into the deaths of children who were known to, or in the care of child protection agencies (van Heugten in 2011a).

During the first decade of the twenty-first century, formal registration was instituted in the UK and in New Zealand. Hopes were held that the public would be encouraged to better trust social workers if they knew that registered social workers held qualifications and were assessed competent to practice, and that there were avenues for deregistering workers proven to be incompetent. However, concerns have begun to emerge about the extent to which the focus of registering bodies, such as the General Social Care Council in Britain and the Social Workers Registration Board in New Zealand, is on prosecuting individual practitioners. This is not matched by attention to risky workplaces, or risky government policies that deprive human service organizations and communities of resources (van Heugten in 2011a).

The expectations placed on social workers point to misunderstandings about their role and about their ability to prevent all risk. More recently, attempts have been made to improve the education of the public, other professionals, and politicians about the role of social workers. In the UK, the Social Work Task Force (2009) has recommended that efforts should be made to raise the positive public profile of social workers by emphasizing the good work that is done and the complex context in which it has to be undertaken. The British Association of Social Workers (2010) launched 'The Social Work Bill' in a renewed effort to explain social work and improve its status.

In New Zealand, efforts at community re-education have borne some fruit. Rachel thought that on balance, she could discern improvements in public perceptions of child protection social workers, and also in responsibility sharing by other professions. She said, 'I think there's more understanding' and noted that, 'There's been a huge amount done' to ensure that the public and other professions understand that child protection is a community responsibility. Nevertheless, 'Social workers still feel that pressure.'

Social workers facing complaints

Despite the best efforts of social workers and the concerns of employers, distressing outcomes sometimes occur. These do not all lead to complaints being made. There are many reasons for this, including the difficulties and obstacles that may be in the way of service users gaining access to complaint mechanisms and articulating their concerns via formal channels. Other reasons include the fact that service users and their families will often understand that a distressing outcome was not foreseeable or preventable by the worker. Resolutions may be arrived at via face-to-face discussions that involve frank disclosure, coupled with explanations of improvements that have been made to prevent similar future outcomes. Mediation can also assist in restoration of relationships with agencies if not with the worker.

Threats of complaint about real or perceived errors and harm are also more common than actual complaints. Some writers have suggested that threats of complaint action may be more distressing to social workers than threats of violence. This is thought to be so because the identity of the worker is closely linked to caring work with service users. The possibility of being found seriously lacking with respect to that work is then quite destabilizing. It may feel as if all of the good work that one has ever done can be negated with just one complaint (Smith 2007). At such a time supervisors and colleagues play an important role in ensuring that workers are reminded to take a broader view of their practice.

Compassionate support is essential, whether there are good grounds for complaint or not. In addition, in my experience, workers facing complaint action are better served when they have at least some supporters with whom they can frankly discuss their doubts about being a good enough practitioner. This offers more opportunities for working through problems and growing from the experience, than does being supported entirely by people who are willing to overlook any part you may have played in a poor outcome.

Despite all of the efforts outlined above, and despite, for example child homicides having decreased in the UK and in New Zealand, complaints, especially against child and family social workers, continue to rise. In mid 2010, Marcia Lawrence-Russell, the head of the British Association of Social Workers' Advice and Representation Service noted that social workers 'tremble' at the thought of complaints and that significantly more social workers were seeking help from the service (Higgs 2010).

When formal complaints are made, the time taken to resolve them is often lengthy. The period from threat to formal complaint can be so long and distressing, that sometimes the formality comes as a relief. The time from first receipt of the notice of complaint to receiving the outcomes of one or more hearings is variable but it is not uncommon for this to take more than a year (Strom-Gottfried 2003).

Complaints may be made to employers, professional associations, registration bodies and human rights organizations. Most bodies will have guidelines stipulating where complaints should be directed, for example that they should be made to an employing organization or a registration board in the first instance. These rules are in place to prevent people being subjected to multiple complaints over the same matter. Nevertheless, complainants may engage in long-running efforts to seek redress via every legal avenue, as they are of course entitled to do.

If you are facing a complaint, legal advice is essential to help you step through the maze of rules. These rules differ in different localities, and they change and are interpreted differently over time as precedents are set. Although you may have access to legal advice under your employer's insurance cover, your interests and those of your employer may not always coincide. This is why it is wise to carry your own professional indemnity insurance. When you first become aware that a complaint may be made against you, it is very important that you notify your insurer and your professional organization. Yes, it feels exposing, but not to do so could cost you your cover.

When organizations are faced with complaints that may impact on their reputation, they may appear to close ranks, or begin to apply bureaucratic rules without reference to a value base or ethical considerations. Service users often experience this as being the case and this can be very distressing to them. Indeed, they may feel forced to follow a formal route and formal processes, when in fact they just want to be heard.

Workers can be equally surprised by the bureaucratic turn their agency takes in its approach (Hsieh, Thomas and Rotem 2005). Rules and guidelines may seem overly rigidly applied, and support may feel to be lacking. For the workers being complained against, processes seem slow, and whilst the situation feels like an emergency to them, this is not necessarily how it is responded to by others.

Bodies handling complaints will have time frames within which they are expected to notify respondents of steps in their processes. These dates are not always met, and especially when there are a large number of cases, a backlog can occur. You are entitled to be informed about progress on your case in a timely manner. There should be a contact person who is not involved in decision-making about your case, but who will understand your need for responses and reply to your requests for updates.

It is important to be well-supported, including by peers and supervisors. Supervisory relationships may be implicated in the complaint and it may be necessary to make alternative arrangements where this is the case. Legal advice is essential, but legal advice is expensive and lawyers are not generally in a position to provide you with the kind of emotional support that you may need. You may therefore also need counselling and this may be funded by your workplace under employee support schemes.

When you are responding to a formal complaint it may be difficult to put it aside because the case forces you to continue to sharpen your memory around the facts and details of your actions and to constantly revisit the events as they unfolded at the time. It is therefore natural to dwell on this. I sometimes think that formal complaint processes force complainants and respondent social workers to remain fixed in a psychological state akin to PTSD, as details must remain clear and concrete, and grievances unmitigated rather than being allowed to soften with time. If you express uncertainty or ambivalence, this may appear to weaken your case, and you may be encouraged to quash these. For this reason too, some psychological methods for resolving your distress that might otherwise be considered helpful, such as Eye Movement Desensitization and Reprocessing (EMDR) or hypnosis, may not be advisable because these may fade or change your memories of events.

As a consequence of all this, you may find yourself dwelling overly much, and your existence at work and at home becomes consumed by the complaint. It may be helpful to set aside time for documentation, but structure and limit the time you spend on dealing with the case. Make sure this takes up a smaller portion than the time you allocate for other things such as work, family, friends and activities that you enjoy.

Some people find it useful to employ visualization techniques, for example putting the complaint in a box to open and shut as necessary. Others are helped by cognitive methods that challenge common hindsight biases such as: 'I *could* have done something different and that would have been better with hindsight, therefore I *should* have known and done that.' Again others meditate or use mindfulness-based techniques. Walking, swimming or other exercise and eating well may help prevent depression. As already mentioned above, seeking help via confidential counselling services is a sensible plan. It is highly likely you will need to call on this at least periodically over the duration of a formal complaint.

Ultimately, difficult though this is to bear, any complaint about your work is part of your working life, and it should be contained there, and not be allowed to eat up your personhood. Yes, it may be true that someone else lost their life and it may seem unfair that you will ultimately benefit and learn from that. There may be people who will never forgive you for your failings. But you will not be truly honouring a client who died, their family and friends, your profession, yourself or your loved ones by avoiding the learning opportunities that emerge for you.

If you are able and willing to continue in your job, you will need support to do so, and to retrieve your sense of competence and self-belief which will almost certainly be dented. If you are not continuing as a social worker or human service worker, perhaps because others have judged you to be incompetent and you have been deregistered, then again, your life is bigger than just this occupation, and you are entitled to fair and compassionate help to enable you to retrieve your self-esteem.

The toolkit for building resilience in the face of criticism

The following recommendations relate specifically to dealing with errors, near misses and complaints and build on the resilience enhancing tools discussed in previous chapters.

- Is there a planned approach to the reporting of errors and near misses? Is the main aim of the reporting system to detect systems failings, and work out how these may be overcome to prevent future mistakes? Does your organization reward and affirm people who report harmful outcomes and find ways of overcoming the likelihood of their recurrence?

- Do you have a protocol for supporting service users and workers following preventable negative outcomes?

- Do you have adequate insurance? It is becoming increasingly unlikely, especially in child and family work, that you will avoid a complaint being made against you at some time. Defending even an entirely unfounded complaint can be costly, and you may not be able to rely on your employer's insurance to provide you with legal representation to adequately protect you. Your employer's interests and yours may not coincide.

- Perhaps more than any other situation you may face, a complaint against you challenges your belief in the value of your central investment of self in work. You may need personal counselling or psychotherapy to help you deal with this. You will certainly need supportive supervision. You will not benefit from a supervisor or counsellor who is merely a champion for you, and you are ideally served by experienced supervisors who have knowledge of complaints processes. Your agency or your association should be able to assist you in establishing support.

Additional resource
Malpractice and liability

Reamer, F. G. (2003) *Social Work Malpractice and Liability: Strategies for Prevention*, 2nd edn. New York: Columbia University Press.

Chapter 9

Towards Balance in Practice

Introduction

This final chapter draws together major themes from the book to make some final recommendations. Its overarching aim is to inspire you to value yourself and your fellow human service workers. Workers who strive to make a better world deserve to be well looked after rather than burned out and the goal here is to encourage you to take practical steps toward achieving that.

In considering models of workplace stress, we saw that stress increases when complex demands and challenges combine with a lack of control over how we can do our work, and when there is insufficient support for workers. For human service workers, stress reaches critical proportions when they believe that there are injustices in decision-making around how scarce resources are distributed or how service users are treated.

The impact of stress overload makes itself felt beyond the individual worker's physical and psychological health when it impacts on colleagues and clients, and in the worker's private sphere. Work–life balance deteriorates when heavy workloads intrude on family life. Coping with traumatic experiences such as violence and bullying at work can badly interfere with enjoyment across all domains.

Supportive supervision was noted to be a key resource that helps social workers to build on their strengths. Supervisors and line managers who understand social work's mission and the need for adequate resources, are able to bring these to attention at an organizational level.

Some of the interventions that were recommended in the earlier chapters require investments to be made by employers and the state. The following suggestions instead focus on immediate improvements we can make in our working lives by taking small steps at a grassroots level. The first part of this discussion considers the importance of being able to make meaning out of our work. The question raised here is how human service workers can continue to believe that their efforts to help people are valuable in a context where resources are scarce and economic imperatives may be rated above human needs.

Next, the need for day-to-day self-care is addressed, with some examples of how we can build nurturance into our daily lives. The section on supportive supervision speaks more broadly to supervisors and managers and considers the ways in which leaders may model better boundaries around the demands of work.

Finally, moral distress is still infrequently mentioned in relation to social work, and yet this may be the most debilitating of all of the pressures we face. It has led some of the book participants to leave agencies or to consider leaving social work.

Meaning making and mindfulness

In earlier chapters I discussed the importance of meaning making, whereby social workers are able to make sense of the important contributions they make in their role alongside the necessity of self-care. I also suggested that the practice of mindfulness may improve our capacity to attune to others and ourselves without exposing us to stress overload. These concepts are linked in that although mindfulness does not encourage a desperate search for meaning, a mindful approach will often inspire feelings of compassion and connectedness. I explore these ideas a little more below.

Val had struggled with depression and burnout, and had at times doubted the value of her work. She explained that one story in particular helps her remember that her efforts are worthwhile, in spite of the fact that it is not possible to help everyone in need. The story tells of a man who walks along a beach upon which the high tide has deposited thousands of starfish. He encounters a person throwing the starfish back into the sea one by one, and points out that this is a pointless exercise since there are too many to save. In this version the star thrower is a boy, who picking up yet another starfish holds it up and says, 'No, but I can save this one.'

The story that comforts Val is widely known and narrated in various forms in different countries. The original author is the poet scientist Loren Corey Eiseley. The story is entitled 'The Star Thrower' and was first published in *The Unexpected Universe* (Eiseley 1969) and later republished in a collection of stories that carries its name *The Star Thrower* (Eiseley 1978).

In Loren Eiseley's original story, the star thrower is not a boy but a weather beaten man, and the visitor to the mythical seaside resort of Costabel who encounters him is the writer Eiseley himself. As Eiseley walks along the beach he first encounters scavengers who gather shellfish and other sea creatures that are boiled alive so that the shells can be sold to tourists. Eiseley at first thinks the star thrower is mad and he returns to his accommodation. That night, however, he is unable to sleep and eventually, as day breaks, the insistence of his conscience leads him to join the star thrower in taking action. This joining overcomes a moral and spiritual isolation, and gives hope that collaboration between compassionate human beings can overcome self-interested destructiveness.

The story is retold in motivational seminars and workshops, often without reference to Eiseley. He died in 1977, and when he is remembered, he is sometimes idealized as a visionary. His life was, however, far from idyllic (Wisner 2005).

One of Eiseley's predominant struggles, which is reflected in *The Star Thrower*, was his search for meaning in a brutal and destructive Darwinian world where only the fittest survive. Central to his quest, we can discern a debate about the place of pragmatic economics versus values, and about science versus the arts and humanities.

In this writing, Eiseley emphasized the importance of being in the moment, to observe and consider the beauty that surrounds us. He thought this consideration might then inspire us, so that we would use all resources available to us, whether they come from the sciences or the arts, to step beyond selfish preoccupation into a spontaneous caring for the value of all life. Eiseley did not call this capacity for observation and consideration 'mindfulness' but the similarities are obvious, and there are Buddhist and Christian symbols embedded in his 16 page essay (Lioi 1999).

In reality, of course, our capacity for being in the moment, let alone to feel inspired, will wax and wane. As I recovered from breast cancer treatment, my awareness of beauty in the world was heightened, and I thought I would never again take life for granted. All too soon, however, I returned to my ordinary state of being wherein colours are less vivid and I overlook or dismiss small miracles. Similarly, following an earthquake, communities join together, but over time most people return to their daily lives and the intensity of neighbourly connections fades.

Nevertheless, the memory that a sharper appreciation is possible remains and this state can be revisited. The basic principles of breathing and being aware of our bodies, of nature and the people around us, can be learned, for example as part of mindfulness training. This learning needs to be reinforced if it is to remain easily called upon. We can discover what works best for us, whether it is being physically still in meditation or prayer, or engaging in movement such as dance, swimming, gardening or walking. Eiseley, for example, would spend hours outdoors, quietly observing nature around him. It is helpful to integrate the practice of mindfulness into our everyday lives.

Often when we are harried, being in the moment is pushed aside and we need something or someone to jolt us back into renewing our commitment. What jolts us is not always an outwardly big event.

At the end of a working day, which almost never ends before six, I am greeted by my nine-year-old daughter. In her hands are two badminton rackets, purple for her and red for me. 'I've been waiting since four o'clock. You promised to play today so come on!' Her dad says, 'Let your mum eat first.' I say, 'But the book.' The look on her face is formidable however, and I am soon out there. At the start of spring we seemed to be spending much time picking the shuttlecock up, rather than returning it to one another, but our daily efforts have paid off. Picking up involves cartwheels on Hanna's part, a walk, and sometimes a groan on mine.

One evening, as I lean over to pick up the shuttlecock, Hanna says, 'ah, the day is ending.' 'Why do you say that just now?' I ask her. 'The daisies of course, they are all closing.' As I look around at my daisy filled lawn, I am filled with wonder. In this moment, for the first time in my life, I observe that daisies close their petals as the sun goes down. It may be knowledge that everyone else has long held, but to me it is a wondrous sight and I feel grateful that I am lucky enough to have this pointed out to me by a cartwheeling little girl who makes me stop work to play outside.

In Chapter 5 on trauma, I suggested that the practice of mindful awareness may offer a means of buffering ourselves from emotional contagion. Emotional contagion may occur if we become overly involved in the feelings of another person, and in that process lose awareness that we are separate beings. In addition to assisting us to remain reflective, and as Eiseley's story suggests, also linking us with a sense of greater purpose, the practice of being and doing in the moment may encourage us to savour leisure time activities and apply better self-care.

Physical and psychological self-care

Social work is stressful, even if we develop a calmer capacity to engage in our work. Our bodies, including our brains, need rest to recover from exertion. This is why participants talked about the importance of setting boundaries around work by not taking work home and taking holidays. Several found their work–life balance improved when they worked four days a week.

Stress is not bad, but a constant pressure, even positively charged, can wear us down. Like damage done by smoking, the damage from stress can be largely unseen and unfelt until it reaches critical levels. Some of us are very resilient and manage for long periods under high pressure but we may still be harmed.

In 2007, I attended a five day, live-in, New Zealand Women in Leadership programme, an initiative established to foster women's participation in leadership activities in the universities, where participation rates in senior ranks and roles remain low relative to men. My most valued experience on the course occurred by chance at a dinner, where I was seated next to a non-participant sleep expert. Sleep had been pushed aside for me while my partner was ill, and over time I had come to dismiss my need for much of it. After all, if Maggie Thatcher could get by on four hours, why not I? It is not uncommon for women in midlife with multiple responsibilities to cut back on their sleep.

I don't remember the exact damage the sleep expert outlined would occur to my brain over time. Nor do I remember her name or wherefrom she hailed. I know her research credentials were good, but what her role was precisely I have also forgotten. I do vividly recall my fright as her message hit home. By trying to make up for lost daytime hours after midnight, I was harming my brain, and in the long run that might impact more permanently on my capacity to embed and process information. I went home, and instituted an immediate change. Eventually, I discovered my memory lapses were not, after all, due to perimenopause, but due to lack of sleep and too much multitasking.

Humour and laughter can also seem unnecessary or frivolous, but they were found to be of enormous benefit by participants at work and outside of it. Participants valued jokes, workplace baking competitions and other fun events that fostered enjoyable social connections.

As I come closer to finishing my book, my son Jack coincidentally determines that I need humour lessons. He charges ten cents a week, on principle rather than the size of his effort. I receive points for trying, but falter to build a stock of good 'comebacks' (retorts), to the jokes of others. I am told I need to practise these as I have been diagnosed to be a 'humour victim' who is always willing to laugh at my own expense but never ready with a repartee. I am advised to test myself with 'light' jokes as I am still learning, and in any case heavy jokes can make people cry, or told in the wrong setting, could lead me to lose my job. 'Never tell a joke that hurts others.' 'Never spoil someone else's joke by reinforcing it [repeating the punch line], or explaining why it is funny.' This will lead people to avoid telling jokes around me. Also, 'Never laugh at an overheard joke because people will think you are eavesdropping.' Those are just some of the interpersonal guidelines for joke making discerned by my 10-year-old, who understands the place of fun in communicating a nuanced engagement with other human beings better than I.

If you are out of practice in relation to applying basic self-care, a small step forward may mean getting into bed just half an hour earlier, or challenging your unkind self-talk, or identifying one person who will help you introduce more fun into your life. One small step is better than no step at all. Overdoing your efforts, like starting with a heavy joke, or an hour-long jog, may well backfire, make your muscles ache, or otherwise dishearten you so that you fall back into old habits of self-neglect.

Interestingly, and reinforcing of this notion that a gentle approach to self-care is still worthwhile, a survey of 40,401 residents of Norway showed that even light exercise can reduce depression. Moreover, it is not the biological activity, but the *leisure*-based context and in particular the *social* connections that surround the exercise that were found to make the most beneficial impact (Harvey *et al.* 2010).

Being kind and gentle in our attitude toward ourselves can be especially difficult when our best efforts to achieve good outcomes for clients seem in vain, and we worry about our abilities. Val recommended that we should prepare for such difficult times.

> **Val:** Another thing that's really important is to have a 'feel good folder', like one of those clear file folders. Every time you get something positive about your practice, so whether it is a good report from someone or a letter to say, 'Thank you for what you did', or whatever, you know, or even a note, 'Good work', because you do get those things, save them in one place. ... Being able to say, 'I know I changed that person's life', that's why we're in the business, we're in the business to make people's lives better. So having specific evidence to say that you did it is really important on the days when you know how bad you are. Because there are always going to be those days, but you need to have something that reminds you that, actually, you're *wrong*. Because, you know, we all are subject to those skewed views of ourselves at times.

Physical, psychological, spiritual and social self-care are interlinked, and a practical step in one of these domains will have a positive flow-on effect in the others.

Supportive supervision

Ideally, we also have supportive supervisors and mentors to remind us of the good work we do, and to help us to remain grounded in our capacities. Like good teachers, they identify where we are in our development and help us work out how we can build on our strengths to set and achieve even higher standards. They tend to call our weaknesses our 'growing edge' and when they say that they actually mean it.

For decades now, we have known that punishments and shaming putdowns do not help people to develop. There is research in abundance that tells us this, yet we appear afraid to reward and compliment and instead continue to focus on fault-finding. We leap in with risk management strategies, before we have properly attended to staff members' concerns about the impacts of changes, and the need for support of workers and service users. We fail to properly involve them in developing policies and protocols. The information in this book supports a reversal of such approaches.

Sometimes an act of managerial bravery jumps out at us. Participants spoke of managers who go an extra mile to understand and relieve stresses workers face at home by easing workloads or hours. They recounted stories of bosses who helped workers to lead balanced lives by encouraging them to take time off to coach a school sports team, or to accompany an ageing parent to a doctor's appointment. We may read or hear about inspirational managers, but often they seem to stay just out of our reach. Few of us encounter them in our workplaces. Perhaps our managers also read inspirational books, but encounter scepticism and are dragged back down to ordinariness. Perhaps they need to know that these simple actions mean a lot.

Supervisors and mentors are clearly principal conduits for messages about self-care to workers, but are not always aware of the extent of the influence of their actions. When we, as managers or leaders, fail to care for ourselves, for example by working long hours, the potential damage spreads contagiously because we model 'expected' organizational behaviour even if we do not intend to.

Recently, at a New Zealand Women in Leadership alumni reunion, several participants, including myself, resolved to make a small achievable change in our working lives – to stop sending work-related emails in weekends and evenings. We decided this because we wanted to put better boundaries around our working lives to protect our time at home from constant intrusions. We also did it because we realized that by emailing as we did, we were making matters worse for others, by establishing a context in which private time is no longer the norm for women, or men, who want to achieve success at work.

Email overload is a typical problem for academics. While this particular issue may be less common in frontline practice, the intrusion of work into personal time is a pervasive problem. Several participants talked about staying behind after hours to write reports, or to make telephone calls. Excessive requirements to be on call were particularly disruptive. Taking steps to model the recognition that these are not reasonable or fair expectations may lead to a social movement that makes a difference.

Coping with moral distress

Social workers experience moral distress when they are unable to assist service users to make positive life affirming choices. This inability may be due to a lack of resources, such as a lack of out of home placement options for children and young persons, or a lack of dignified care options for a person who is terminally ill. It is important to recognize that social work and other human service work is emotional labour, and that workers are empathic people who will feel distress when they cannot help others who are in evident need.

By and large, we are able to make peace with our consciences because we have done our best, and although with hindsight we might think we could have done better, our motives were not malign.

Supervisors who are attuned to the issue of moral distress are unlikely to approach social workers' struggles by citing coded ethical requirements. They recognize instead that social workers' values are set in a background of cultural and familial experiences and beliefs. At times the journey to find a balance between personal and professional or organizational values is likely to be particularly challenging, and during such times experienced supervisors with specific expertise, for example cultural expertise, may be essential. Experienced cultural supervisors may help workers to determine whether there is a true problem with job or organizational fit, or whether an appropriate accommodation can be wrought. In New Zealand, bicultural education and supervision are often recommended as a means of assisting non-Māori workers to develop skills to practise with Māori service users, but Rewa suggested Māori workers setting out in a social work career have a need for in-depth cultural support.

66 **Rewa:** If you're of Māori descent ... you've got to keep your cultural identity because it's important to you. And sometimes the two value bases don't meet. And so how do you do that without trading off? And that's really really important because if you trade off your value base then where does your passion for your profession fit? What we should have, is good cultural supervisors ... that assist us

to know how to … keep the balance of our own values and beliefs, and still be seen as a professional social worker, adhering to all the rules and regulations that are required of us, but not to lose our own cultural identity. **”**

Most often, appropriate assistance will help workers negotiate a comfortable integration of personal and professional values since the latter are grounded in principles of human rights and justice. However, the question of organizational fit may be more problematic. For example, in previous chapters social workers talked about how their employing organizations had become overly output driven or even manipulated waiting lists in an effort to gain or retain lucrative contracts. They felt that the actions and activities expected of them were no longer aligned with appropriate social work goals and values. When challenging such situations is not viable, or is to no avail, we may decide to leave and work elsewhere. Moral distress that continues unabated is traumatizing. At worst, we begin to depersonalize clients in order to cope and this is an outcome we should be assisted to avoid.

The toolkit for balance in practice

A toolkit stored on a shelf is of little benefit. The points outlined below are all practical steps aimed at inspiring balance.

- Identify your core values and principles and check back regularly to ensure your work efforts remain aligned to these. Being clear about your core principles may enable you to relax and let go of less important issues. You may also begin to think more creatively about how to achieve the things that are most important.

- Ensure that your mentors and supervisors work from a strengths perspective, and will be honest with you about your developmental needs. There is much evidence that positive regard is most helpful and shaming approaches are not beneficial. If your supervisor doesn't work from a strengths perspective, he or she may be able to be re-educated. Meanwhile, however, the supervisee's needs should come first and it may be time to make alternative arrangements to get those met.

- People appointed to supervise or manage staff should have undertaken education to prepare them to undertake these important roles. In addition, it may be helpful to provide workers with opportunities to seek specialist supervision, such as cultural supervision, to meet their professional development needs.

- Turn up the dial on noticing positive events and opportunities for growth, and turn down the dial on negative critique. This doesn't mean we should fail to address wrongs, but the balance should fall toward constructive communications.

- If you supervise or manage staff, make an effort to build positive self-esteem by outwardly recognizing their efforts and good work.

- Ensure you have uninterrupted leisure time. Do not allow work to invade every corner of your private space. Risk a total break from work-related interruptions during weekends and vacations.

- Consider what replenishes you and if you have let those practices lapse, reintroduce them. Alternatively, learn something new that is unrelated to your work. Perhaps you always wanted to sing, draw, or dance? All of these activities naturally encourage mindfulness. If the activity also involves you in some social contact this may be especially beneficial in relation to overcoming stress.

- Turn to your children, your partner, your siblings, your parents or friends and check in with them. Are they alright? Is your work heavy for them? If so, make a plan to relieve them.

- Draw on all professions and disciplines who share core human service values. If we can pull together in developing strategic approaches to support our work, we will achieve much more.

- Remember that it is meaningful to save just one star.

- Finally, social workers and human service workers are worth investing in.

Fourteen experienced practitioners reached out and committed their time and efforts to contribute to this endeavour. They did this in the hope that their insights will help others, and ensure others will not feel alone, as they themselves have sometimes felt. Despite having faced some dark times, they all retain their capacity to be awed by service users who achieve goals against the odds. They continue to find their work meaningful, and are filled with hope. This does not mean that they have stopped finding their work distressing at times, though this is now less often the case, but they have learned how to restore balance when it threatens to become lost.

At the end of my book, I return to my garden, where the weeds are about to set seed, gather my sense of humour around me, and see that these are not a waste of time but serve a core restorative function for me and my family.

Additional resource

Eiseley, L. C. (1978) *The Star Thrower*. London: Harcourt Brace.

References

Abdallah, T. (2009) 'Prevalence and predictors of burnout among Palestinian social workers.' *International Social Work 52*, 2, 223–233.

Acker, G. M. (2009) 'The challenges in providing services to clients with mental illness: Managed care, burnout and somatic symptoms among social workers.' *Community Mental Health Journal 46*, 6, 591–600.

Acquavita, S. P., Pittman, J., Gibbons, M. and Castellanos-Brown, K. (2009) 'Personal and organizational diversity factors' impact on social workers' job satisfaction: Results from a national internet-based survey.' *Administration in Social Work 33*, 2, 151–166.

Adams, K. B., Matto, H. C. and Harrington, D. (2001) 'The Traumatic Stress Institute Belief Scale as a measure of vicarious trauma in a national sample of clinical social workers.' *Families in Society 82*, 4, 363–371.

Alexander, C. and Charles, G. (2009) 'Caring, mutuality and reciprocity in social worker-client relationships: Rethinking principles of practice.' *Journal of Social Work 9*, 1, 5–22.

Allen-Meares, P. (2007) 'Cultural competence: An ethical requirement.' *Journal of Ethnic and Cultural Diversity in Social Work 16*, 3 & 4, 83–92.

Aotearoa New Zealand Association of Social Workers (1993) *Code of Ethics*. Dunedin, New Zealand: ANZASW.

Aotearoa New Zealand Association of Social Workers (2008) *Code of Ethics*, 2nd edn. rev. Dunedin, New Zealand: ANZASW.

Arnd-Caddigan, M. and Pozzuto, R. (2008) 'Use of self in relational clinical social work.' *Clinical Social Work Journal 36*, 3, 235–243.

Badger, K., Royse, D. and Craig, C. (2008) 'Hospital social workers and indirect trauma exposure: An exploratory study of contributing factors.' *Health and Social Work 33*, 1, 63–71.

Baginsky, M., Moriarty, J., Manthorpe, J., Stevens, M., MacInnes, T. and Nagendran, T. (2010) *Social Workers' Workload Survey: Messages from the Frontline*. Findings from the 2009 Survey and Interviews with Senior Managers. London: Social Work Task Force.

Baillien, E. and De Witte, H. (2009) 'Why is organizational change related to workplace bullying? Role conflict and job insecurity as mediators.' *Economic and Industrial Democracy 30*, 3, 348–371.

Baker, C. N. (2007) 'The emergence of organized feminist resistance to sexual harassment in the United States in the 1970s.' *Journal of Women's History 19*, 3, 161–184.

Baker, E. K. (2003) *Caring for Ourselves: A Therapist's Guide to Personal and Professional Well-being*. Washington, DC: American Psychological Association.

Banks, S. (2008) 'Critical commentary: Social work ethics.' *British Journal of Social Work 38*, 6, 1238–1249.

Beale, D. and Hoel, H. (2010) 'Workplace bullying, industrial relations and the challenge for management in Britain and Sweden.' *European Journal of Industrial Relations 16*, 2, 101–118.

Beddoe, L. (2009) 'Creating continuous conversation: Social workers and learning organizations.' *Social Work Education 28*, 7, 722–736.

Beddoe, L., Appleton, C. and Maher, B. (1998) 'Social workers' experience of violence.' *Social Work Review 10*, 1, 4–11.

Bell, H. (2003) 'Strengths and secondary trauma in family violence work.' *Social Work 48*, 4, 513–522.

Bell, H., Kulkarni, S. and Dalton, L. (2003) 'Organizational prevention of vicarious trauma.' *Families in Society 84*, 4, 463–470.

Ben-Porat, A. and Itzhaky, H. (2009) 'Implications of treating family violence for the therapist: Secondary traumatization, vicarious traumatization, and growth.' *Journal of Family Violence 24*, 7, 507–515.

Bennett, P., Evans, R. and Tattersall, A. (1993) 'Stress and coping in social workers: A preliminary investigation.' *British Journal of Social Work 23*, 1, 31–44.

Bentley, T., Catley, B., Cooper-Thomas, H., Gardner, D., O'Driscoll, M. and Trenberth, L. (2009) *Understanding Stress and Bullying in New Zealand Workplaces.* Final report to OH&S Steering Committee. Accessed on 23 November 2010 at www.massey.ac.nz/massey/fms//Massey News/2010/04/docs/Bentley-et-al-report.pdf

Berceli, D. and Napoli, M. (2006) 'A proposal for a mindfulness-based trauma prevention program for social work professionals.' *Complementary Health Practice Review 11,* 3, 153–165.

Black, K. (2007) 'Health care professionals' death attitudes, experiences, and advance directive and communication behavior.' *Death Studies 31,* 6, 563–572.

Boscarino, J. A., Figley, C. R. and Adams, R. E. (2004) 'Compassion fatigue following the September 11 terrorist attacks: A study of secondary trauma among New York City social workers.' *International Journal of Emergency Mental Health 6,* 2, 57–66.

Brady, J. L., Guy, J. D., Poelstra, P. L. and Brokaw, B. F. (1999) 'Vicarious traumatization, spirituality, and the treatment of sexual abuse survivors: A national survey of women psychotherapists.' *Professional Psychology-Research and Practice 30,* 4, 386–393.

Branch, R. and Willson, R. (2007) *Cognitive Behavioural Therapy Workbook for Dummies.* Chichester, Sussex: John Wiley & Sons.

Branch, S., Ramsay, S. and Barker, M. (2007) 'Managers in the firing line: Contributing factors to workplace bullying by staff – an interview study.' *Journal of Management and Organization 13,* 3, 264–281.

Breslau, N. (2009) 'The epidemiology of trauma, PTSD, and other posttrauma disorders.' *Trauma, Violence, and Abuse, 10,* 3, 198–210.

British Association of Social Workers (2010) *The Social Work Bill.* Accessed on 12 November 2010 at http://dl.dropbox.com/u/3522570/socialworkbill/baswsocworkbill.pdf

Bronstein, L., Kovacs, P. and Vega, A. (2007) 'Goodness of fit: Social work education and practice in health care.' *Social Work in Health Care, 45,* 2, 59–76.

Brough, P. and Williams, J. (2007) 'Managing occupational stress in a high-risk industry: Measuring the job demands of correctional officers.' *Criminal Justice and Behavior 34,* 4, 555–567.

Buchbinder, E. (2007) 'Being a social worker as an existential commitment: From vulnerability to meaningful purpose.' *The Humanistic Psychologist 35,* 2, 161–174.

Cairo, J. B., Dutta, S., Nawaz, H., Hashmi, S., Kasl, S. and Bellido, E. (2010) 'The prevalence of posttraumatic stress disorder among adult earthquake survivors in Peru.' *Disaster Medicine and Public Health Preparedness 4,* 1, 39–46.

Canfield, J. (2005) 'Secondary traumatization, burnout, and vicarious traumatization: A review of the literature as it relates to therapists who treat trauma.' *Smith College Studies in Social Work 75,* 2, 81–99.

Carmel, M. J. S. and Friedlander, M. L. (2009) 'The relation of secondary traumatization to therapists' perceptions of the working alliance with clients who commit sexual abuse.' *Journal of Counseling Psychology 56,* 3, 461–467.

Carpenter, J., Schneider, J., Brandon, T. and Wooff, D. (2003) 'Working in multidisciplinary community mental health teams: The impact on social workers and health professionals of integrated mental health care.' *British Journal of Social Work 33,* 8, 1081–1103.

Carver, C. S. (1998) 'Resilience and thriving: Issues, models, and linkages.' *Journal of Social Issues 54,* 2, 245–266.

Caverley, N. (2005) 'Civil service resiliency and coping.' *International Journal of Public Sector Management 18,* 5, 401–413.

Chouliara, Z., Hutchison, C. and Karatzias, T. (2009) 'Vicarious traumatisation in practitioners who work with adult survivors of sexual violence and child sexual abuse: Literature review and directions for future research.' *Counselling and Psychotherapy Research 9,* 1, 47–56.

Christie, A. and Weeks, J. (1998) 'Life experience: A neglected form of knowledge in work education and practice.' *Practice 10,* 1, 55–68.

Coffey, M., Dugdill, L. and Tattersall, A. (2004) 'Stress in social services: Mental well-being, constraints and job satisfaction.' *British Journal of Social Work 34,* 5, 735–746.

Cohen, M. and Gagin, R. (2005) 'Can skill-development training alleviate burnout in hospital social workers?' *Social Work in Health Care 40,* 4, 83–97.

Colarossi, L., Heyman, J. and Phillips, M. (2005) 'Social workers' experiences of the World Trade Center disaster: Stressors and their relationship to symptom types.' *Community Mental Health Journal 41,* 2, 185–198.

Collings, J. A. and Murray, P. J. (1996) 'Predictors of stress amongst social workers: An empirical study.' *British Journal of Social Work 26,* 3, 375–387.

Collins, S. (2008) 'Statutory social workers: Stress, job satisfaction, coping, social support and individual differences.' *British Journal of Social Work 38*, 6, 1173–1193.

Collins, S. and Parry-Jones, B. (2000) 'Stress: The perceptions of social work lecturers in Britain.' *British Journal of Social Work 30*, 6, 769–794.

Congress, E. P. (2000) 'What social workers should know about ethics: Understanding and resolving practice dilemmas.' *Advances in Social Work 1*, 1, 1–25.

Congress, E. P. (2001) 'Dual relationships in social work education: Report on a national survey.' *Journal of Social Work Education 37*, 2, 255–266.

Connolly, M. and Doolan, M. (2007) 'Responding to the deaths of children known to child protection agencies.' *Social Policy Journal of New Zealand 30*, 1–11.

Conrad, D. and Kellar-Guenther, Y. (2006) 'Compassion fatigue, burnout, and compassion satisfaction among Colorado child protection workers.' *Child Abuse and Neglect 30*, 10, 1071–1080.

Cortina, L. M. and Magley, V. J. (2003) 'Raising voice, risking retaliation: Events following interpersonal mistreatment in the workplace.' *Journal of Occupational Health Psychology 8*, 4, 247–265.

Coyle, D., Edwards, D., Hannigan, B., Fothergill, A. and Burnard, P. (2005) 'A systematic review of stress among mental health social workers.' *International Social Work 48*, 2, 201–211.

Crabtree, D. A. (2002) 'Vicarious traumatization in therapists who work with juvenile sex offenders.' Unpublished Doctoral Project, Pace University, New York.

Crawshaw, L. (2007) *Taming the Abrasive Manager: How to End Unnecessary Roughness in the Workplace.* San Fransisco, CA: Jossey-Bas.

Cronin, M. S., Ryan, D. M. and Brier, D. (2007) 'Support for staff working in disaster situations: A social work perspective.' *International Social Work 50*, 3, 370–382.

Cunningham, M. (1999) 'The impact of sexual abuse treatment on the social work clinician.' *Child & Adolescent Social Work Journal 16*, 4, 277–290.

Curry, D., McCarragher, T. and Dellmann-Jenkins, M. (2005) 'Training, transfer, and turnover: Exploring the relationship among transfer of learning factors and staff retention in child welfare.' *Children and Youth Services Review 27*, 8, 931–948.

Dane, B. and Chachkes, E. (2001) 'The cost of caring for patients with an illness: Contagion to the social worker.' *Social Work in Health Care 33*, 2, 31–51.

Davys, A. and Beddoe, L. (2010) *Best Practice in Professional Supervision: A Guide for the Helping Professions.* London: Jessica Kingsley Publishers.

Dawood, S. R. S. (2010) 'Perception and nature of workplace bullying among the voluntary sector workforce: A qualitative analysis.' *Journal of Health, Safety and Environment 26*, 3, 233–247.

Dekel, R., Hantman, S., Ginzburg, K. and Solomon, Z. (2007) 'The cost of caring? Social workers in hospitals confront ongoing terrorism.' *British Journal of Social Work 37*, 7, 1247–1261.

Demir, A., Ulusoy, M. and Ulusoy, M. F. (2003) 'Investigation of factors influencing burnout levels in the professional and private lives of nurses.' *International Journal of Nursing Studies 40*, 807–827.

Department of Labour (2008) *Work-Life Balance and Flexibility in New Zealand: A Snapshot of Employee and Employer Attitudes and Experiences in 2008.* Wellington, New Zealand: DoL.

Dhooper, S. S. and Byars, L. F. (1989) 'Stress and the life satisfaction of black social workers.' *Affilia 4*, 1, 70–78.

Dickens, J. (2006) 'Care, control and change in child care proceedings: Dilemmas for social workers, managers and lawyers.' *Child and Family Social Work 11*, 1, 23–32.

Diener, E., Emmons, R. A., Larsen R. J. and Griffin, S. (1985) 'The Satisfaction With Life Scale: A measure of global life satisfaction.' *Journal of Personality Assessment 49*, 71–75.

Dill, K. (2007) 'Impact of stressors on front-line child welfare supervisors.' *The Clinical Supervisor 26*, 1 & 2, 177–193.

Dollard, M. F., Dormann, C., Boyd, C. M., Winefield, H. R. and Winefield, A. H. (2003) 'Unique aspects of stress in human service work.' *Australian Psychologist 38*, 2, 84–91.

Duncan, S., Hyndman, K., Estabrooks, C., Hesketh, K. *et al.* (2001) 'Nurses' experience of violence in Alberta and British Columbia hospitals.' *Canadian Journal of Nursing Research 32*, 4, 57–78.

Dwyer, S. (2007) 'The emotional impact of social work practice.' *Journal of Social Work Practice 21*, 1, 49–60.

Earthquake Commission and GNS Science (2010) *GeoNet.* Accessed on 22 November 2010 at www.geonet.org.nz

Edward, K.-L. (2005) 'The phenomenon of resilience in crisis care mental health clinicians.' *International Journal of Mental Health Nursing 14*, 2, 142–148.

Eidelson, R. J., D'Alessio, G. R. and Eidelson, J. I. (2003) 'The impact of September 11 on psychologists.' *Professional Psychology: Research and Practice 34*, 2, 144–150.

Einarsen, S. (1999) 'The nature and causes of bullying at work.' *International Journal of Manpower 20*, 1 & 2, 16–27.

Einarsen, S., Hoel, H., Zapf, D. and Cooper, C. L. (2003) 'The Concept of Bullying at Work: The European Tradition.' In S. Einarsen, H. Hoel, D. Zapf and C. L. Cooper (eds) *Bullying and Emotional Abuse in the Workplace.* London: Taylor and Francis.

Einarsen, S. and Mikkelsen, E. G. (2003) 'Individual Effects of Exposure to Bullying at Work'. In S. Einarsen, H. Hoel, D. Zapf and C. L. Cooper (eds) *Bullying and Emotional Abuse in the Workplace.* London: Taylor and Francis.

Eiseley, L. C. (1969) *The Unexpected Universe* London: Harcourt Brace.

Eiseley, L. C. (1978) *The Star Thrower.* London: Harcourt Brace.

Ellett, A. J. (2009) 'Intentions to remain employed in child welfare: The role of human caring, self-efficacy beliefs, and professional organizational culture.' *Children and Youth Services Review 31*, 1, 78–88.

Employment Act (2008) London: HMSO.

Employment Relations (Flexible Working Arrangements) Amendment Act (2007) Wellington: NZ Parliament.

Employment Relations Act (2000) Wellington: New Zealand Parliament.

Ennis, L. and Horne, S. (2003) 'Predicting psychological distress in sex offender therapists.' *Sexual Abuse: Journal of Research and Treatment 15*, 2, 149–157.

Erdoğan, S., Kılıç, C., Aker, T., Tural, Ü. and Önder, E. (2006) 'Prevalence of psychiatric disorders three years after the 1999 earthquake in Turkey: Marmara Earthquake Survey (MES).' *Social Psychiatry and Psychiatric Epidemiology 41*, 11, 868–874.

Eriksson, C. B., Vande Kemp, H., Gorsuch, R., Hoke, S. and Foy, D. W. (2001) 'Trauma exposure and PTSD symptoms in international relief and development personnel.' *Journal of Traumatic Stress 14*, 1, 205–212.

Evans, S. and Huxley, P. (2009) 'Factors associated with the recruitment and retention of social workers in Wales: Employer and employee perspectives.' *Health and Social Care in the Community 17*, 3, 254–266.

Evans, S., Huxley, P., Gately, C., Webber, M. *et al.* (2006) 'Mental health, burnout and job satisfaction among mental health social workers in England and Wales.' *British Journal of Psychiatry 188*, 1, 75–80.

Evans, S., Patt, I., Giosan, C., Spielman, L. and Difede, J. (2009) 'Disability and posttraumatic stress disorder in disaster relief workers responding to September 11, 2001 World Trade Center disaster.' *Journal of Clinical Psychology 65*, 7, 684–694.

Exline, J. J. and Lobel, M. (1999) 'The perils of outperformance: Sensitivity about being the target of a threatening upward comparison.' *Psychological Bulletin 125*, 3, 307–337.

Fair Work Act (2009) Canberra: Parliament of Australia.

Figley, C. R. (ed) (1995) *Compassion Fatigue: Coping with Secondary Traumatic Stress Disorder in Those Who Treat the Traumatized.* New York: Brunner/Mazel.

Firdaus, S. D. (2009) 'A hassle a day may keep the pathogens away: The fight-or-flight stress response and the augmentation of immune function.' *Integrative and Comparative Biology 49*, 3, 215–236.

Fish, R. and Culshaw, E. (2005) 'The last resort? Staff and client perspectives on physical intervention.' *Journal of Intellectual Disabilities 9*, 2, 93–107.

Fitzgerald, L. F., Buchanan, N. T., Collinsworth, L. L., Ramos, A. M. and Magley, V. J. (1999) 'Junk logic: The abuse defense in sexual harassment litigation.' *Psychology, Public Policy, and Law 5*, 3, 730–759.

Fitzgerald, L. F., Swan, S. C. and Fischer, K. (1995) 'Why didn't she just report him? The psychological and legal implications of women's responses to sexual harassment.' *Journal of Social Issues 51*, 1, 117–138.

Fox, S. and Stallworth, L. E. (2005) 'Racial/ethnic bullying: Exploring links between bullying and racism in the US workplace.' *Journal of Vocational Behavior 66*, 3, 438–456.

French, J. R. P., Caplan, R. D. and Van Harrison, R. (1982) *The Mechanisms of Job Stress and Strain.* New York: Wiley.

Freudenberger, H. J. (1974) 'Staff burnout.' *Journal of Social Issues 30*, 1, 159–165.

Gall, T. L., Charbonneau, C., Clarke, N. H., Grant, K., Joseph, A. and Shouldice, L. (2005) 'Understanding the nature and role of spirituality in relation to coping and health: A conceptual framework.' *Canadian Psychology – Psychologie Canadienne 46*, 2, 88–104.

Gately, L. A. and Stabb, S. D. (2005) 'Psychology students' training in the management of potentially violent clients.' *Professional Psychology: Research and Practice 36*, 6, 681–687.

General Social Care Council (2010a) *Codes of Practice for Employers of Social Care Workers.* Accessed on 20 December 2010 at www.gscc.org.uk/cmsFiles/Registration/Codes%20of%20Practice/CodesofPracticeforEmployersofSocialCareWorkers.pdf

General Social Care Council (2010b) *Codes of Practice for Social Care Workers.* Accessed on 20 December 2010 at www.gscc.org.uk/cmsFiles/Registration/Codes%20of%20Practice/CodesofPracticeforSocialCareWorkers.pdf

Goddard, C. and Stanley, J. (2002) *In the Firing Line: Relationships, Power and Violence in Child Protection Work.* Victoria, NSW: John Wiley & Sons.

Grainger, H. and Fitzner, G. (2007) *The First Fair Treatment at Work Survey: Executive Summary – Updated.* London: Department of Trade and Industry.

Gray, M. and Gibbons, J. (2007) 'There are no answers, only choices: Teaching ethical decision making in social work.' *Australian Social Work 60*, 2, 228–238.

Gray, M. M., Wuest, J., MacIntosh, J. and Cronkhite, M. (2010) 'Workplace bullying in health care affects the meaning of work.' *Qualitative Health Research 20*, 8, 1128–1141.

Green, R. and Lonne, B. (2005) '"Great lifestyle, pity about the job stress": Occupational stress in rural human service practice.' *Rural Society 15*, 3, 252–266.

Gregerson, M. B. (2007) 'Creativity enhances practitioners' resiliency and effectiveness after a hometown disaster.' *Professional Psychology: Research and Practice 38*, 6, 596–602.

Griffin, M. L., Hogan, N. L., Lambert, E. G., Tucker-Gail, K. A. and Baker, D. N. (2010) 'Job involvement, job stress, job satisfaction, and organizational commitment and the burnout of correctional staff.' *Criminal Justice and Behavior 37*, 2, 239–255.

Gustafsson, G., Eriksson, S., Strandberg, G. and Norberg, A. (2010) 'Burnout and perceptions of conscience among health care personnel: A pilot study.' *Nursing Ethics 17*, 1, 23–38.

Halpern, J., Gurevich, M., Schwartz, B. and Brazeau, P. (2009) 'Interventions for critical incident stress in emergency medical services: A qualitative study.' *Stress and Health 25*, 2, 139–149.

Hanley, G., Bryant, M. and Buttigieg, D. (2009) 'Poor bullying prevention and employee health: Some implications.' *International Journal of Workplace Health Management 2*, 1, 48–62.

Hanrahan, P. M. (1997) '"How do I know if I'm being harassed or if this is part of my job?" Nurses and definitions of sexual harassment.' *NWSA Journal 9*, 2, 43–63.

Hardina, D. (2005) 'Ten characteristics of empowerment-oriented social service organizations.' *Administration in Social Work 29*, 3, 23–42.

Harvey, S. B., Hotopf, M., Øverland, S. and Mykletun, A. (2010) 'Physical activity and common mental disorders.' *The British Journal of Psychiatry 197*, 5, 357–364.

Hatcher, R. and Noakes, S. (2010) 'Working with sex offenders: The impact on Australian treatment providers.' *Psychology Crime and Law 16*, 1 & 2, 145–167.

Heames, J. and Harvey, M. (2006) 'Workplace bullying: A cross-level assessment.' *Management Decision 44*, 9, 1214–1230.

Hershcovis, M. S. and Barling, J. (2010) 'Towards a multi-foci approach to workplace aggression: A meta-analytic review of outcomes from different perpetrators.' *Journal of Organizational Behavior 31*, 1, 24–44.

Hesse, A. R. (2002) 'Secondary trauma: How working with trauma survivors affects therapists.' *Clinical Social Work Journal 30*, 3, 293–309.

Higgs, L. (2010, 20 May) 'BASW concerned over sharp rise in complaints about social workers.' *Children and Young People Now.* Accessed on 11 November 2010 at www.cypnow.co.uk/news/ByDiscipline/Social-Care/1004672/BASW-concerned-sharp-rise-complaints-social-workers

Hodge, D. R. (2002) 'Conceptualizing spirituality in social work: How the metaphysical beliefs of social workers may foster bias toward theistic consumers.' *Social Thought 21*, 1, 39–61.

Hodge, D. R. and Bushfield, S. (2006) 'Developing spiritual competence in practice.' *Journal of Ethnic and Cultural Diversity in Social Work 15*, 3 & 4, 101–127.

Hoel, H., Sparks, K. and Cooper, C. L. (2001) *The Cost of Violence/Stress at Work and the Benefits of a Violence/Stress-Free Working Environment.* Report Commissioned by the International Labour Organization (ILO). Geneva, Switzerland: ILO.

Høgh, A., Pejtersen, J. H., Olsen, O. and Ortega, A. (2009) 'Prevalence of workplace bullying and risk groups: A representative population study.' *International Archives of Occupational and Environmental Health 82*, 3, 417–426.

Horwitz, M. J. (2006) 'Work-related trauma effects in child protection social workers.' *Journal of Social Service Research 32*, 3, 1–18.

House of Commons Health Committee (2003) *The Victoria Climbié Inquiry Report. Sixth Report of Session 2002–03.* London: HMSO.

Hsieh, S. Y., Thomas, D. and Rotem, A. (2005) 'The organisational response to patient complaints: A case study in Taiwan.' *International Journal of Health Care Quality Assurance 18*, 4, 308–320.

Hunt, C. M., Davidson, M. J., Hoel, H. and Fielden, S. L. (2010) 'Reviewing sexual harassment in the workplace – an intervention model.' *Personnel Review 39*, 5, 655–673.

Hunter, S. V. and Schofield, M. J. (2006) 'How counsellors cope with traumatized clients: Personal, professional and organizational strategies.' *International Journal for the Advancement of Counselling 28*, 2, 121–138.

Huxley, P., Evans, S., Gately, C., Webber, M. *et al.* (2005) 'Stress and pressures in mental health social work: The worker speaks.' *British Journal of Social Work 35*, 7, 1063–1079.

Ilies, R., Hauserman, N., Schwochau, S. and Stibal, J. (2003) 'Reported incidence rates of work-related sexual harassment in the United States: Using meta-analysis to explain reported rate disparities.' *Personnel Psychology 56*, 3, 607–631.

Janson, G. R., Carney, J. V., Hazler, R. J. and Insoo, O. (2009) 'Bystanders' reactions to witnessing repetitive abuse experiences.' *Journal of Counselling and Development 87*, 3, 319–326.

Janson, G. R. and Hazler, R. J. (2004) 'Trauma reactions of bystanders and victims to repetitive abuse experiences.' *Violence and Victims 19*, 2, 239–255.

Janusz, B. D. (2010) 'Bully-free workplaces.' *Our Times 29*, 3, 16–20.

Jaskyte, K. (2005) 'The Impact of organizational socialization tactics on role ambiguity and role conflict of newly hired social workers.' *Administration in Social Work 29*, 4, 69–87.

Jayaratne, S., Croxton, T. A. and Mattison, D. (2004) 'A national survey of violence in the practice of social work.' *Families in Society 85*, 4, 445–453.

Jeffrey, A. and Austin, T. (2007) 'Perspectives and practices of clinician self-disclosure to clients: A pilot comparison study of two disciplines.' *American Journal of Family Therapy 35*, 2, 95–108.

Juby, C. and Scannapieco, M. (2007) 'Characteristics of workload management in pulic child welfare agencies.' *Administration in Social Work 31*, 3, 95–109.

Kahn, W. L. and Harkavy-Friedman, J. M. (1997) 'Change in the therapist: The role of patient-induced inspiration.' *American Journal of Psychotherapy 51*, 3, 403–414.

Kapp, C. (2009) 'Barbara Hogan: South Africa's Minister of Health.' *The Lancet 373*, 9660, 291.

Karasek, R. A. (1979) 'Job demands, job decision latitude, and mental strain: Implications for job redesign.' *Administrative Science Quarterly 24*, 2, 285–307.

Karasek, R. A. and Theorell, T. (1990) *Healthy Work: Stress, Productivity, and the Reconstruction of Working Life*. New York: Basic Books.

Knaus, W. J. (2008) *The Cognitive Behavioral Workbook for Anxiety: A Step-by-Step Program*. Oakland, CA: New Harbinger Publications.

Kootte, A. F. (2001) 'Death anxiety, occupational stress and burnout in hospice social workers.' Unpublished PhD Dissertation, The Florida State University, Gainesville, FL.

Koritsas, J., Coles, J. and Boyle, M. (2010) 'Workplace violence towards social workers: The Australian experience.' *British Journal of Social Work 40*, 1, 257–271.

Kosny, A. A. and Eakin, J. M. (2008) 'The hazards of helping: Work, mission and risk in non-profit social service organizations.' *Health, Risk and Society 10*, 2, 149–166.

Krumer-Nevo, M., Slonim-Nevo, V. and Hirshenzon-Segev, E. (2006) 'Social workers and their long-term clients: The never-ending struggle.' *Journal of Social Service Research 33*, 1, 27–38.

Kyonne, J. (2007) 'The role of teamwork in public child welfare caseworkers' intentions to leave.' Unpublished PhD Dissertation, University of Missouri, Columbia.

Lackie, B. (1983) 'The families of origin of social workers.' *Clinical Social Work Journal 11*, 4, 309–322.

Lai, T. J., Davidson, J. R. T., Connor, K. M., Chang, C. M. and Lee, L. C. (2004) 'Full and partial PTSD among earthquake survivors in rural Taiwan.' *Journal of Psychiatric Research 38*, 3, 313–322.

Lait, J. and Wallace, J. E. (2002) 'Stress at work: A study of organizational-professional conflict and unmet expectations.' *Relations Industrielles – Industrial Relations 57*, 3, 463–490.

Lambert, E. G., Hogan, N. L. and Tucker, K. A. (2009) 'Problems at work: Exploring the correlates of role stress among correctional staff.' *The Prison Journal 89*, 4, 460–481.

Lambert, E. G. and Paoline, E. A., III. (2008) 'The influence of individual, job, and organizational characteristics on correctional staff job stress, job satisfaction, and organizational commitment.' *Criminal Justice Review 33*, 4, 541–564.

Landau, R. (1997) 'Terrorism and the social worker.' *Practice 9*, 4, 5–12.

Landy, F. J. and Conte, J. M. (2007) *Work in the 21st Century: An Introduction to Industrial and Organizational Psychology*, 2nd edn. Oxford, UK: Blackwell.

Lasalvia, A., Bonetto, C., Bertani, M., Bissoli, S. *et al.* (2009) 'Influence of perceived organisational factors on job burnout: survey of community mental health staff.' *British Journal of Psychiatry 195*, 6, 537–544.

Lazarus, R. S. and Folkman, S. (1984) *Stress, Appraisal and Coping*. New York: Springer.

Le Fevre, M., Matheny, J. and Kolt, G., S. (2003) 'Eustress, distress, and interpretation in occupational stress.' *Journal of Managerial Psychology 18*, 7 & 8, 726–744.

Lee, S.-H., Juang, Y.-Y., Su, Y.-J., Lee, H.-L., Lin, Y.-H. and Chao, C.-C. (2005) 'Facing SARS: Psychological impacts on SARS team nurses and psychiatric services in a Taiwan general hospital.' *General Hospital Psychiatry 27*, 5, 352–358.

Lehrer, P. M., Woolfolk, R. L. and Sime, W. E. (eds) (2007) *Principles and Practice of Stress Management*, 3rd edn. New York: Guilford Press.

Leka, S. and Jain, A. (2010) *Health Impact of Psychosocial Hazards at Work: An Overview*. Geneva, Switzerland: World Health Organization.

Lewis, M. A. (2006) 'Nurse bullying: Organizational considerations in the maintenance and perpetration of health care bullying cultures.' *Journal of Nursing Management 14*, 1, 52–58.

Leymann, H. (1996) 'The content and development of mobbing at work.' *European Journal of Work and Organizational Psychology 5*, 2, 165–184.

Lietz, C. A. (2010) 'Critical thinking in child welfare supervision.' *Administration in Social Work 34*, 1, 68–78.

Linzer, N., Sweifach, J. and Heft-LaPorte, H. (2008) 'Triage and ethics: Social workers on the front line.' *Journal of Human Behavior in the Social Environment 18*, 2, 184–203.

Lioi, A. (1999) 'Coasts demanding shipwreck: Love and the philosophy of science in Loren Eiseley's "The Star Thrower".' *Interdisciplinary Studies in Literature and Environment 6*, 2, 41–61.

Littlechild, B. (2002) 'The effects of client violence on child-protection networks.' *Trauma, Violence, and Abuse 3*, 2, 144–158.

Littlechild, B. (2005a) 'The nature and effects of violence against child-protection social workers: Providing effective support.' *British Journal of Social Work 35*, 3, 387–401.

Littlechild, B. (2005b) 'The stresses arising from violence, threats and aggression against child protection social workers.' *Journal of Social Work 5*, 1, 61–82.

Littlechild, B. (2008) 'Child protection social work: Risks of fears and fears of risks – Impossible tasks from impossible goals?' *Social Policy and Administration 42*, 6, 662–675.

Lloyd, C., King, R. and Chenoweth, L. (2002) 'Social work, stress and burnout: A review.' *Journal of Mental Health 11*, 3, 255–266.

Lloyd, C., McKenna, K. and King, R. (2005) 'Sources of stress experienced by occupational therapists and social workers in mental health settings.' *Occupational Therapy International 12*, 2, 81–94.

Lonne, R. L. (2003) 'Social Workers and Human Service Practitioners.' In M. F. Dollard, A. H. Winefield and H. R. Winefield (eds) *Occupational Stress in the Service Professions*. London: Taylor and Francis.

Lowe, T. B. and Korr, W. S. (2007) 'Workplace safety policies in mental health settings.' *Journal of Workplace Behavioral Health 22*, 4, 29–47.

Luckyj, A. and Campbell, P. (2009) 'Times are tough: Can you handle the pressure?' *Beyond Numbers 479*, 12–14.

Lymbery, M. E. F. (2003) 'Negotiating the contradictions between competence and creativity in social work education.' *Journal of Social Work 3*, 1, 99–117.

Macdonald, G. and Sirotich, F. (2001) 'Reporting client violence.' *Social Work 46*, 2, 107–114.

Macdonald, G. and Sirotich, F. (2005) 'Violence in the social work workplace: The Canadian experience.' *International Social Work 48*, 6, 772–781.

Mari, M., Costa, A., Priebe, S., Petrelli, F., Grappasonni, I. and Dewey, M. (2009) 'Posttraumatic stress disorder six months after an earthquake: Findings from a community sample in a rural region in Italy.' *Social Psychiatry and Psychiatric Epidemiology 44*, 5, 393–397.

Marin, A. J. and Guadagno, R. E. (1999) 'Perceptions of sexual harassment victims as a function of labeling and reporting.' *Sex Roles: A Journal of Research 41*, 11 & 12, 921–940.

Martin, G. P., Phelps, K. and Katbamna, S. (2004) 'Human motivation and professional practice: Of knights, knaves and social workers.' *Social Policy and Administration 38*, 5, 470–487.

Maslach, C. and Jackson, S. E. (1986) *The Maslach Burnout Inventory Manual*, 2nd edn. Palo Alto, CA: Consulting Psychologist Press.

Maslach, C. and Leiter, M. P. (1997) *The Truth About Burnout: How Organizations Cause Personal Stress and What to Do About It*. San Francisco, CA: Jossey-Bass.

Matthieu, M. M., Ivanoff, A., Lewis, S. and Conroy, K. (2007) 'Social work field instructors in New York City after 9/11/01: Impact and needs resulting from the World Trade Center disaster.' *The Clinical Supervisor 25*, 1 & 2, 23–42.

Mayhew, C. and Chappell, D. (2007) 'Workplace violence: An overview of patterns of risk and the emotional/stress consequences on targets.' *International Journal of Law and Psychiatry 30*, 4 & 5, 327–339.

McCann, I. L. and Pearlman, L. A. (1990) 'Vicarious traumatization: A framework for understanding the psychological effects of working with victims.' *Journal of Traumatic Stress 3*, 1, 131–149.

McCormick, J. (2003) 'Professional Workers and Stress.' In C. L. Peterson (ed) *Work Stress: Studies of the Context, Content and Outcomes of Stress: A Book of Readings*. Amityville, NY: Baywood Publishing.

McDermott, S. (2010) 'Professional judgements of risk and capacity in situations of self-neglect among older people.' *Ageing and Society, 30*, 6, 1055–1072.

McDonald, C. (2007) '"This is who we are and this is what we do": Social work education and self efficacy.' *Australian Social Work 60*, 1, 83–93.

McGowan, B. G., Auerbach, C. and Strolin-Goltzman, J. S. (2009) 'Turnover in the child welfare workforce: A different perspective.' *Journal of Social Service Research 35*, 3, 228–235.

McKay, L. (2007) *Understanding and Coping with Traumatic Stress: Headington Institute Online Training Resources for Humanitarian Workers.* Accessed on 21 November 2010 at www.headington-institute.org/Default. aspx?tabid=1783

McLean, J. and Andrew, T. (1999) 'Commitment, satisfaction, stress and control among social services managers and social workers in the UK.' *Administration in Social Work 23*, 3 & 4, 93–114.

McLean Parks, J., Ma, L. and Gallagher, D. G. (2010) 'Elasticity in the "rules" of the game: Exploring organizational expedience.' *Human Relations 63*, 5, 701–730.

Meier, A. (2002) 'An online stress management support group for social workers.' *Journal of Technology in Human Services 20*, 1 & 2, 107–132.

Messinger, L. (2004) 'Out in the field: Gay and lesbian social work students' experiences in field placement.' *Journal of Social Work Education 40*, 2, 187–204.

Monnickendam, M., Savaya, R. and Waysman, M. (2005) 'Thinking processes in social workers' use of a clinical decision support system: A qualitative study.' *Social Work Research 29*, 1, 21–30.

Moosmann, S. (2000) 'The effect of trauma work on the spirituality of the counsellor: A critical incident analysis.' Unpublished MA Thesis, University of British Columbia, Vancouver.

Moriarty, J. and Murray, J. (2007) 'Who wants to be a social worker? Using routine published data to identify trends in the number of people applying for and completing social work programmes in England.' *British Journal of Social Work 37*, 4, 715–733.

Morley, C. (2004) 'Critical reflection in social work: A response to globalisation?' *International Journal of Social Welfare 13*, 4, 297–303.

Moulden, H. M. and Firestone, P. (2007) 'Vicarious traumatization: The impact on therapists who work with sexual offenders.' *Trauma Violence and Abuse 8*, 1, 67–83.

Munro, E. (1998) 'Improving social workers' knowledge base in child protection work.' *British Journal of Social Work 28*, 1, 89–105.

Murdach, A. D. (1994) 'Avoiding errors in clinical-prediction.' *Social Work 39*, 4, 381–386.

Namie, G. and Namie, R. (2009) *The Bully at Work: What You Can Do to Stop the Bully and Reclaim Your Dignity on the Job,* 2nd edn. Naperville, IL: Sourcebook Inc.

Narayan, G. S. (2005) 'Social workers in management: Work/family stress and issues of self-care.' *Social Work 41*, 1, 1–16.

Nelson-Gardell, D. and Harris, D. (2003) 'Childhood abuse history, secondary traumatic stress, and child welfare workers.' *Child Welfare 82*, 1, 5–26.

Newhill, C. E. and Wexler, S. (1997) 'Client violence toward children and youth services social workers.' *Children and Youth Services Review 19*, 3, 195–212.

Nissly, J. A., Mor Barak, M. E. and Levin, A. (2005) 'Stress, social support, and workers' intentions to leave their jobs in public child welfare.' *Administration in Social Work 29*, 1, 79–100.

O'Donohue, W. T., Avina, C., Mosco, E. A. and Bowers, A. H. (2006) 'Sexual harassment as diagnosable PTSD trauma.' *Psychiatric Times 23*, 1, 50.

Oliver, J. and Brough, P. (2002) 'Cognitive appraisal, negative affectivity and psychological well-being.' *New Zealand Journal of Psychology 31*, 1, 2–7.

Olson, C. J. and Royse, D. (2006) 'Early-life adversity and choice of the social work profession.' *Journal of Evidence Based Social Work 3*, 2, 31–47.

Osofsky, J. D. (2008) 'In the aftermath of Hurricane Katrina: A personal story of a psychologist from New Orleans.' *Professional Psychology: Research and Practice 39*, 1, 12–17.

Overholser, J. C. and Fine, M. A. (1990) 'Defining the boundaries of professional competence: Managing subtle cases of clinical incompetence.' *Professional Psychology: Research and Practice 21*, 6, 462–469.

Pal, S. and Saksvik, P. Ø. (2008) 'Work-family conflict and psychosocial work environment stressors as predictors of job stress in a cross-cultural study.' *International Journal of Stress Management 15*, 1, 22–42.

Parzefall, M.-R. and Salin, D. M. (2010) 'Perceptions of and reactions to workplace bullying: A social exchange perspective.' *Human Relations 63*, 6, 761–780.

Petrovich, A. (2008) 'Lessons learned in the sandwich.' *Affilia 23*, 3, 223–230.

Phelps, A., Lloyd, D., Creamer, M. and Forbes, D. (2009) 'Caring for carers in the aftermath of trauma.' *Journal of Aggression, Maltreatment and Trauma 18*, 3, 313–330.

Pollack, D. (2010) 'Social work and violent clients: An international perspective.' *International Social Work 53*, 2, 277–282.

Pope, K. S. and Feldman-Summers, S. (1992) 'National survey of psychologists' sexual and physical abuse history and their evaluation of training and competence in these areas.' *Professional Psychology: Research and Practice 23*, 5, 353–361.

Poulin, P. A., Mackenzie, C. S., Soloway, G. and Karayolas, E. (2008) 'Mindfulness training as an evidenced-based approach to reducing stress and promoting well-being among human services professionals.' *International Journal of Health Promotion and Education 46*, 2, 72–80.

Press, The (2010a) 'Doctors issue "hype" warning.' 11 September, p.11.

Press, The (2010b) 'Staunch Cantabs sure of recovery.' 27 September, p.A5.

Quick, J. C. and Nelson, D. L. (1997) 'Job Stress.' In L. H. Peters, S. A. Youngblood and C. R. Greer (eds) *The Blackwell Dictionary of Human Resource Management*. Oxford, UK: Basil Blackwell.

Quine, L. (1999) 'Workplace bullying in NHS community trust: Staff questionnaire survey.' *British Medical Journal 318*, 7178, 228–232.

Quine, L. (2002) 'Workplace bullying in junior doctors: Questionnaire survey.' *British Medical Journal 324*, 7342, 878–879.

Rabin, S., Feldman, D. and Kaplan, Z. (1999) 'Stress and intervention strategies in mental health professionals.' *British Journal of Medical Psychology 72*, 2, 159–169.

Ramon, S., Campbell, J., Lindsay, J., McCrystal, P. and Baidoun, N. (2006) 'The impact of political conflict on social work: Experiences from Northern Ireland, Israel and Palestine.' *British Journal of Social Work 36*, 3, 435–450.

Reamer, F. G. (1998) 'The evolution of social work ethics.' *Social Work 43*, 6, 488–500.

Reamer, F. G. (2008) 'Social workers' management of error: Ethical and risk management issues.' *Families in Society 89*, 1, 61–68.

Reid, Y., Johnson, S., Morant, N., Kuipers, E. *et al.* (1999) 'Explanations for stress and satisfaction in mental health professionals: A qualitative study.' *Social Psychiatry and Psychiatric Epidemiology 34*, 6, 301–308.

Renner, L., Porter, R. and Preister, S. (2009) 'Improving the retention of child welfare workers by strengthening skills and increasing support for supervisors.' *Child Welfare 88*, 5, 109–127.

Rhodes, C., Pullen, A., Pitsis, A., Vickers, M. H. and Clegg, S., R. (2010) 'Violence and workplace bullying: What are an organization's ethical responsibilities?' *Administrative Theory and Praxis 32*, 1, 96–115.

Risley-Curtiss, C. and Hudson, W. W. (1998) 'Sexual harassment of social work students.' *Affilia 13*, 2, 190–110.

Roberts, A. R., Monferrari, I. and Yeager, K. R. (2008) 'Avoiding malpractice lawsuits by following risk assessment and suicide prevention guidelines.' *Brief Treatment and Crisis Intervention 8*, 1, 5–14.

Robinson, J. (2006) 'Academic affairs: A report from the front lines.' *Chronicle of Higher Education 52*, 35, B.11.

Roscigno, V. J., Lopez, S. H. and Hodson, R. (2009) 'Supervisory bullying, status inequalities and organizational context.' *Social Forces 87*, 3, 1561–1589.

Rose, S., Bisson, J., Churchill, R. and Wessely, S. (2002) 'Psychological debriefing for preventing post traumatic stress disorder (PTSD).' *Cochrane Database of Systematic Reviews 2002*, Issue 2. Art. No.: CD000560. DOI: 10.1002/14651858.CD000560.

Rosoff, P. M. (2008) 'The ethics of care: Social workers in an influenza pandemic.' *Social Work in Health Care 47*, 1, 49–59.

Rothschild, B. and Rand, M. L. (2006) *Help for the Helper: The Psychophysiology of Compassion Fatigue and Vicarious Trauma*. New York: W.W. Norton.

Salin, D. (2003) 'Ways of explaining workplace bullying: A review of enabling, motivating and precipitating structures and processes in the work environment.' *Human Relations 56*, 10, 1213–1232.

Salin, D. and Hoel, H. (2011) 'Organizational Causes of Workplace Bullying.' In S. Einarsen, H. Hoel, D. Zapf and C. L. Cooper (eds) *Bullying and Harassment in the Workplace: Developments in Theory, Research and Practice*, 2nd edn. London: Taylor and Francis.

Salston, M. and Figley, C. R. (2003) 'Secondary traumatic stress effects of working with survivors of criminal victimization.' *Journal of Traumatic Stress 16*, 2, 167–174.

Savaya, R., Monnickendam, M. and Waysman, M. (2006) 'Extent and type of worker utilization of an integrated information system in a human services agency.' *Evaluation and Program Planning 29*, 3, 209–216.

Saxon, C., Jacinto, G. A. and Dziegielewski, S. F. (2006) 'Self-determination and confidentiality: The ambiguous nature of decision making in social work practice.' *Journal of Human Behavior in the Social Environment 13*, 4, 55–72.

Schneider, K. T., Swan, S. and Fitzgerald, L. F. (1997) 'Job-related and psychological effects of sexual harassment in the workplace: Empirical evidence from two organizations.' *Journal of Applied Psychology 82*, 3, 401–415.

Scully, M. and Rowe, M. (2009) 'Bystander training within organisations.' *Journal of the International Ombudsman Association 2*, 1, 1–9.

Selye, H. (1976) *The Stress of Life*, 1956 rev. edn. New York: McGrawHill.

Sex Discrimination Act 1975 (Amendment) Regulations (2008) London: HMSO.

Shamai, M. (2005) 'Personal experience in professional narratives: The role of helpers' families in their work with terror victims.' *Family Process 44*, 2, 203–215.

Shamai, M. and Ron, P. (2009) 'Helping direct and indirect victims of national terror: Experiences of Israeli social workers.' *Qualitative Health Research 19*, 1, 42–54.

Shepherd, M. (2006) 'Using a learning journal to improve professional practice: A journey of personal and professional self-discovery.' *Reflective Practice 7*, 3, 333–348.

Sherman, E. and Siporin, M. (2008) 'Contemplative theory and practice for social work.' *Journal of Religion and Spirituality in Social Work 27*, 3, 259–274.

Shields, G. and Kiser, J. (2003) 'Violence and aggression directed toward human service workers: An exploratory study.' *Families in Society 84*, 1, 13–20.

Shubs, C. H. (2008) 'Countertransference issues in the assessment and treatment of trauma recovery with victims of violent crime.' *Psychoanalytic Psychology 25*, 1, 156–180.

Siebert, D. C. (2001) 'Work and well being: A survey of distress and impairment among North Carolina social workers.' Unpublished PhD Dissertation, University of North Carolina, Chapel Hill.

Siebert, D. C. and Siebert, C. F. (2007) 'Help seeking among helping professionals: A role identity perspective.' *American Journal of Orthopsychiatry 77*, 1, 49–55.

Siegrist, J. (1996) 'Adverse health effects of high-effort/low-reward conditions.' *Journal of Occupational Health Psychology 1*, 1, 27–41.

Simon, C. E., Pryce, J. G., Roff, L. L. and Klemmack, D. (2005) 'Secondary traumatic stress and oncology social work: Protecting compassion from fatigue and compromising the worker's worldview.' *Journal of Psychosocial Oncology 23*, 4, 1–14.

Slate, R. N. and Vogel, R. E. (1997) 'Participative management and correctional personnel: A study of the perceived atmosphere for participation in correctional decision making and its impact on employee stress and thoughts about quitting.' *Journal of Criminal Justice 25*, 5, 397–408.

Smith, J. C. (2001) *Advances in ABC Relaxation: Application and Inventories*. New York: Springer.

Smith, M. (2007) 'Smoke without fire? Social workers' fears of threats and accusations.' *Journal of Social Work Practice 21*, 3, 323–335.

Smith, M. and Nursten, J. (1998) 'Social workers' experiences of distress – moving towards change?' *British Journal of Social Work 28*, 3, 351–368.

Smith, M., Nursten, J. and McMahon, L. (2004) 'Social workers' responses to experiences of fear.' *British Journal of Social Work 34*, 4, 541–559.

Social Work Reform Board (2010) *Building a Safe and Confident Future: One Year On*. Progress Report from the Social Work Reform Board. London: SWRB.

Social Work Task Force (2009) *Building a Safe, Confident Future*. The Final Report of the Social Work Task Force. London: SWTF.

Spencer, P. C. and Munch, S. (2003) 'Client violence toward social workers: The role of management in community mental health programs.' *Social Work 48*, 4, 532–544.

Stanley, N., Manthorpe, J. and White, M. (2007) 'Depression in the profession: Social workers' experiences and perceptions.' *British Journal of Social Work 37*, 2, 281–298.

Stanley, T. (2010) '"Child in Need" plans: Tools for family empowerment.' *Practice 22*, 3, 155–165.

Steed, L. and Bicknell, J. (2001) 'Trauma and the therapist: The experience of therapists working with the perpetrators of sexual abuse.' *Australasian Journal of Disaster and Trauma Studies, 1*. Accessed on 20 November 2010 at http://search.ebscohost.com/login.aspx?direct=true&db=psyh&AN=2001-03478-003&site=ehost-live

Stevens, M. (2008) 'Workload management in social work services: What, why and how?' *Practice 20*, 4, 207–221.

Stevens, M. and Higgins, D. J. (2002) 'The influence of risk and protective factors on burnout experienced by those who work with maltreated children.' *Child Abuse Review 11*, 5, 313–331.

Stockdale, M. S., O'Connor, M., Gutek, B. A. and Geer, T. (2002) 'The relationship between prior sexual abuse and reactions to sexual harassment: Literature review and empirical study.' *Psychology, Public Policy, and Law 8*, 1, 64–95.

Strand, V. and Bosco-Ruggiero, S. (2010) 'Initiating and sustaining a mentoring program for child welfare staff.' *Administration in Social Work 34*, 1, 49–67.

Stroebe, M. and Schut, H. (1999) 'The dual process model of coping with bereavement: Rationale and description.' *Death Studies 23*, 3, 197–224.

Strom-Gottfried, K. (2000) 'Ethical vulnerability in social work education: An analysis of NASW complaints.' *Journal of Social Work Education 36*, 2, 241–252.

Strom-Gottfried, K. (2003) 'Understanding adjudication: Origins, targets, and outcomes of ethics complaints.' *Social Work 48*, 1, 85–94.

Tehrani, N. (2011) 'Workplace Bullying: The Role for Counselling'. In S. Einarsen, H. Hoel, D. Zapf and C. L. Cooper (eds) *Bullying and Harassment in the Workplace: Developments in Theory, Research and Practice*, 2nd edn. London: Taylor and Francis.

Tham, P. (2007) 'Why are they leaving? Factors affecting intention to leave among social workers in child welfare.' *British Journal of Social Work 37*, 7, 1225–1246.

Tham, P. and Meagher, G. (2009) 'Working in human services: How do experiences and working conditions in child welfare social work compare?' *British Journal of Social Work 39*, 5, 807–827.

Thomas, C. H. and Lankau, M. J. (2009) 'Preventing burnout: The effects of LMX and mentoring on socialization, role stress, and burnout.' *Human Resource Management 48*, 3, 417–432.

Thorpe, G. L., Righthand, S. and Kubik, E. K. (2001) 'Brief report: Dimensions of burnout in professionals working with sex offenders.' *Sexual Abuse: A Journal of Research and Treatment 13*, 3, 197–203.

Ting, L., Jacobson, J. M. and Sanders, S. (2008) 'Available supports and coping behaviors of mental health social workers following fatal and nonfatal client suicidal behavior.' *Social Work 53*, 3, 211–221.

Tosone, C. (2007) 'Therapeutic intimacy: A post-9/11 perspective.' *Smith College Studies in Social Work 76*, 4, 89–98.

Tracy, S. J., Myers, K. K. and Scott, C. W. (2006) 'Cracking jokes and crafting selves: Sensemaking and identity management among human service workers.' *Communication Monographs 73*, 3, 283–308.

Trotter, J., Crawley, M., Duggan, L., Foster, E. and Levie, J. (2009) 'Reflecting on what? Addressing sexuality in social work.' *Practice 21*, 1, 5–15.

Turner, K. (2009) 'Mindfulness: The present moment in clinical social work.' *Clinical Social Work Journal 37*, 2, 95–103.

Turner, L. M. and Shera, W. (2005) 'Empowerment of human service workers: Beyond intra-organizational strategies.' *Administration in Social Work 29*, 3, 79–94.

Vagg, P. R. and Spielberger, C. D. (1998) 'Occupational stress: Measuring job pressure and organizational support in the workplace.' *Journal of Occupational Health Psychology 3*, 4, 294–305.

Van Deusen, K. M. and Way, I. (2006) 'Vicarious trauma: An exploratory study of the impact of providing sexual abuse treatment on clinicians' trust and intimacy.' *Journal of Child Sexual Abuse 15*, 1, 69–85.

van Dyk, A. C. (2007) 'Occupational stress experienced by caregivers working in the HIV/AIDS field in South Africa.' *African Journal of AIDS Research 6*, 1, 49–66.

van Heugten, K. (1999) 'Social workers who move into private practice: A study of the issues that arise for them.' Unpublished PhD Thesis, University of Canterbury, Christchurch, New Zealand.

van Heugten, K. (2002) 'Social workers who move into private practice: Ideological considerations as a factor in the transition.' *Families in Society 83*, 5 & 6, 465–473.

van Heugten, K. (2004) 'Co-worker violence toward social workers: Too hard to handle?' *Social Work Review 16*, 4, 66–73.

van Heugten, K. (2007) 'Workplace bullying of social workers.' *Aotearoa New Zealand Social Work Review 19*, 1, 14–24.

van Heugten, K. (2010) 'Bullying of social workers: Outcomes of a grounded study into impacts and interventions.' *British Journal of Social Work 40*, 2, 638–655.

van Heugten, K. (2011a) 'Registration and social work education: A golden opportunity or a Trojan horse?' *Journal of Social Work*.

van Heugten, K. (2011b) 'Theorising active bystanders as change agents in workplace bullying of social workers ' *Families in Society*.

van Heugten, K. and Jones, J. (2007) 'Women's rights officers and women-only spaces: Addressing women's oppression on tertiary campuses.' *Te Awatea Review 5*, 1, 3–6.

van Heugten, K. and Rathgen, E. (2003) 'From studentship to professional social worker: Factors in a successful transition.' *Social Work Review 15*, 1 & 2, 13–17.

Vandekerckhove, W. and Commers, M. S. R. (2003) 'Downward workplace mobbing: A sign of the times?' *Journal of Business Ethics 45*, 1 & 2, 41–50.

Vandervort, F. E., Gonzalez, R. P. and Faller, K. C. (2008) 'Legal ethics and high child welfare worker turnover: An unexplored connection.' *Children and Youth Services Review 30*, 5, 546–563.

Vartia, M. A. (2001) 'Consequences of workplace bullying with respect to the well-being of its targets and the observers of bullying.' *Scandinavian Journal of Work, Environment and Health 27*, 1, 63–69.

Wasti, S. A. and Cortina, L. M. (2002) 'Coping in context: Sociocultural determinants of responses to sexual harassment.' *Journal of Personality and Social Psychology 83*, 2, 394–405.

Webster, L. and Hackett, R. K. (1999) 'Burnout and leadership in community mental health systems.' *Administration and Policy in Mental Health 26*, 6, 387–399.

Westbrook, T., M., Ellis, J. and Ellett, A., J. (2006) 'Improving retention among public child welfare workers: What can we learn from the insights and experiences of committed survivors?' *Administration in Social Work 30*, 4, 37–64.

Whitehead, J. T. (1985) 'Job burnout in probation and parole: Its extent and intervention implications.' *Criminal Justice and Behavior 12*, 1, 91–110.

Wiener, S. (2006) 'Role conflict, role ambiguity and self-efficacy among school social workers.' Unpublished DSW Thesis, Adelphi University, New York.

Williams, C. C. (2007) 'Mixed-method evaluation of continuing professional development: Applications in cultural competence training.' *Social Work Education 26*, 2, 121–135.

Wimpfheimer, S. (2004) 'Leadership and management competencies defined by practicing social work managers.' *Administration in Social Work 28*, 1, 45–56.

Winstanley, S. and Hales, L. (2008) 'Prevalence of aggression towards residential social workers: Do qualifications and experience make a difference?' *Child and Youth Care Forum 37*, 2, 103–110.

Wisner, W. H. (2005) 'The perilous self: Loren Eiseley and the reticence of autobiography.' *Sewanee Review 113*, 1, 84–95.

Woodward, A. (2009) 'Engaging frontline workers in times of organizational change.' *Public Administration Review 69*, 1, 25–28.

Work and Families Act (2006) London: HMSO.

Yin, R. T. (2004) 'Innovations in the management of child protection workers: Building worker resilience.' *Social Work 49*, 4, 605–608.

Yip, K.-S. (2006) 'Self-reflection in reflective practice: A note of caution.' *British Journal of Social Work 36*, 5, 777–788.

Young, C. M. (1999) 'Vicarious traumatization in psychotherapists who work with physically or sexually abused children.' Unpublished PhD Dissertation, The California School of Professional Psychology at Alameda, Alameda, CA.

Zapf, D., Escartin, J., Einarsen, S., Hoel, H. and Vartia, M. (2011) 'Empirical Findings on Prevalence and Risk Groups of Bullying in the Workplace: Developments in Theory, Research and Practice.' In S. Einarsen, H. Hoel, D. Zapf and C. L. Cooper (eds) *Bullying and Harassment in the Workplace: Developments in Theory, Research and Practice*, 2nd edn. London: Taylor and Francis.

Subject Index

abuse, vicarious trauma 112, 124
acceptance-based approach 55
Active Bystander Training 171
addictions work 94
additional resources 31
administrative demands 35–7,
    105–6
advocacy 96, 125
agency setting 98–9, 124
aggression, from service users 43
    see also violence
alcohol misuse 64
alienation 39
anger 142–3, 162–3
anti-harassment culture 155
anxiety 64
assertiveness 28
attention 55
attitude 55
autonomy 18
awareness, of stress overload 23–4

balance in practice 193–4, 202–3
behavioural effects 17, 24
being in the moment 195–6
benefits, of stress 22–3
blame 178
boundaries
    emotional 127–8
    regard for 37
    sexual 154
    work and home 71, 72–3, 76,
        124–5, 197
breathing techniques 125
British Association of Social
    Workers 187
buddies 119
bullying 43, 151, 193
    advice 168
    causes 164–7
    codes and policies 168
    and culture 168
    cyber-bullying 161
    defining 156–61
    effects of 161–4
    ethics 169
    legislation 158, 168

and organizational change
    165–6
perpetrators 157–8
prevalence 157
prevention and intervention
    167–72
record-keeping 167
research into 157
research method 158–9
resilience 170
and restructuring 165–6
role of bystanders 170–1
support 162, 167
toolkit 172–5
wider effects 164
burnout 17, 25, 26–7
    avoiding 34
    contributory factors 30, 40
    dimensions of 56
    environmental sources 27–8
    and ethical problems 102
    organizational effects 27
    protective factors 28
    working with sex offenders 92
busy-ness 35
bystanders, and bullying 170–1

caseloads, size and complexity 32
challenges, responding to 17
change 20, 49
change processes, involving
    workers in 53
child protection 83–90
    burnout 27
    increasing complexity 88–9
    interagency working 87–8
    levels of stress 33
    reflection 89–90
    staff turnover 34–5
    supervisory support 89
    support 89
    training and development
        89–90
    trauma in 123–4
    workload management 99
Christchurch earthquake 108–11
client groups, diversity 102

client problems, complexity of 35
clients, depersonalization of 41
codes of ethics 169, 181
cognitive appraisal 21
cognitive approaches 54–5, 120,
    127
cognitive behavioural interventions
    30
cognitive effects, of stress overload
    23, 24
cognitive restructuring 54–5
cohesion 29, 52
collegial violence 150–1, 172–5
    see also bullying; sexual
        harassment
collusion 105
comfort, physical and emotional
    20
communication, improving 53
community development workers
    136
community disasters 114–15
community re-education 187
comparative levels of stress 33–5
compassion fatigue 25–6, 83, 92
compassion satisfaction 83
competence 86, 178–80, 181
complaints
    bureaucracy 189
    coping with stress 190–1
    counselling 190–1
    ethical conduct 181
    facing 187–91
    guidelines for 188–9
    legal advice 189, 190
    sexual harassment 156
    support for workers 188, 190
complexity, of client problems 35
confidentiality, research
    participants 14–15
conscience 102
consent, research participants 15
consultation, on education 48
contexts of practice, impact of
    98–9
continuing education 49
control 18, 41–2
coping strategies 17, 19

Author Index